AN HONOURABLE CALLING:
POLITICAL MEMOIRS

An Honourable Calling

Political Memoirs

ALLAN BLAKENEY

UNIVERSITY OF TORONTO PRESS
Toronto Buffalo London

ISBN: 978-0-8020-9891-7

Printed on acid-free paper

Library and Archives Canada Cataloguing in Publication

Blakeney, Allan
An honourable calling : political memoirs / Allan Blakeney.

Includes index.
ISBN 978-0-8020-9891-7

1. Blakeney, Allan.   2. Saskatchewan – Politics and government – 1971–1982.
3. Canada – Politics and government – 20th century.   4. Federal-provincial
relations – Canada – History – 20th century.   5. Prime ministers –
Saskatchewan – Biography.   I. Title.

FC3527.1.B43A3 2008   971.24′03092   C2008-903916-5

Photographs courtesy of Allan Blakeney.

University of Toronto Press acknowledges the financial assistance to its
publishing program of the Canada Council for the Arts and the
Ontario Arts Council.

University of Toronto Press acknowledges the financial support for its publishing
activities of the Government of Canada through the Book Publishing Industry
Development Program (BPIDP).

Contents

Illustrations follow page 134

Preface

In the following pages I have set down some thoughts on issues of public concern that I have encountered in my years of public life. I have included a good number of autobiographical details so that the reader can get a better idea of where these thoughts have come from. Whether we acknowledge it or not, we are all shaped by how, when, and in what circumstances we grew up and got an education.

I deal with issues which I encountered in a life in government, as a public servant and as an elected official over a period of some thirty-eight years. What I have not done is try to give a sense of the 'inside' life of a politician. There are many difficulties about giving details of what took place in meetings of cabinets and party caucuses. There are a number of matters on which I would have liked to give my slant on the issue. I think particularly of caucus meetings prior to the resignation of Woodrow Lloyd as leader of the New Democratic Party in Saskatchewan. But then there are real questions of confidentiality. If we agree that proceedings in caucus and cabinet will be confidential, then I think it best to respect that confidentiality. Certainly, some liberties could be taken, but it hardly seems worthwhile. The result is that I have included very little about my relations with cabinet and caucus colleagues. This distorts the story. These relations are key to what was accomplished and the way things happened. My memories of my cabinet and caucus relations are among the fondest memories of my life. I grew up in a small business environment. I was a public servant, I engaged in the private practice of law and I enjoyed a life in politics, and I can say that the people I rubbed shoulders with in politics, measured by standards of integrity, ability, loyalty, and selflessness, were every bit as competent and honourable as I met in my other fields of endeavour. The people I worked with in politics were good people.

And I am proud to call some hundreds of them friends, almost to a person.

I had cabinet colleagues and especially a deputy leader, Roy Romanow, whom I trusted unhesitatingly. I felt comfortable in sharing with them all the information I had and giving them all the public profile they could obtain, without once feeling that my position as leader might be undermined. I doubt that many leaders are so fortunate. It was a great relationship. In a sense I'm sorry that I've decided not to include the many stories of how these people interacted and how they came to respect one another. They will have to wait for another day and perhaps another author.

So, my remarks are a little bloodless. I hope they give some sense of the ideas and issues we wrestled with. They don't give the sense of the day-to-day interchange of a lively group of people which made doing my job such a pleasure. Not many people are fortunate enough to have a job where they use a large part of their talents a great part of the time. Being a minister is such a job, as is being a premier. It is a job that is hard, mean, fun, and, I believe, important.

I hope to be able to convey to you a truth which my father taught me: in a democratic society where people are struggling to govern themselves, politics matter.

Acknowledgments

I wish to thank a number of people who, over far too long a period of time, have helped me with their research and secretarial skills for this project. They include Tania Sarkar, Russell Isinger, Penny Yaeger, Jennifer Boutin, Tanis Halpepe, Iffat Ritter, and Courtney Kirk.

Specialized research on resource issues was provided by Erin Weir and John Burton. Gwevril Kirk provided her skill in reviewing the typescript and in preparing the index, while Dennis Gruending offered detailed editorial suggestions.

The staff at University of Toronto Press provided guidance on organization of the manuscript and a foil for lively arguments about grammar and punctuation.

Writing these memoirs has provided me an opportunity to relive some of the more controversial parts of my public life and on occasion to foist on people around me my particular memories of distant events. This added to the enjoyment if not the speed of the research.

To all those I have mentioned and others who have helped me, I express my appreciation for their assistance and their forbearance.

AN HONOURABLE CALLING:
POLITICAL MEMOIRS

1

Winning Office

On a sweltering night in June 1971, amid the bustle of an election eve, at our headquarters in a vacant supermarket building in Regina, thoughts were rolling through my head.

When I was in high school, the yearbook editor had predicted that I would become a lawyer and a politician. I had graduated from Dalhousie Law School in Halifax and had been elected to the Saskatchewan legislature. Now, as the night wore on, it became clear that the major step in my political career was about to happen. I was to be premier of Saskatchewan.

My life in politics had two or three personal high points. One was the victory in the doctors' strike of July 1962. Another was being elected to lead a government and be premier in June 1971. Each of these peaks was followed by some hard slogging but slogging that brought many occasions when there was a real sense of accomplishment.

The election called by Premier Ross Thatcher in May for 23 June 1971 was by no means a sure thing for the NDP. I hoped to win my own constituency of Regina Centre fairly handily, but results across the province were another matter. Premier Thatcher had been a forceful leader, making friends and enemies, but leaving no doubt about who was in charge.

There was trouble in the farm sector leading to some unpopular federal government measures, and a new militancy among teachers and trade unionists. For whatever reason, the public had decided to dispose of the Thatcher government. The New Democrats had run a good campaign and we had some solid policy proposals, but I don't think either elected us.

When the dust had settled, the New Democrats had gained 55 per cent of the vote, and 42 per cent went to the governing Liberals. The seat count was 45 and 15. I recall speaking to our supporters in the supermarket building. I had prepared a speech to give if we lost. I didn't bother to prepare one to use if we won. No one would listen anyway. So I was off the cuff. I remember saying, 'We've changed the government – now let's change the province.' And that was very much our state of mind. We felt we were carrying on in the footsteps of Tommy Douglas and Woodrow Lloyd. They had pioneered in many ways. Now it was our turn to restore some things that had been dismantled – 'repair the damage of the wrecking crew,' as we put it in our partisan way – and to go on to build on the Douglas-Lloyd legacy and to do our own pioneering. Perhaps those were less cynical times, but we really did believe that we could make major and useful changes for Saskatchewan and its people.

Seven days later, on June 30, I was sworn in as premier. There followed two or three months of whirlwind activity: choosing a small cabinet, recruiting new people for the public service, and unwinding industrial deals for an iron mine and a pulp mill made by the previous government. These industrial projects involved large sums of public money and were, I thought, improvident or environmentally hazardous or both. So I decided that neither should go forward.

We convened a special session of the legislature for late July to get started on our election platform. We had called the platform New Deal for People, and the initials were not lost on either the Opposition or the public. The party had worked out the platform over a couple of years, using policy groups set up by our leader, Woodrow Lloyd, a greatly underrated public figure. We had over a hundred specific proposals, and during the next four years we were able to deliver on most of them, and all the major ones. To get us on our way we had to convey an impression of immediate action. We called a session to start less than four weeks after assuming office.

The major steps taken were to repeal legislation severely limiting the right to strike, doing away with user fees under the medicare plan, and abolishing the charges against the estates of patients who had received treatment for mental illness. Our party had fought against those laws when they were introduced by the Thatcher government, and had campaigned against them during the 1971 election. We lost no time in repealing them without any opposition from the Liberals who had championed them just a few short years before. One of the satisfactions of politics is to advance an idea, campaign on that idea, get elected, and act on it promptly. The position we took on each of these issues stood for thirty-five years under governments of different stripes.

Before long I was introduced into the arcane world of federal-provincial relations.

In August, Prime Minister Trudeau invited me to lunch and a *tête à tête* at 24 Sussex Drive and we had a chance to size up each other. He was charming and casual. My recollection is that I was a little wary.

My first federal-provincial conference was in the early fall of 1971. Among the new premiers were Bill Davis of Ontario and Peter Lougheed of Alberta. Lougheed and I became collaborators and warm friends. We clearly had policy differences, but we had similar styles of administration. He was anxious to use the government of Alberta to diversify the economy of his province as we were attempting to do in Saskatchewan. Later we had similar problems with the way the federal government was dealing with oil and gas production, pricing, and taxation. We worked hard to see that our provinces gained benefits from their natural resources.

Mr Thatcher had operated a bare bones government. We needed to staff and organize for an activist government. Key people were engaged. I think of Murray Wallace, Garry Beatty, and Wes Bolstad, but there were others. New agencies were organized. Among them were departments of Continuing Education, Consumer Affairs, Culture and Youth, Environment, and Northern Saskatchewan, as well as an Independent Electoral Boundaries Commission, an Ombudsman's Office, and a Human Rights Commission. Each of these represented an idea we wanted to push.

Medicare needed to be protected and expanded. We saw an urgent need to overhaul teacher collective bargaining and generally to improve educational opportunities in rural Saskatchewan. We felt a need to deal with issues of the environment, although the word was hardly used in 1971. In our election material we talked about pollution. I saw an opportunity to build on the many and varied backgrounds and cultural roots of Saskatchewan people.

We wanted to pursue our vision of a new revitalized rural Saskatchewan consisting of the largest possible number of family farms. In Saskatchewan agricultural issues are always near the top of the agenda. But on the farm, times were relatively good for the years after 1973. So we devoted our attention to heading off any dismantling of the Crow's Nest Pass freight structure and any wholesale abandoning by the railway companies of the thousands of miles of branch lines, which are the arteries and veins that nourish our dispersed farm economy. But with these issues we were defending the status quo and if nothing happened, we were happy. We introduced some plans to bring a bit more stability to farm incomes and to deal with the tough problem of financing the rollover of farm ownership to the next generation. We introduced a number of new ideas, which were important but not as vital as the Crow Rate and rail-line abandonment. I'll say more about our moves in agriculture later.

We saw the need for Saskatchewan to make a new start on building better relations between Aboriginal and non-Aboriginal people. I had seen Ross Thatcher make an honest and determined try and had seen his efforts fail. We needed to try again. I will say more on this subject presently.

Working people had been roughly dealt with during the Thatcher years. We had many ideas for what we saw as progressive labour legislation which we hoped to proceed with.

It was indeed to be an effort to change the province, our own quiet revolution based heavily on roots that went deep into Saskatchewan's history and hopes, its dynamics and its dreams.

I served as Saskatchewan's premier for eleven years. It was a great privilege. I have long felt that Saskatchewan has exerted an influence out of all proportion to its size in making Canada the tolerant and relatively just society that it has become.

Canada has much to offer the world because of our unique experience and design as a federal state. Despite our difficulties and failings, the English and French have learned how to get along with one another, and with the Aboriginal people who were here for thousands of years prior to European settlement. People of many other backgrounds have found peace, tolerance, and prosperity in Canada. We have developed ways to discuss our problems and have devised an economy and system of governance that are widely admired.

Most politicians lose an election sooner or later. After three terms in office my government was defeated decisively by the Conservatives in 1982. I felt that it was my duty to remain and rebuild the party for the next election. When it came in 1986, we won the popular vote but not the seat count. I retired as leader of the NDP in 1987 and was replaced most capably by Roy Romanow, an accomplished politician who had served as deputy premier throughout our eleven years in government.

I retired from the legislature in 1988, but I have never lost my keen interest in public issues. I have served as a visiting professor at York University and later at the University of Saskatchewan. I believe that my relationship with a new generation of students and exceedingly competent academics has allowed me to remain current on many important issues and sensitive to their nuances. I have also served on a variety of boards, including those of Cameco Corporation, Crown Life, SaskTel, Greystone Capital Management, and Algoma Steel.

Perhaps most satisfying has been my work with emerging democracies, notably in South Africa, but also Russia and Kyrgyzstan. Canada's unique brand of federalism and our secular and tolerant civic nationalism provide a useful model in a world beset by religious, tribal, and ethnic rivalries. Despite the daunting problems related to globalization, inequity, and institutionalized violence, we can make the world a better place, and Canadians can be among the helpful agents in that transformation.

I have participated in public life, in Saskatchewan, in Canada, and to a far lesser extent in other countries for more than fifty years. I have never ceased believing that public life is an honourable calling, because it deals in the most basic way with the well-being of each individual in our society, national and global. I believe that I have learned some valuable lessons along the way – about democracy, about the economy, and about how best to structure and use government for the benefit of citizens, both in Canada and abroad. I hope in the pages to follow to share with you some of what I think I have learned.

2

An Unlikely Chap

In many ways I was an unlikely person to become Saskatchewan's premier. I was neither born in Saskatchewan nor educated in Saskatchewan. Indeed, when I became minister of education in 1960, I used to joke that I was qualified to be fair and impartial since I had never spent a day of my life at any educational institution in Saskatchewan as either a teacher or a student.

I was born in Nova Scotia. My father's people sailed from their home in the Belfast area of Northern Ireland in the 1760s to settle in South Carolina. They were supporters of the Loyalist side in the American War of Independence and were summarily pushed off their land. They came to Nova Scotia as United Empire Loyalists in 1782. Perhaps that is why I have always been, and remain, a Canadian nationalist even though that term is in some disfavour in an era whose buzzwords are 'globalization' and 'deep integration.'

My wife's ancestors came from New England to Liverpool, Nova Scotia, in 1760. They were part of a considerable number of people who moved up from New England to Nova Scotia after the expulsion of the Acadian settlers from the Annapolis Valley of Nova Scotia in 1755 and particularly after the capture by the British of the French stronghold of Quebec by General Wolfe in 1759 and the fall of Montreal in 1760.

My father's family had its ups and downs. My grandfather was a reasonably successful merchant with a couple of stores and a small ship, but he suffered business reverses and health problems. He died at age sixty. My father, the fifteenth of sixteen children, was left with few resources and only six grades of formal schooling. He joined the Canadian forces during the First World War. The war was not kind to him. He suffered frozen feet – 'trench feet' as it was termed – and shrapnel wounds in his hand

and arm. He was invalided to Britain. While in hospital there, he met a nurse, Bertha May Davies, from the Rhondda valley, a mining valley in South Wales. They were married in 1919 in Wales and came to Canada shortly thereafter.

I was their second child and their first son, born in 1925. By this time my father had set up a wholesale fruit business serving a stretch of the south shore of Nova Scotia from Halifax to Shelburne, a distance of about two hundred kilometres that included communities such as Hubbards, Chester, Mahone Bay, Lunenburg, Bridgewater, Liverpool, Shelburne, and a host of smaller villages.

In 1931 my brother John was born. When he was young, he developed pneumonia and empyema. He was in the local hospital – the Dawson Memorial – and was not going to make it. Many children died of pneumonia before the days of sulpha drugs and penicillin. As I have noted, my mother had been an army nurse during the First World War and was a very strong-willed woman. No son of hers was going to die. She simply would not permit it. She brought John home, engaged a housekeeper to look after the household including my father, my sister, and me, and established John in a room where she stayed and nursed him twenty-four hours a day. It looked as though an iron will might not be enough. Hugh Fraser was a young doctor new to the town. With my mother assisting, he operated on John in our house, removing a portion of his rib and draining his lungs. John survived, became a healthy young boy, and lived for close to seventy years, with a bit of a hole in his back.

The Second World War meant an increased workload for my father. My mother, meanwhile, had contracted Paget's disease, a degenerative disease of the bone, and spent a full year in bed. My sister Beryle was away at university, and I became a home-helper, scrubbing floors and doing assorted jobs. Mother graduated to crutches, then canes, then leg braces and remained active for most of her life. She died at eighty-two.

My father worked hard, especially in the summer months, which was the time to sell fruit. We had no summer cottage, nor did my mother want one. She and my father liked to travel, usually by car and usually in the fall. In 1939 I went with my parents to Boston – a common destination – and then on to New York to attend the New York World's Fair. It was a great adventure for me – to go to Yarmouth, Nova Scotia, by car, then to Boston by ship, to stay with relatives, and on by bus to Providence, Rhode Island, and then by ship down Long Island Sound and into New York harbour and the sights, sounds, and smells of the great port. We stayed at a hotel in the Bronx (different then than it has become since) and each day took the subway out to Flushing Meadows, where the fair was located. General Motors had a display of the highways of the future – a spaghetti of overpasses now all too familiar in cities such as Los Angeles, Atlanta, and Montreal. General Electric created artificial lightning using ten million volts of power (or so they said). We, of course, toured New York, the Bowery, Central Park, and the Empire State Building – then, and perhaps again, the tallest building in New York.

We lived in Bridgewater, where I studied at the local schools, attended church and Sunday school, and participated in the life of a small town of something over three thousand people. I suppose many people look back on the place where they grew up with uncritical nostalgia. I certainly have fond memories of my birthplace. Bridgewater was not as rich a town as neighbouring Lunenburg, which had a good number of wealthy fishing and shipping families. But ours was a good town. The school had teachers of very high quality. The principal for all of my twelve years was A.G.G. Hirtle, a science graduate of Acadia University and a sports enthusiast. Our literature teacher was Lawrence Hancock, a fine teacher and a scholar. During the Second World War, when opportunities opened up, Mr Hancock moved on and was the first full-time director of the Maritime School of Social Work. Other teachers were outstanding in their own way. Athletic coaching was rudimentary, and music and art instruction were not strong. But in the fundamentals – language and literature, history, geography, math, physics, and chemistry – I found that I was well prepared when I later arrived at Dalhousie University.

Churches and church activities played a major part in the life of the town. There were six 'regular' churches. The largest was the Lutheran Church, as was fitting in the county of Lunenburg, peopled by settlers from Hanover, Germany, and other parts of Western Europe in 1753. The next in size was the Baptist Church. Many of the people who moved up from New England – after mainland Nova Scotia became British following the Treaty of Utrecht in 1713 – were Baptist. The trickle of New Englanders became a wave following the expulsion of the Acadians. Well-developed farmland was there for the taking as Britain tried to shore up its position in Nova Scotia before the war brewing with France erupted. That war was not long delayed. It led to the capture by New Englanders, with British help, of Louisbourg in 1758. Quebec fell in 1759 and Montreal in 1760.

We had a lively Sunday school, which I attended regularly from as early as I can remember until I went off to university at age seventeen. My father attended church regularly and sometimes attended men's Bible class. He supported the philosophy and ethics of the church but clearly had difficulty with some of the theology. I don't know whether he was ever baptized. He did not urge me to be baptized and I never have been. At Sunday school the older boys were taught by Mr George Hubley, a leading dry goods merchant in town, a fine, fair, quiet man, and closet philanthropist. I still have the Bible he presented to me when I went off to university. His message was one of decency and duty. He has made his mark on generations of Bridgewater boys.

My father, despite his lack of formal education, read widely. I particularly remember a periodical called *Saturday Night*, edited by B.K. Sandwell, which contained literate articles on national affairs. My father was interested in politics and talked with me about issues. He was no admirer of W.L. Mackenzie King. He favoured R.B. Bennett but, as the Depression wore on, switched his support in the 1935 federal election to the new Reconstruction Party of H.H. Stevens. What I learned from my father was that political issues mattered.

Bridgewater had an active tennis club with five good-quality clay courts. I've seen some fine tennis there. I can recall the Eastern Canadian championships. I remember seeing the men's doubles between Commander Edwards of the Canadian Navy and Hugh MacLennan, the author, on one team from Halifax and, as I recall, LeClair and Deschenes from Montreal on the other team. We had excellent women players, including Jean Wright, a summer visitor from the United States, Elsie Harrington, a local woman, and, during the Second World War, Dorothy Round Little, who had moved from Britain for the duration of the war and who had, as Dorothy Round, been Wimbledon Champion in 1934 and 1937.

I played lots of tennis with my schoolmates and occasionally with local players, including Robert MacGregor Dawson, the distinguished political scientist who taught at the University of Toronto. He was born in Bridgewater, spent summers there and, after retirement, lived and died there.

The scout-guide movement thrived in Bridgewater. We had our own scout cabin in a wooded area close to town. I was a wolf cub and later a scout and patrol leader of the Owl patrol. Scouting taught good lessons and as boys we took them seriously.

I can remember a week-long camp under canvas in the woods. We set up our camp with all the 'gadgets' beloved by boys. I had a problem as a boy. I was plagued by bed-wetting and I was fearful of going camping and sleeping in a tent with five or six other boys. But I went. I hoped that I could avoid an accident, but it was not to be. I was embarrassed. The leaders in a quiet way made it clear that I was not to be made fun of, and I wasn't. I put my bed out in the sun to dry – without comment. Another boy, Robert, was sometimes the butt of jokes. In some way the leaders arranged for Robert to stay overnight, on his own, in the woods on a bed he had made of boughs. He returned to camp. When the leaders asked if one of us wanted to go off on our own for a night there were no takers. We were subtly invited to admire Robert for his courage, and he was no longer made fun of. It was only later that I came to appreciate that these were effective ways of teaching us what it meant to be, as the scout law says, a brother to every other scout. Those may have been simple times, but they were not without their strengths.

A great event of summer when I was a boy was the Baptist Sunday school picnic. On these occasions almost all the small boys in Bridgewater were Baptists. I recall for one picnic the *OK Service*, a coastal motor vessel of a few hundred tons, was chartered and all were taken aboard for a trip down the LaHave River for about twelve miles to Dublin Shore. At Dublin Shore (named after some Irish settlers who came in the early 1800s), the usual games were played and quantities of food and drink (including a red drink called sarsaparilla) were consumed. Then we all returned up the river in the serenity of the twilight. When I think of it, I don't suppose that anyone today would risk taking a large number of eight-, ten-, and twelve-year-olds on a ship without elaborate precautions, which would probably have been impossible to arrange. We seem to have lost our innocence. Liability lawyers have a lot to answer for.

I graduated from high school in 1942 when I was sixteen years old and was off to Dalhousie University in Halifax. In 1942 the Second World War was in full swing. Before the Japanese attack on Pearl Harbor, Hawaii, in 1941, the United States was a neutral nation. There were many restrictions on what could be shipped from the United States to countries participating in the European war. Halifax became an extremely busy port for the shipment of goods from North America to Britain. The harbour was clogged with ships awaiting convoy to Britain. I have counted more than a hundred ships at anchor in that part of Halifax Harbour known as Bedford Basin.

While I was at Dalhousie, the war had an immediacy not shared by most Canadians. That is not surprising. Halifax was not only a place from which men and goods were sent to war, it was a place to which war came. The Second World War transformed the city. This city of some sixty thousand people had about an equal number of servicemen about the city.

Streetcars were jammed. Restaurants and theatres had line-ups. And the memories of the First World War were still fresh. In 1917 when the harbour was filled with merchant ships, as it was in 1942, two ships had collided and one had caught fire. The burning ship, the *Mont Blanc*, was filled with explosives, which exploded with almost unimaginable force. It has been called the largest man-made explosion in the history of the world up until the atomic bomb that struck Hiroshima in 1945. The city of some 50,000 was devastated. More than 1,600 people were killed, 9,000 seriously injured, and 25,000 – half the residents – were made homeless, all in an instant. The force of the blast tossed the cannon of the *Mont Blanc* some six kilometres from the harbour. Windows were shattered over an 80-kilometre radius. The many stories of tragedy and distress were imprinted on the minds of the residents of Halifax and were still fresh in 1942. War was serious business and the possibility of disaster never far from people's thinking.

I saw the great passenger ships of the world – the *Queen Elizabeth*, the *Queen Mary*, the *Empress of Britain*, and others – in port loading thousands of servicemen for transport to Europe. The streets of Halifax were again full of servicemen and merchant sailors from every part of the world. The possibility of air attack was real, and we had regular blackouts and air-raid drills at Pine Hill residence, where I stayed.

At Dalhousie I settled in to enjoy the history and political science courses. Dr R.A. MacKay taught some of the political science courses. In history I had Dr George Earl Wilson.

I took a class in logic from Dr H.L. Stewart and I found it very useful. Most of us feel that we can think straight, but we often lack a framework by which to detect the flawed reasoning used in so many arguments in the public arena. We all see these flawed arguments every day. Horses have tails. Birds have tails. Therefore, birds are horses. That's not too convincing. Communists oppose private ownership of railways. Jones opposes private ownership of railways. He toes the party line. Therefore, Jones is a communist. A little more convincing, but no more logical. Jones may be a communist, but that argument doesn't support it.

Getting one's powers of logical thinking in order is good training for many walks of life, including law and politics.

On this point I remember my first year of law school. The method of study was to be given a list of cases to read. Often they were English cases argued before England's highest court, the House of Lords. I recall reading one case in which several judges wrote judgments. I read one judgment, tightly argued and written in beautiful prose. I concluded that the judge's conclusion was clearly right and almost inescapable. I went on to read what the next judge wrote – again I read and was totally convinced until it began to dawn on me that this second judge was going to reach a different conclusion than the first judge, a conclusion I found equally convincing. I reread the two judgments to pinpoint where the two had parted company. It was the different shade of meaning that they gave to a key word. That was a good lesson. Arguments can be cogent, persuasive, and wrong – or, at least, another opinion can be equally cogent and persuasive and reach a different result. This impressed upon me the need to bring both a sceptical mind and an analytical approach to all arguments put to me. This is especially true if I am inclined to agree with the conclusion reached on other grounds. It's easy and dangerous to accept the strength of an argument simply because you agree with the conclusion reached by the argument.

At Dalhousie I was elected to the student council for the 1944–5 and 1946–7 years. I recall one issue that came before the council. The CCF party proposed to organize a club on the campus – a branch of a national organization – the Cooperative Commonwealth University Federation (CCUF). There were no other political clubs on campus, and some members of council felt that it was not wise to have partisan political clubs on campus. One member, Molly Schwartz, was of that view. I clearly was not. I had no objection to a non-partisan approach to public issues. Indeed, another student and I had organized a non-partisan public affairs group called the Round Table Club. But I felt there was room as well for clubs affiliated with political parties. That position was accepted, and a fledgling CCUF club was organized on campus. By now I had departed from my Conservative upbringing and had come to embrace the basic principles of social democracy. I became the first vice-president of the CCUF club.

Molly and I came to know each other. I spent lots of time at the Schwartz home, and after I completed my studies, Molly and I were married in 1950.

Professor George Wilson – an interesting lecturer, a wise man, but with a melancholy view of life – taught most of my history courses at Dalhousie. Since I was, and still am, an almost irrepressible optimist, I was able to get a great deal out of George Wilson's courses without succumbing to his sad and somewhat cynical pessimism. It is easy to be pessimistic about the human condition, and if we are completely honest, we probably will be pessimistic and perhaps even cynical. But if we regard life with all of its warts as a great adventure, and if we embrace the idea of the possibility, if not the inevitability, of progress toward a happier condition for all the human inhabitants of this planet, then I think we can pursue knowledge and wisdom without feeling that the enterprise is inevitably doomed to failure.

George Wilson put out a little book in his later years entitled *All for Nothing?* It is honest, wise, but sad. He sees all of us as individuals, lonely and seeking fulfilment and freedom, but too often being led astray by the search for power or wealth or pleasure and by accepting the standards of the world, by believing that success is measured by the judgment of the world, and as the world is judged, our life would so be judged. He felt that it was only as a person forgets himself, loses himself in the worship of knowledge, of truth, and of beauty, and as he feels the sadness of the world and is filled with sympathy for all of those who suffer, that he can find himself and enter the kingdom of the wise.

I found this message compelling but incomplete. All should seek knowledge of truth and beauty and should be sensitive to those who suffer. But in the journey of life we are not alone. There are many brothers and sisters who accompany us. We are called to recognize our common humanity and our common fragility and to see what we can do to ease the burdens of our fellow travellers and to relieve the suffering of those less fortunate than us. If we can do these things with humility, we are likely to come to appreciate some other aspects and shades of our common condition.

For those who are uncertain about the life hereafter or about whether, in that life, one's condition will be determined or influenced by how one lived in our world, there is another definition of eternity. Between the time that humans rose from the primordial ooze to the time when we split the atom, a comparatively short period has elapsed. During this period humans have been developing ideas and thoughts about what humankind should be; they have been developing a spiritual universe. It is our contribution to this spiritual universe that defines whether our life has been a success. We all contribute by precept and example; contribute positively or negatively. Some great thinkers have shaped how our children will think and act. Some great doers have shaped how our children will think and act.

There are some who would say that the aim in life is to be free of the world, its temptations, snares, and delusions, so that one can pursue knowledge and beauty. Except for a very few scholars who will be able to tell their fellow humans about their insights into knowledge and beauty, I think this is a self-centred pursuit. For those who have the choice of being part of the world with all its dangers, or of withdrawing from the world to pursue knowledge of truth and beauty, I hope we have developed our spiritual universe to the point that it imposes upon all who are fortunate enough to have this choice a duty to be of the world, a duty to be of assistance to those who suffer, a duty to add positively to the capital of our spiritual universe. Of course we are flawed. Of course our reach must exceed our grasp. But just as surely if we march with our fellow humans toward what we now think is right, there is good reason to believe that we will find the journey fulfilling and our children and theirs will benefit from what we have added to the sum total of human achievements.

We will all cross the river Jordan, and all cross it alone. What is on the other side will remain a mystery or a product of faith. Our path on this side is ours to choose. Our choices should be guided primarily by being in company with our fellow humans and all those whose lives we can touch.

George Wilson asked us to think. For that I am grateful to him. The fact that I may have disagreed with him is not relevant.

R.A. MacKay taught political science with knowledge and flair. He had served on the Rowell-Sirois Commission, on (as we would say today) federal-provincial relations. We in Canada have a Constitution, which gives to the provincial governments' law-making jurisdiction over most of the things that affect the lives of our citizens. Our economy has developed so that the ability of provinces to raise revenue varies greatly from province to province. We have spent a great deal of the energies of our political leaders in devising ways for the federal government to use its tax-raising abilities to finance many of the activities that fall under the law-making power of the provinces and for the federal government to do this in a way that reduces the disparities among Canadians living in different regions of Canada. We have equalization payments whereby the federal government raises money by using its taxing powers and distributes the money to provinces whose taxing ability is lower than the national average. We have shared-cost programs under which the federal government pays part of the cost of important services delivered to Canadians in such fields as hospital and medical care and legal aid.

It is easy to represent federal-provincial negotiations on equalization and cost-shared programs as fractious and acrimonious. And they sometimes are. But the system has worked remarkably well. It has allowed a large measure of equality of services for all Canadians while permitting local administration and local variation to accommodate the many differences that exist across our broad land.

I remember a particular story that Professor MacKay used to illustrate to us how *habeas corpus* could be used to protect civil rights. He recounted the story of one Peter Verigin (the younger), who was the leader of the Doukhobor community in Saskatchewan. The Doukhobor community had been invited to come to Canada from Russia by the Canadian government. It is widely reported that the great Russian novelist Leo Tolstoy facilitated the movement of a substantial number of Doukhobors from Russia to Canada.

Peter Petrovich Verigin was the son of Peter Vasilivich Verigin (called Peter the Lordly), who migrated to Canada with help from Tolstoy. In 1899 about 7,500 Doukhobors came to western Canada. Many settled in east central Saskatchewan in an area soon to be known as the Verigin district.

The Doukhobors were given certain assurances that they could come to Canada and live in peace – that they would not be conscripted for service in the armed forces and would be able to live their communal way of life. Inevitably, difficulties arose. During the First World War there was an enormous slaughter of men in the trenches. Eventually conscription was enacted in Canada in 1917. It was not possible to require Doukhobor men to serve in the armed forces and, at the same time, honour the commitments made to Doukhobors when they came to Canada. And such was the loss of life among Canadians serving in Europe that ordinary Canadians were not willing to make exceptions based upon those commitments. Friction between the Doukhobors and Canadian governments increased. Difficulties arose also about how the Doukhobors could own their farmland communally when our land-holding system in Saskatchewan (as elsewhere in Canada) is designed for owners to be either individuals or corporations.

Peter Verigin (the younger) was born in Russia and came to Canada in 1927. He fell afoul of the law and was convicted of perjury. In the early 1930s while Verigin was in Prince Albert Penitentiary, Dr J.T.M. Anderson, Saskatchewan's Conservative premier, and Conservative prime minister R.B. Bennett decided secretly to return Verigin to Soviet Russia. To accomplish this, they pardoned Verigin before government agents took him to a train headed from Prince Albert to Halifax. From there he was to be deported.

A reporter at Saskatoon's daily newspaper, the *Star Phoenix*, got wind of the plan, and her city editor called Peter Makaroff, a Saskatoon lawyer who acted for Verigin. Makaroff appealed to Prime Minister Bennett and the federal minister of immigration to no avail. Makaroff then raced for

Halifax, travelling by auto to the United States and using aircraft of all types to get to Halifax. With the help of a Halifax lawyer, Makaroff appeared before a crusty old judge, Humphrey Mellish. As recounted by Professor MacKay, Mellish issued writs of *habeas corpus* directed to wardens of local prisons, masters of ships in the harbour, and others who might be detaining Verigin.

Verigin was to have been carried away from Canada on a ship, the *Montcalm*. But the writs produced their desired effect and Verigin was brought before Judge Mellish. Once it became clear that Verigin had, in fact, been pardoned, there were no lawful grounds for his further detention, and Makaroff returned to Saskatoon with his client, now a free man.

It was a colourful story that stuck in my mind. When I moved to Saskatchewan in 1950, I soon met Peter Makaroff, then still practising law in Saskatoon and still a stout defender of civil liberties. He was in practice with Roger Carter and his wife, Mary Carter. Roger later served as dean of law at the University of Saskatchewan, and Mary was, for over twenty years, a judge of the Court of Queen's Bench. I became warm friends of the Carters.

When I took my first year at Dalhousie law school, the whole school, students and staff, would not have filled a bus. We had, as I recall it, seventeen students in first year and six or eight in each of years two and three. There were two full-time professors, Dean Vincent MacDonald and Professor George Curtis. Each, in his own way, was an exceptional teacher. Dean MacDonald, later Mr Justice MacDonald of the Nova Scotia Supreme Court, taught constitutional law, torts, and agency, among other subjects. His lectures were clear and coherent, and his views were equally clear. When pressed as to whether matters were quite that clear (they rarely are in law), he replied that we had received the gospel according to St Vincent.

Professor George Curtis was a superb teacher. He encouraged everyone to participate. It was almost impossible to make a fool of oneself in his class. Every answer, however wrong or misguided, 'raised an interesting issue.' He would then restate the issue and, with a deft switch, get the discussion back on track and continue the barrage of questions. It was the Socratic Method used with great success.

Unfortunately for us, George Curtis left after our first year to go to Vancouver as the first dean of law at the new law school at the University of British Columbia. He later served Canada with great distinction at a series of conferences dealing with international agreements on the law of the sea. He died in 2005 when in his hundredth year.

In later years Moffatt Hancock and James Milner joined Dean Mac-Donald. Both were distinguished scholars. Dr Hancock later went to Stanford University, where he had a brilliant career. Jim Milner taught us corporate law and later became a well-known authority on municipal law when he taught at the University of Toronto.

My legal studies taught me law, taught me to think and to use language, but did not teach me much about the wisdom of the ages. I graduated from law school with a sound technical education in law and an introduction to some broader intellectual pathways.

I recall my student years as ones filled with activity and new experiences. I was younger than most of my classmates – I had a B.A. before I was twenty and an LL.B. before I was twenty-two. I remember in my final year setting myself a kind of wish list. I hoped to get the University Medal in Law for highest marks, a particular award for student activity, a Rhodes Scholarship, and to have success in my relations with Molly Schwartz. I certainly did not deserve the student award and did not get it. I did get the University Medal and the Rhodes Scholarship, and Molly and I deepened our friendship.

After graduation I was off to Oxford to study philosophy, political science, and economics. I felt that this was a better way to prepare myself for a career in public life than taking further legal studies. It was a great two years. I travelled fairly extensively, sometimes with the University of Oxford's ice hockey team, sometimes with the university badminton team, and sometimes privately. On one occasion we played hockey in the Spengler Cup competition at Davos, Switzerland, and on another we played a team from the U.S. Army at the handsome arena built by Hitler at Garmisch-Partenkirchen, Germany, for the 1936 Olympic Games. As I have mentioned above, my mother grew up in the Rhondda valley of South Wales, and many of her relatives still lived there. I had an opportunity to visit extensively with them and get a feel for the particular culture surrounding coal mining in Britain.

The instruction at Oxford was by the tutorial method. This brought the student in close contact with some lively minds. My economics tutor at The Queen's College was Charles Hitch, an American. He went on to become president of the University of California, a huge institution with now close to two hundred thousand students.

I marvelled at the intellectual ferment that was Oxford. It was the reverse of the ivory tower. Economics and political science professors were constantly on the move to London to work with the government for a stretch ('he's off to Whitehall') and then returning to Oxford. In one of my courses, almost the only prescribed reading was the *London Times*, a leading newspaper and the *Economist*, then (and now) a front-rank periodical. We occasionally referred to the *New Statesman* and *Nation*, a somewhat more left-leaning periodical. If (say) a budget had been tabled in Parliament, our job was to read those journals, consider what we had learned elsewhere, and write a critique of the budget. Would it do for Britain what ought to be done? This would produce a lively discussion with the tutor, who might take any position favouring or opposing parts of the budget.

While the tutorial method was the basic approach to instruction, there were lectures, which one was free to attend, or not. They would not be the subject of examination but were for background. At the time, there was a lively public controversy about whether the British government should nationalize the steel industry as they had the coal industry. Two series of lectures were running. One was given by a Manchester School economist who poured scorn on the whole idea. He opined that the government couldn't even say what they meant by the steel industry, let alone know how they would go about nationalizing it. The other was by the distinguished political economist G.D.H. Cole, who was a warm supporter of the proposal. The two professors refrained from any personal references, but they certainly took roundhouse swings at the ideas advanced by the other, all couched in elegant but sharp prose. In many ways Oxford was more like a boxing ring than an ivory tower.

In the last weeks of my time in Europe, four other students from Queen's and I acquired an ancient automobile and trailer and drove to Budapest for a student festival. The five of us were all studying philosophy, politics, and economics. We were three from England, one English by ethnic background but from East Africa, and me, a Canadian. At Oxford I had the common experience of becoming very conscious of being a Canadian and of the similarities and differences between English, American, Australian, and Canadian students. I recall a tiny incident when a British student, an American student, and I were talking about our systems of government. As I talked and listened, I became aware that, without in any way being consciously jingoistic, both the Brit and the American assumed that their system of government was the best in the world and that this would be readily conceded by the others. I harboured no such assumption about Canadian government. At the time, few Canadians believed that anything we did in Canada, perhaps except playing hockey, was the best in the world. Certainly we didn't start with that assumption. We've become more confident since.

When our 1931 Austin and trailer had taken us through devastated cities in West Germany and through Prague and Bratislava to Budapest, we met students from both sides of the Iron Curtain. There were many cultural performances but next to no conversation on political issues. There were a few lectures which were clearly inspired by the communist government of Hungary and were simplistic in their approach. Perhaps they suffered in translation. Perhaps not. It was a great adventure and an educational one even if not in a formal sense. A curious follow-up to this story is that in 2005 I was contacted by a student in Hungary who was doing some research on the Budapest festival of 1949, who had obtained my name from some list or other, and had managed to track me down. I was not avoiding contact, but it occurred to me that with modern technology there is no place to hide.

Looking back, it was an adventure that I thought was great fun at the time, is pleasant to remember, but that I would not wish to repeat today. Sleeping in a sleeping bag in a field beside the road or in the back of our small trailer; travelling unmarked roads (road signs had often been removed during the war years and not replaced) and getting lost; all in a car with an electrical system that could not run the motor and the lights at the same time, and with brakes that could not be relied upon to stop the car and trailer on any downhill slope: this was great fun for five young men in their early twenties, and therefore invincible.

We were travelling at a time when there was great tension between the communist government of Mátyás Rákosi of Hungary and the independent communist government of Marshal Tito in Yugoslavia. When we got to the Yugoslav border, our car was stripped, seats removed, our luggage examined down to the last tent peg, and a person assigned to ride with us through the country. Fortunately he spoke some German and we were able to communicate. He insisted that we drive and not stop. We explained that when darkness fell, we would have no lights. He was not persuaded, so we drove until the lights stopped functioning. We were able to stop at the top of a hill. In the morning we were able to unhitch the trailer, push the car down the hill to get it started (the battery was all but dead), and drive it enough to get the battery marginally functional. And so, after returning for the trailer and the passengers, we were off again. When we reached Ljubljana, now the capital of the new country of Slovenia, our escort left us and was replaced by a uniformed military type, who carried a side arm and spoke no language but Slovene. We continued on until we reached what was then the free city of Trieste and our escort 'saw us off the premises,' so to speak. That was my introduction to Yugoslavia.

Marshal Josef Broz Tito was the durable and talented leader of Yugoslavia who developed his own brand of communism. He was able to keep the fractious ethnic groups that composed his country united and reasonably prosperous. Sadly, following his death, the country has not survived and after several wars, deep divisions remain. While he was alive and while the East-West Cold War persisted, Tito was from time to time courted by both East and West. As a result, when he died his funeral was an occasion for world leaders to be seen.

Prime Minister Trudeau asked Premier Hatfield of New Brunswick and me to join the Canadian party headed by Governor General Ed Schreyer and Mrs Schreyer. Very rarely has there been such a collection of dignitaries. For security reasons almost all of them were housed in one hotel. When we were being transported to the football stadium where the funeral ceremonies were to take place, the departure was choreographed. We were leaving later, so we retired to the hotel lobby to watch the performance. The dignitaries were transported in identical Mercedes Benz automobiles, which were lined up in the parking lot. I counted over 270. The procedure was that the dignitary came down in the elevator and walked through the lobby to the front door, where the designated limousine was waiting. Dick Hatfield and I were among the crowd in the lobby, and the game was to see if one could identify the leader. Many appeared in resplendent uniforms: 'Who's that?' 'I think it's the King of Sweden.' 'I think it's Denmark,' and on and on. I noted one curious thing – the way the bodyguards acted. An Eastern European leader would emerge from the elevator flanked by two bodyguards. A cameraman stepped out to take a photo, and the bodyguards on each side moved forward to get between the photographer and the leader. Then the chancellor of Germany, Willy Brandt, came along with the bodyguards. The photographer stepped out, and the two bodyguards melted backwards and away so as not to spoil the photo. The contrast was marked. President Carter was unable to come, but his then famous mother, Lillian, was there with the American delegation. We spoke with her in the elevator, and when she found we were Canadian she was effusive in her friendliness. Shortly before the Tito funeral there had been an ugly incident involving Americans at the embassy in Tehran, Iran, and the Canadian ambassador to Iran, Ken Taylor, had been able to help the Americans by sheltering some of them in the Canadian embassy. At least for the time being, Canadian officials were seen as good guys.

I saw but did not talk to many foreign leaders – the premier of China, Margaret Thatcher, and Prince Philip – and many more.

Aside from the unequalled international pageant, the reaction in Belgrade was surprising. The line-up of ordinary people to go past the bier where Tito's body was lying in state was miles long. It was as if they felt that the stability of the Tito years was threatened. If such was the case, their feeling was certainly prescient.

All this was many years in the future as we made our way from Hungary and across Slovenia to Trieste and on to Venice. I've returned to Venice several times and never cease to experience it as a magical city. I recall on a recent visit Anne and I arrived in the evening. We were staying at a modest hotel near the railway station. After checking in, we took a *vaporetto* (water taxi) down to the Piazza San Marco. It was dusk. A mist was in the air. There was hardly a soul in the great square, which is usually teeming with humanity. Through the light haze we could see the great cathedral, the Doges' Palace, and the buildings around the square. It looked like a scene from a fairy tale. When I visit distant places which we have seen in pictures and movies, I'm often a little disappointed when I recognize that they are places where people live and work and that there is therefore bustle and crowds and not a serene, silent postcard atmosphere. But on that occasion Venice and the great square seemed to be there for us and us alone.

Our Oxford-Budapest odyssey took us from Venice, across northern Italy and the French Riviera, north up the valley of the Rhone to Paris, and thence to England and Oxford.

Soon I was bidding goodbye to my friends from Queen's and returning to Canada. I've kept in touch with them and had several reunions when I visited Britain, as I did frequently over the years. Three of us are left.

Upon my return to Canada I set about to get myself admitted to the bar in Nova Scotia. I soon decided that I would like to see more of Canada. I contacted law firms extensively in Vancouver and Edmonton and got in touch with a Dalhousie law graduate with the government of Saskatchewan to see whether there were any opportunities there. My preference was to go to Saskatchewan for a relatively brief time.

At this point I had travelled fairly extensively in Europe – England, Scotland, Ireland, Wales, Belgium, Holland, France, Germany, Switzerland, Czechoslovakia, Hungary, Yugoslavia, and Italy – and had been to Boston and New York a couple of times as well as Philadelphia and Washington. I had even visited Montreal and Quebec City, but not Ottawa or Toronto or anything west – if, indeed, there was anything west of Toronto.

I had seen the name 'Saskatchewan' on maps in my schoolbooks, and heard of Peter Verigin, so I assumed there was a place with that name.

Not only had I not been to the Prairies, I had no sense of everyday life there. I remember an incident when I was in grade school studying geography. There were some questions at the end of each chapter in our text. One of the questions was 'When did the first elevator come to your town?' I had ridden an elevator in Eaton's department store in Halifax. I knew that the local grocery wholesalers had an elevator to move goods in their warehouse, complete with ropes and pulleys. But I couldn't see why this would fit into the lesson. The grain elevator, so familiar to any lad growing up in Saskatchewan, was totally unknown to me.

The responses I received from Saskatchewan and from Vancouver were discouraging. From Edmonton they were encouraging. I decided to article in Edmonton and made the journey by train across Canada in February of 1950 to commence articles with a law firm now known as Emery Jamieson LLP. A few months later an opening occurred in Saskatchewan, and I decided to work for a time with the Tommy Douglas government of that province to see what social democracy was like at close range.

The government of Saskatchewan in 1950, at least at the senior officials' level, seemed to be a small band of happy warriors. I remember my first days on the job. I was taken around to meet Tommy Douglas, who was very warm and charming even with a new and relatively junior employee. Somehow it helped a young lad from the Maritimes to see that the premier stood in line with everyone else in the legislative cafeteria in Regina, that he always ordered the same lunch of poached eggs, toast, and milk, and that he ate sitting at tables along with public servants and politicians of high and low estate.

My job was to be the secretary to the board of directors and lawyer for a string of small Crown corporations. Two corporations had their own legal staff, the Saskatchewan Power Corporation and the Saskatchewan Government Insurance Office. The others relied upon my services or the services of lawyers in private practice. These included the telephone utility, our inter-urban bus line, a charter and scheduled air service in northern Saskatchewan, a plant manufacturing brick and tile, a printing plant, a producer of sodium sulphate, a company operating a fur auction service, a marketer of freshwater fish, an operator of northern trading posts, a corporation harvesting and marketing timber, and operating a sawmill and a box factory, as well as one operating a mill producing wool products, primarily blankets and wool textiles.

I spent a good bit of time with the person who headed up the holding company for the corporations, George Cadbury. He was a scion of the

British family famous for manufacturing chocolates, Bird's custard, and other staples of the British diet. He was in early middle age, independently wealthy, and had a background in management of some of the Cadbury companies. He had come to Saskatchewan in 1947 to see whether he could give a hand to the Douglas government, which was trying to get some secondary industry operating in an overwhelmingly agricultural economy. He was personally charming, shrewd and self-confident, and a great mentor for me.

One might well ask what it was about Saskatchewan that would attract a man of Cadbury's calibre, or, for that matter, what it was that so interested me. A big part of the answer is that Saskatchewan had become one of the most active social laboratories in Canada. I believe this stems from the characteristics that developed in Saskatchewan because of its unique settlement pattern.

Back in 1670 the British Crown gave rights over the territory which is now Saskatchewan to the Hudson's Bay Company. Trading in furs was their major business, and it served the commercial interests of the company to keep the area free from non-Aboriginal settlement so that the company could trade with the Aboriginals who harvested furs.

This state of affairs continued until the settlement of the West in the United States threatened to produce waves of colonists pouring north into what is now Canada. The new Dominion, created in 1867, acquired the lands of the Hudson's Bay Company in 1869. There was a perceived need for rapid settlement. This set the stage for the settling of the Prairies, particularly of the lands that are now Saskatchewan and Alberta, and this process has set its stamp on these provinces.

The federal government had a railway built from the settled areas of Montreal and Toronto, across what are now northern Ontario and the Prairie provinces, and through the mountains to the Pacific coast at Vancouver. The Canadian Pacific Railway was completed in 1885. Settlers were offered free land; opportunities for settlement were advertised widely throughout North America and Europe. Over the last two decades of the 1800s and the first two decades of the 1900s, people trickled, and sometimes flooded, in. There were people of English, Scandinavian, and German extraction who came up from the United States. Many thousands – French, Scottish, Irish, and English – came from eastern Canada on the new railway. They were joined shortly thereafter by many who came directly from Europe – from Germany, Ukraine, Poland, Hungary, Romania, Serbia, and other lands.

Saskatchewan is replete with names drawn from the map of Europe. It was settled by a rich mix of ethnic and religious groups set down in a fertile land, but with a harsh climate and next to none of the means of transportation and communication that are now thought to be essential for human settlement. These people came and they prospered, but with many hardships. Then in the 1930s, Saskatchewan was hit harder than any other place in Canada by the double disasters of worldwide economic depression and a drought lasting almost a decade. Crops were meagre. Livestock had to be slaughtered. Prices for all farm products were ruinously low.

I believe these extraordinary circumstances have given Saskatchewan a distinctive character. These settlers from many cultures and backgrounds were driven to co-operate. They worked together or they perished. Since there was no established leadership core, they learned to lead themselves. There was no established economic elite except a few old families in the small cities. The economic leaders – the people who were masters of the economic engines that controlled the lives of the settlers – all lived outside the province. The banks, the mortgage companies, farm machinery manufacturers, railway companies, the grain exchange, and commodity traders all had their major offices outside the province. As these economic forces had no strong voice within Saskatchewan, the settlers were united, not only against the harsh climate, but also against their economic overlords.

The only power that they exercised over their lives, the only tool they had, was government. And they soon learned to use the tool of government as a counter to the economic power they so grievously lacked. And soon they learned to create a new tool – the co-operative movement.

As I have noted, in its formative years the province was distinctive in having no established social elite and no resident economic elite. There was a rich ethnic variety, with the people of British and French origin combined making up less than 50 per cent of the population; a harsh climate, which all but forced co-operation; and a one-industry economy in which virtually everybody shared the same economic interests.

There was a further element. A number of the early political leaders who emerged had strong roots in the United Kingdom and had no fear of either co-operatives or governments as tools to build a new society.

With this background it is not surprising that the history of the development of institutions and facilities to provide health care for this diverse population is a history of self-help and of enlisting provincial and local governments to play a major role. These governments proved to be highly responsive to the needs of the people.

My job as board secretary of the Crown corporations meant that I spent a large part of my time at board meetings. The boards were all chaired by a cabinet minister, and my job was to help the chairman get on with his work and to manage the relations between the non-executive chairman and the chief executive officers, then referred to as general managers. The chairmen (they were all male) were a diverse lot. Some had little business experience; some, like the provincial treasurer, Clarence Fines, were hugely competent; and some, like J.H. Brockelbank, had limited business experience, but high intelligence and a good deal of worldly wisdom. The job took me to most corners of the province and was a great introduction to Saskatchewan life.

In 1955 I moved to be chairman of the Saskatchewan Securities Commission, which deals with regulating how securities are sold to the public. The knowledge I gained about prospectuses, public offerings, and puts and calls stood me in good stead when dealing with business people in my years as premier.

At this time I began to ponder my future. I'd come to Saskatchewan without any intention of living my life there. I'd enjoyed all my years in public service, but I'd always had it in the back of my mind that I wanted to enter elected politics. What I now decided was that I would give this path a try in Saskatchewan.

After 1956, I began to prepare myself to seek a nomination for the 1960 election. But then disaster struck. Molly and I had found a good community in Regina. Along with five other people, we formed a cooperative and built houses for each of us, hiring most of the labour. Molly and I moved into our house at 3135 Montague Street in early 1953, and Barbara, our first child, was born in May. Our son Hugh was born in 1955. We had developed a range of very congenial friends. We enjoyed our new bungalow and our growing family. We had just spent a happy Christmas in 1957 when Molly was struck with a heart ailment and died very suddenly. I was numbed. We had no relatives in the province to help us through these black days. But our friends rallied round in the best Saskatchewan fashion, and somehow we survived and moved on. I delayed my move to private practice until I had my bearings.

Within a year or so I renewed an acquaintanceship with Anne Gorham, who was a friend of Molly's from Halifax. Anne was teaching at Victoria College, which was soon to become the University of Victoria in British Columbia. She and I were married in May 1959, and she took on the task of being mother to two children. Barbara, being older, has some recollection of Molly, but Hugh recalls only Anne as his mother. We have been happily married for almost fifty years.

Despite the tragic setback that had befallen our young family, I was still determined to seek a political nomination. I felt that I should not do so while I was a public servant and particularly while I was chairman of a quasi-judicial body such as the Saskatchewan Securities Commission. Prior to my marriage to Anne, in 1959, I left the public service and joined a small law firm, which became Davidson, Davidson & Blakeney. It took me a little while to get into the swing of the private practice of law, but I enjoyed both the work and the associations. C.R. Davidson was a fine lawyer, the firm was congenial, and the Regina Bar was welcoming.

From that comfortable perch, I stood for nomination as a candidate for the CCF for one of the four members of the legislature to be elected in Regina in 1960. Before deciding to stand as a candidate, I talked with several people. Tommy Douglas urged me to run, as did Clarence Fines, who had served in every Douglas administration as Saskatchewan's incomparable treasurer. Clarence proposed to retire from politics, and I suspected that he did some quiet organizing on my behalf, using his many contacts with Regina constituency organizations.

3

Nomination and the 1960 Election Campaign

The CCF nominating convention for Regina City was held in April 1960 in the Trianon ballroom. There were probably 1,700 people there. Regina was to be represented by four candidates all representing one constituency. One sitting member, provincial treasurer Clarence Fines, was retiring, and the two other sitting members, Charlie Williams, who was minister of labour, and Marjorie Cooper, would be nominated easily. The race therefore was for the two remaining nominations. Four contestants emerged. In addition to me they were Henry Baker, the mayor of Regina; Ed Whelan, who had been the president of the Regina CCF constituency and had many contacts within the party; and George Smith, who was the nominee of the Regina Labour Council. As expected, Charlie Williams and Marjorie Cooper were nominated quickly on the first ballot, and future ballots were confined to selecting the remaining two nominees. I ran well and was nominated as the third candidate. The battle for the fourth slot was very close with Ed Whelan eventually winning at the end of a long hot evening.

I remember that Tommy Douglas was the guest speaker. He agreed to interrupt his speech to have the results of ballots announced and further ballots taken. Once that ballot was completed, he would take up his speech again. This must surely be about the most difficult way to speak to a crowd of 1,700 people. But Douglas was up to almost any speaking challenge. I asked him how he could handle this kind of situation. His answer was, 'It doesn't matter, if it's a piece of baloney it doesn't matter how many times you slice it.'

The four nominated candidates set to work immediately on election planning because we anticipated that there would be a provincial election in June. We were hardly into the campaign when it became clear that there was only one issue – the government's proposal to introduce a comprehensive medical care insurance plan. Four parties contested the election, each with a significant body of support. They were the governing CCF, the Liberals, who were the official Opposition under their new leader Ross Thatcher; the Progressive Conservatives; and the Social Credit Party, which had, surprisingly, elected three members in the 1956 campaign.

It soon emerged that a fifth group, the Saskatchewan College of Physicians and Surgeons, had entered the fray. They were not running any candidates, but they did wage a vitriolic attack against any candidates who supported the idea of a comprehensive medical care insurance plan, 'state medicine,' as the College called it. Since the other three parties were equivocal in their support or opposition to public medical care insurance, the guns of the College were aimed at the CCF candidates. The College spent more money, had more television and radio ads, and generally had more written material than any one of the traditional parties. I have contested eight provincial elections in Saskatchewan and am familiar with the campaigns in three or four more. The 1960 election was the most bitterly contested in my experience. Others were contested with as much vigour, but none was contested with more venom. It was my first campaign and a lively introduction to electoral politics.

The College mobilized some doctors to give public speeches and presentations about the dangers of state medicine. They got some of their election material from the Canadian Medical Association and some, I suspect, from the American Medical Association. They certainly received support from both of those bodies. Some of their material was almost a godsend for my fellow candidates and me. I remember a sample speech they sent out to doctors for possible use on the campaign trail. It contained a passage approximately as follows: 'What will you do when state medicine comes to Saskatchewan. All the local doctors will leave. British doctors will not come. They know from experience about state medicine. You will be left with nothing but the garbage of Europe.'

The College circulated other literature that was equally scurrilous. In a book written in 1973, Ken MacTaggart quoted a College publication as saying, 'A government controlled plan offers a latent but potential threat to certain dogmas and views of the Roman Catholic Church relating to maternity, birth control, and the state.'[1]

---

1 Ken MacTaggart, *The First Decade: The Story of the Birth of Canadian Medicare in Saskatchewan and Its Development during the Following Ten Years* (Toronto: Southam Murray, Canadian Medical Association, 1973), 81.

The College provided a kit to physicians for their use in talking to individuals and groups during the election campaign. It was entitled 'Women and Their Personal Doctor,' and it said this: 'During a woman's change in life, she is subjected to many disturbances which she doesn't understand. She goes to her personal doctor and the doctor will spend whatever time it takes to overcome the situation. It could very easily be that this type of condition must be referred to a psychiatric clinic or a mental hospital, a situation that we as your personal physician would deplore.'

In a province like Saskatchewan, the phrase 'garbage of Europe' was not a happy one. Fewer than half of the people of the province trace their origins to British or French backgrounds. Close to half would, at that time, have had more recent roots in Germany, Ukraine, Poland, Scandinavia, and other continental European countries. I remember taking this speech with me when I spoke at the Ukrainian, Romanian, and Hungarian halls. The College used the slogan 'Political medicine is bad medicine.' My remarks would go something like this: 'The College says that political medicine is bad medicine. I say that public medicine is good medicine. And I say another thing. I say that medical politics is bad politics. Here are some of the things they are saying.' I would then read the passage ending with the quote 'the garbage of Europe.'

The people who filled the Romanian and Ukrainian halls were not amused. If any political group tried to use that sort of language today, the crowd would simply laugh. But in 1960 there was still enough sensitivity to produce a reaction, not of amusement, but of anger. I rather doubt that any local doctors would have used that sort of language in any public speech. But the fact that their out-of-province public relations consultants circulated that material for use was a stain on the campaign waged by the College.

I have always felt that it was entirely improper for the College of Physicians and Surgeons to enter the political fray as it did in 1960. The College of Physicians and Surgeons was and is the statutory licensing body authorized by the legislature to register physicians and to discipline them. All doctors are forced by law to belong to the organization, but not all doctors share the same political views. The political work of the medical profession should be done by bodies like the Saskatchewan Medical Association or the Canadian Medical Association. A doctor does not have to belong to these organizations to lawfully practise his profession. Nonetheless, the College of Physicians and Surgeons used the powers given to it by the legislature – to regulate the medical profession in the public interest – for the purpose of raising money by a levy on all doctors and for waging a highly partisan political campaign.

I have heard no one deny that the Canadian Medical Association made large cash contributions toward the 1960 campaign. It is more difficult to establish the level of assistance from the American Medical Association, but I entertain no doubts about their involvement.

The tenor and tone of the campaign waged by the College in 1960 presaged an even more vigorous and scurrilous campaign waged by the College and its allies in 1962, at the time of the introduction of the medical care plan. I'll have more to say on this later.

Despite the resources mobilized against us in 1960, and the venom that characterized the campaign, the government was re-elected, winning 37 seats out of a total of 55 and taking 40 per cent of the vote in a four-party contest. The CCF regarded the election as a mandate to move forward with medical care insurance.

Minister of Education

Soon after the election Premier Douglas asked me to join the cabinet as minister of education and minister in charge of the Saskatchewan Government Insurance Office.

I understood better than most new candidates how government operated. I had worked in the public service for eight years, and in my job as secretary to the boards of a string of Crown corporations, I had worked closely with the chairpersons of those corporations, all cabinet ministers. My role as minister of education, however, was more foreign to me. As I have noted above, I used to joke that I must be the only minister of education in the recent history of Saskatchewan who had never spent a day of his life in any educational institution in Saskatchewan, either as a student or as a teacher.

I took to my duties with relish. The previous minister, Woodrow Lloyd, was a warm friend, and he wrote me a little note wishing me well. Woodrow was a philosopher of education as well as a practitioner of it and was widely recognized for his erudition, wisdom, and common sense.

I look back on my days at the Department of Education with warm nostalgia. The deputy minister was Allan McCallum, a wise man of many talents. He had a fund of stories and he could sing about forty verses, some of them scatological, of the great party song 'The Ball of Kerrymuir.' He knew Saskatchewan like the back of his hand.

He had field men across Saskatchewan. They were there to help teachers and school trustees deal with the many changes that were coming about, because the province had, in the preceding ten or so years, transformed itself from a province with thousands of little red schoolhouses to a province of consolidated schools operated by elected bodies governing larger school units. The increase in educational opportunities for the students was huge, but so too were the social disruptions, as were the changes in patterns of rural life, which were often centred around the local schoolhouse and the local teacher.

One of the jobs of the field men was to identify any areas of discontent and try to deal with them as rapidly as possible. McCallum's knowledge of his turf was awesome. I can recall delegations of citizens coming to meet with me, usually to protest some decision made by the board of one of the larger school units. McCallum would brief me, advising me who were in the delegation, the general arguments they would raise, and the appropriate response that we might make. Sometimes he even informed me of the likely position that each member of the delegation might take. I have often contrasted this standard of performance with that delivered by some other departments, in which the senior officials seemed to take the view that it was the job of the politicians to deal with the public when they were unhappy with the department's policies, and, indeed, that the politicians should deal in a peremptory way with members of the public who had the temerity to question the wisdom of the policies being pursued by the officials. That was certainly not the McCallum approach.

I attended dozens of school graduations and openings of new schools. Often my wife, Anne, would come with me. We used to chuckle about how she would be greeted in different communities. I remember one school opening where she was greeted effusively, given a bouquet of flowers, and seated on the stage while I was making my remarks. In another community, upon our arrival, I was taken off to meet the members of the board of the larger school unit (all of them male), while she was invited to join the women in the kitchen, where they were preparing lunch to serve to the audience at the completion of the formal ceremonies. Anne was equally at home in either situation.

I went into northern Saskatchewan. In one community in the northeast, children were just beginning to attend school on any regular basis. Up until that time the Indian band to which they belonged were nomads, following the caribou herd north into the Northwest Territories and then back into Saskatchewan. They had no fixed dwellings and no fixed community where they lived. The band was just beginning to have permanent dwellings in a fixed location under circumstances in which children could go to school. One wonders about the cultural changes which those children would have experienced.

A number of other issues arose during my brief period as education minister. One was the then constant of Saskatchewan politics – the Time Question. This is an issue which does not trouble the mind of most Canadians. Growing up in Nova Scotia, I never doubted that we would be on Atlantic standard time except when it moved to Atlantic daylight time during the summer. When I came to Saskatchewan in 1950, I found that the world was not that simple. Saskatchewan straddles the logical boundary line between central standard time and mountain standard time. The railway companies made decisions on which time would be used, and the results were quite remarkable. I could start off on a given day from Regina on central standard time, come to a community which observed mountain time, proceed further north to one which was on central time, and still further north to one which was on mountain time. All the while, I would not have deviated as much as twenty miles off a north-south line. I learned to make all appointments outside Regina by agreeing to meet at, say, two o'clock and specify central time or mountain time.

All this was further complicated by a good deal of reluctance from many communities to observe daylight saving time, which was left to individual local governments to decide. The opportunities for error were formidable. One might wonder what this had to do with the minister of education. A large number of children, some of them quite young, were transported by school bus over poor roads. Particularly in the winter, this meant that children were being transported in the dark. There was a lively difference of opinion in rural Saskatchewan as to whether it was better to start the children off in the morning in the dark, so that there would be more light on the journey home, or, conversely, whether it was better to have some daylight when the children boarded the bus, even if this meant they were transported home in the dark. There were also arguments surrounding whether or not cows observed daylight saving time in their milking patterns. There were clearly no answers to these questions, but this simply added to the vigour of the debate.

Eventually, six or seven years later, people arrived at a new solution. It called for the whole province, except for a few communities on the Alberta border, to go on central standard time (it was called 'fast time') all year round. No one, except the communities on the Alberta border, was to go on daylight saving time. This is the compromise that has endured and that has led to the puzzlement of other Canadians when Saskatchewan people say they do not go on daylight saving time.

Another persistent issue was the matter of closing rural schools. Rural Saskatchewan had undergone a major transformation in the last fifty or sixty years. In 1941 there were 138,713 farms; by 1951 this had dropped to 112,000; by 2001 there were only 50,598 farms. The number of farm families dropped by more than 2,000 per year in the 1940s and by an average of over 1,000 per year later in the century. And generally families came to have fewer children. The boards of the larger school units set up in the 1940s and '50s had to deal with this depopulation. They had to close not only the little red schoolhouses at the country crossroads but also two-, three-, and four-room schools in villages. There were perfectly sound reasons for closures, which convinced everyone except the people in the villages whose schools were being closed. They insisted, with some force, that to close the school would be to doom their village, and they sent their delegations to meet with the successive ministers of education. The ministers had mounted sound and persuasive arguments that persuaded pretty well everybody – everybody but the people in the villages whose schools were being closed.

People in rural Saskatchewan have not been able to arrive at a vision of what they want society to be like in the future, and to have that vision accepted on a continuing basis by the majority of the people. There is a strong nostalgic pull for the old rural Saskatchewan in which there were smaller farms, more farm families, and a nearby village or small town with a school, a skating rink, a curling rink, a hall, the co-op store and, perhaps, other retailers, a machinery dealer or two, a couple of elevators, a credit union, and, in some, a small hospital or nursing home. As citizens, they embrace that nostalgic vision, but as customers they drive past their local stores and dealerships to go to merchants in larger centres for better selection and better deals. As patients, they ignore their local hospitals to get better services in the hospitals in larger centres.

As an aside, I recall a comment at the time some rural hospitals were closed in the 1990s. One local hospital, which was being closed, had a delivery suite for delivering babies. A reporter asked a prominent local citizen whether it would cause any inconvenience to the community not to have these maternity services available. His comment was, 'Not really. I think my daughter was the last child born in that hospital and she has already totalled two cars.' That is a comment not only on the uses of the local hospital but also on the prevailing rites of passage among rural youth.

The elevator companies in rural Saskatchewan have adopted a policy of wholesale consolidation. Decisions about closure of elevators, stores, hospitals, and other services are being made almost wholly based upon considerations of the market or considerations of efficiency and effectiveness in dealing with specific public services such as education and health services.

Nobody is bringing to bear an overall vision of what rural Saskatchewan should be in the decades to come. Nothing very significant will be done or, indeed, can be done unless rural people agree on a broad vision of what they would like to see. As I write this, it is fair to say that rural people are coalescing around the idea that market forces should be allowed to shape the future. This pertains to matters such as elevator location, absentee ownership of farmland, intensive livestock operations, and, in a different sense of the 'market,' location of schools, hospitals, and nursing homes.

One of my duties as minister of education was to be the link between the government and the University of Saskatchewan. Saskatchewan people take great pride in their universities. The provincial government moved quickly after Saskatchewan became a province in 1905 to establish a new university in Saskatoon. Successive provincial governments have had a long and happy relationship with the university. That continued during my years in the Douglas and Lloyd cabinets, and it was a tribute to the sensitivity and sophistication shown by both parties. Later on, in the 1960s, the university experienced growth and some of the ferment that seeped into Canada from the campuses of American universities, fuelled there by opposition to the Vietnam War. Both the Saskatoon and Regina campuses of the university weathered the ferment quite well. Growth, however, was another matter. How this was handled produced some lively controversy when I served as premier in the 1970s. I'll have more to say on this later.

Provincial Treasurer

I became Saskatchewan's provincial treasurer on 7 November 1961 in what was no ordinary cabinet shuffle. It was in that year we lost Tommy Douglas, our incomparable premier, to federal politics.

In the 1958 federal election, John Diefenbaker all but swept the field. That was a traumatic event for the federal CCF. The party dropped from twenty-five seats in 1957 to eight in 1958. Such party stalwarts as M.J.

Coldwell and Stanley Knowles were defeated. The party regrouped in the House of Commons and chose Hazen Argue as house leader.

Throughout the country, our party leaders felt that it was important to change the structure of the CCF. They looked at social democratic parties in other countries, particularly in Britain and Europe, and noted that the parties that were successful generally had links with other popularly based groups in society, particularly the trade union movement. There were efforts under way after 1958 to found a new political party based upon the CCF, but making common cause with the trade union movement and other progressive groups within society. The leaders of the Canadian Labour Congress, under their president, Claude Jodoin, supported the move. There was a huge founding convention in Ottawa in August 1961 characterized by much enthusiasm and a spirited leadership contest. Delegates came from all parts of Canada and I was one.

The leadership contest featured Hazen Argue, the acting federal leader of the CCF and MP for Assiniboia, against Tommy Douglas. Tommy carried the day. I was serving in his cabinet and was a great admirer of his ability to administer but, more importantly, his ability to energize and inspire those who worked with him.

Though we adopted the name New Democratic Party at our national founding convention, the Saskatchewan wing of the party continued to call itself the CCF. We set about to choose a new provincial party leader. The deputy premier, Woodrow Lloyd, had been a cabinet minister since 1944 and was prepared to stand. Olaf Turnbull, an able young man who had first been elected in 1960, opposed him. Olaf was an attractive candidate, still relatively young and with strong leadership credentials in the co-operative movement, but he was no match for Lloyd's experience as a leader in teachers' organizations, in the party, and in the legislature. Woodrow was sworn in as the ninth premier of Saskatchewan on 7 November 1961, and he asked me to take over his old job as provincial treasurer, or finance minister, as the position is known today.

Saskatchewan had encountered enormous financial problems as a province during the 1930s. The Douglas government, when it came to office in 1944, was determined to reverse the provincial government's troubled financial position, and so, when I became provincial treasurer there was a strong tradition of paying our bills (a habit that I had absorbed while working in my father's wholesale business as a young boy). Unfortunately for the people of Saskatchewan, the Conservative government that succeeded us in 1982 ran a string of deficits that averaged more than one billion dollars per year. The 1980s had some difficult years, but so did the CCF-NDP years from 1944 to 1964, and 1971 to 1982.

One of my challenges as provincial treasurer was dealing with the Interprovincial Pipe and Steel Corporation or IPSCO. Bonds provided the bulk of the money for the Regina steel mill, and the government of Saskatchewan guaranteed them. The steel mill had a rocky start, and by 1962 the company could no longer meet its commitments, nor could it borrow more money. IPSCO approached the government of Saskatchewan for a guarantee of their working capital requirements. We agreed, after some agonizing, to guarantee IPSCO's line of credit at the Royal Bank of Canada. Surprisingly the bank declined to lend more money, even with a guarantee from the province. The bank undoubtedly felt that IPSCO's prospects were dubious, and the regional manager said they believed that the money would be lost. The bank would then have to seek recourse against their good customer, the Province of Saskatchewan, and this would damage their relationship with us. I found this to be a strange approach.

I found myself going to Montreal to see Earle McLaughlin, the chairman and CEO of the bank, to make clear to him that we understood the risks we were assuming and wanted them to provide the funds with our guarantee. They eventually agreed to do so. The bank may have been trying to impress upon the government how great they felt the risk was. In the event, IPSCO became very well established and moved up its steel production from its initial one hundred thousand tons per year to its current capacity of well over three million tons, although a large portion of that is produced in the United States. It has recently been sold to foreign buyers for eight billion dollars.

IPSCO was founded and has succeeded in the face of fierce opposition from groups in eastern Canada. Initially, as I have noted, bonds guaranteed by the province financed the mill. By that time, 1960, Saskatchewan had a good credit rating, but despite that, my recollection is that each one of the then big three brokerage houses – Dominion Securities, Wood-Gundy, and Ames & Company – declined to market the bonds. Instead, we found a small broker to market them, but it was clear the Toronto financial community did not welcome IPSCO.

IPSCO has hardly made Regina the Pittsburgh of the Prairies, but it has provided an industry employing about a thousand people directly and many hundreds indirectly in Regina for over forty years. It is a manufacturing success story in which I take a good deal of quiet satisfaction.

It is today, and will continue to be, very difficult to attract secondary manufacturing to Saskatchewan without government assistance. I mean this as a practical and not an ideological statement. Saskatchewan governments of all political stripes have pursued the policy of offering government assistance to major industries (and minor ones, as well). But we must keep our eyes wide open when we are offering assistance.

The major event of my term as provincial treasurer, and one with which I was closely involved, was not primarily a financial issue. It was what followed after the introduction of The Medical Care Insurance Act – the doctors' strike of July 1962.

4

Medicare

The introduction of The Medical Care Insurance Act in the Saskatchewan legislature in 1961 by Premier T.C. Douglas was a momentous day in
the history of medical care insurance in Saskatchewan and Canada. It
was, in some ways, an accident of fate that placed me in the middle of the
action when the battle for publicly financed health care was fought and
won in Saskatchewan, and it is a story that I am proud to relate.

By any standards Thomas Clement Douglas was a remarkable man.
Born in Scotland in 1904, Douglas came to Winnipeg as a small boy with
his father, a tradesman, who was a skilled iron moulder. Douglas had
some health problems as a boy, and it looked as though he would lose a
leg as a result of osteomyelitis. Reportedly it was saved by the intervention of a Winnipeg physician who rendered care on a charity basis. Douglas went on to become a Baptist minister. His first regular charge was in
Weyburn, Saskatchewan, a community in the heart of the wheatlands of
southern Saskatchewan.

He took up his charge in 1930. Weyburn was the home of one of the
two major mental hospitals in Saskatchewan. He interested himself in
the work at the mental hospital, which was later reflected in events during his early years in office when he encouraged groundbreaking work in
the field of mental health.

Douglas immersed himself in the social problems of the community.
Soon he became interested in the new political party based on the principles of democratic socialism, the Co-operative Commonwealth Federation (CCF). He entered politics on behalf of the newly formed CCF and
was elected as an MP in 1935. He returned to Saskatchewan to become
the provincial leader of the CCF, and when that party won a resounding
victory in the provincial election of 1944, he became premier. When he

formed his cabinet, Tommy Douglas kept the health portfolio for himself. There followed a series of initiatives to break new ground in health care insurance.

I've mentioned earlier the settlement of the West and the unique social conditions that this settlement created. I have highlighted the harshness of the physical conditions and the isolation. I sometimes feel that the sense of isolation is the dominant theme in the political and social history of the province, which is only now being overcome by improvements in transportation and communication.

I'll try to sketch some of the forerunners of public medical care.

Precedents in Health Care

In the early days of settlement there were constant difficulties in attracting doctors to serve in smaller communities throughout the province and more difficulty in retaining them. In 1914 a local rural municipal government surrounding the village of Holdfast decided that they would advertise for a doctor and they would pay him a grant out of the taxes raised on the surrounding farmlands. Their legal authority for doing this was doubtful, but they went ahead and in 1915 the rural municipality of Sarnia engaged Dr Henry Schmitt of Illinois as the first municipal doctor in North America. The Saskatchewan legislature passed legislation in 1916 to provide a legal basis for municipal doctors. At first the doctor was simply paid a grant, but by 1919 legislation allowed rural municipalities to engage physicians on a salary. Later changes permitted the option of paying physicians on a fee-for-service basis from public funds.

Over thirty rural municipalities engaged doctors. Reports suggest that doctors were uneasy about being employees of local politicians but appreciated the security of income, particularly during periods when the farm economy was in decline and money was hard to come by.

During the early years of the twentieth century, tuberculosis developed as a major scourge in Saskatchewan. Poverty and overcrowding of large families in small prairie huts favoured development of the disease. Robert G. Ferguson, a young doctor from North Dakota, moved to Canada and was appointed acting superintendent of the new tuberculosis sanatorium at Fort Qu'Appelle in 1917. He was a competent doctor but also an extraordinary communicator. He took the message to all corners of the province that tuberculosis was everybody's problem.

In the words of Dr C. Stuart Houston, '[Ferguson] harnessed the cooperative spirit needed for survival in a new province with poor roads and harsh winters. Rural communities were fertile ground for his persuasive talents. Under his guidance schoolchildren, teachers, nurses, doctors, service clubs, municipalities, and the provincial government cooperated in a costly but seemingly effective effort, unequalled anywhere else on the continent. The aims were to raise money for the Anti-Tuberculosis League and to keep public concern alive.'[1]

Such were Dr Ferguson's gifts that by 1920 The Rural Municipal Act passed by the legislature required each rural municipality to contribute annually to the support of the sanatorium. By 1923 there were travelling TB clinics. By 1925 urban municipalities were required to contribute, and by 1 January 1929 there was universal free diagnosis and treatment of TB. I well remember that when I first came to Saskatchewan, the radio airwaves were filled with announcements of amateur nights to benefit the ACTTBPF. This was in the days before rampant acronyms. Puzzled, I inquired and found out that this mouthful meant Associated Commercial Travellers Tuberculosis Prevention Fund. Even into the 1950s this service club of commercial travellers was supporting the on-going work to eradicate TB. The development of antibiotic drugs has totally changed the face of the battle against TB in Saskatchewan and elsewhere.

Psychiatric Treatment and Research

Groundbreaking research was being carried on at the psychiatric hospital in Weyburn and by other psychiatrists elsewhere in Saskatchewan during the late 1940s and the 1950s. I recall a conversation I had back in the 1950s with Dr Humphrey Osmond, who was conducting experiments at the Weyburn Mental Hospital. There was ferment in the air. The noted British author and scion of a well-known literary family, Aldous Huxley, had been to Saskatchewan talking with people who were conducting experiments to shed further light on how humans perceive reality, and particularly how people suffering from mental illness perceive reality. Out of his visits came his book *The Doors of Perception*. Dr Osmond and his colleagues were using LSD and peyote to induce a mental state – I suppose we would say a temporary psychosis, perhaps similar to that of a patient with schizophrenia – and trying to see what they could learn

---

1 C. Stuart Houston, *Steps on the Road to Medicare* (Montreal and Kingston, ON: McGill-Queen's University Press, 2002), 45.

from that. They were pursuing the hypothesis that there was a chemical basis for schizophrenia – a proposition not fully accepted at that time – and that chemicals might therefore be used to treat schizophrenia and perhaps other mental illnesses.

Within a short number of years these views were conventional wisdom, and these new chemicals – mood-modifying drugs – allowed the treatment and management of many patients with mental illness in new and different ways, many outside of mental hospitals. Most of the patients would be able to live in the community if we could find a way to treat them with the new drugs and to provide for their social needs. But we would continue to need some treatment facilities for acute and for chronic mental illness. So, early in the 1960s, the decision was made that the big mental hospitals could be all but emptied. Then the issue was what would replace them? There soon arose a lively controversy between the advocates of the idea of small free-standing mental health units attached to general hospitals – championed by Dr Sam Lawson, the director of psychiatric services – and the advocates of simply having mental health wards in general hospitals – led by Dr Griff McKerracher, a professor of psychiatry at the University of Saskatchewan.

There was really not much that separated the two views. But, as it seemed to me, a poor lawyer, this did not stop the psychiatrists from waging a rousing battle. In the end, the view favouring wards in general hospitals largely prevailed.

The huge and exciting process, which continued during the 1960s, was the discharge of many hundreds of patients into the community and the setting up of day centres, emergency reaction teams, and the like, to assist these people to maintain themselves in their communities.

Anyone who has ever spent much time at a large mental hospital of the 1950s must applaud the demise of these institutions. They were not all snake pits by any means. But they were all, or almost all, deadening in their uniformity. So, with not a few challenges on how to deal with some hundreds of people who were only minimally able to care for themselves even though they took their medicines, ways were found to provide the help that people needed. The majority managed remarkably well. I suspect that some would have been just as happy in an institutional setting. We in North America are still struggling with issues concerning a small number of patients in nursing homes who have psychiatric problems and who cause difficulties for other residents of the homes. But looking back, we have reason to be proud of our efforts at finding ways to deal with mental illness, not perfectly, but in ways that were a long step forward from the pre-1950s days.

During the 1960s senior people operating psychiatric services for the Saskatchewan government included Drs Fred Grunberg and Hugh Lafave. In about 1980 I was down in the Caribbean talking to some retired mental health staff from the state of New York. They knew Drs Grunberg and Lafave as the people who had led the move to de-institutionalize the New York State mental health system in the 1970s.

An unresolved issue that continues from the 1960s until today is the conflict between the civil rights of mental patients now in the community, and the right of their families and the public to be protected if patients fail to take their medication and as a consequence become violent, as a small number do. Civil rights and patients' rights advocates maintain strongly that state coercion should not be used to restrain any person, mental patient or not, unless and until he or she becomes violent. Citizens should not be incarcerated because of what they might do tomorrow. Nor should they be forced to take medication against their will. So goes this argument. Family members frequently maintain that as soon as a potentially violent patient fails to take prescribed medication, she or he should be taken into temporary custody until the medication is taken, or until it is clear that the patient is not descending into violence. As MLA and then premier in the 1970s, I have heard both sides of this argument put with passion. 'Oh, so we are going to start locking up people who somebody says might someday become violent ...' or 'He is not taking his medication, are you going to wait until he stabs somebody?'

I see very similar issues arise today with respect to the rights and wrongs of laws which allow adolescents addicted to crystal methamphetamines to be apprehended against their will and confined in detoxification units for some days, on the certificate of two physicians.

We all agree that mature people should be free to use their own judgment about what is best for them. We all agree that when a person is in no position to exercise a rational judgment about what is best for them, society should intervene.

We don't agree on just when society should intervene.

There are no satisfactory answers.

Sometimes, when rights collide, all we can do is the best we can do.

Douglas Takes Action

There is no doubt that when Douglas came to office back in 1944, he had a dream of introducing comprehensive health care insurance for the people of Saskatchewan as soon as it could be managed.

In 1945 the government introduced treatment without cost to the patient for cancer care and an air ambulance service to serve the far-flung population of the province. In 1946 a comprehensive medical, dental, and hospital insurance plan was introduced for the Swift Current Health Region, an area with about fifty thousand residents. This was a first for North America on this scale, and the government hoped that it might be a prototype for the whole province.

On 1 January 1947 the government introduced a plan to insure publicly financed hospital care for all citizens of the province. This was another first for North America.

Health care was provided for people on social assistance and for others who were classed as medically indigent. To do this, arrangements were struck with the College of Physicians and Surgeons to provide medical services at agreed fees paid to physicians directly by government.

Douglas had a vision, but he also believed in financial prudence. For people who had lived through the Depression years, the idea of debt carried not only financial but also psychological baggage. Any number of good people had lost farms and homes because they could not make their mortgage payments. Governments had been hobbled in doing the bare essentials because of their unwillingness to default on debt. The province of Alberta defaulted on interest owing on its bonds. In Saskatchewan the cities of Moose Jaw and Prince Albert defaulted. For decades these cities were hampered in their ability to raise money in the financial markets of North America. As Douglas might have put it, he did not wish Saskatchewan to be beholden to the bankers and bond dealers.

So further advances in introducing health care insurance had to wait until the money was found. In the years following 1947, the hospital insurance plan consumed more and more money. As new hospitals were built, and as developments in medical technology surged forward, the standard of hospital care improved rapidly and so did its cost. Try as it might, the Douglas government could not justify making the next leap forward to offer the people of Saskatchewan insurance for physicians' services.

Then the federal government came to the rescue. In April 1957, the St Laurent government had passed legislation promising that the federal government would cover generally 50 per cent of the cost of provincial government hospital insurance plans once they had been introduced by a majority of the provinces representing a majority of the population of Canada. The Progressive Conservatives under John Diefenbaker won a minority government in the federal election of 1957, and in 1958 they were re-elected with a massive majority. Diefenbaker had grown up in

Saskatchewan and had very strong roots in both urban and rural centres in the province. He sensed how important medical care insurance was to people whose lives had been characterized by isolation and vulnerability. He wanted to be part of the march toward comprehensive medical care insurance. In June 1958, the Diefenbaker government passed legislation to allow the federal government to pay half the cost of hospital care insurance provided by any province that met the minimum tests that the federal government set. Saskatchewan easily met the test.

The stage was set. Douglas saw that by 1959 large sums of money would be coming to Saskatchewan to help pay for hospital costs. He and his cabinet colleagues decided to act, and in April 1959 he announced that if the government was re-elected in 1960, it would introduce comprehensive public insurance to cover doctors' fees. He appointed an Advisory Committee on Medical Care, headed by Dr Walter P. Thompson, former president of the University of Saskatchewan. The committee also had representatives from the College of Physicians and Surgeons, the college of medicine at the university, the Saskatchewan Chamber of Commerce, the Saskatchewan Federation of Labour, the provincial government, and the public. The Thompson Committee began its work immediately in an atmosphere of dark suspicion on the part of the representatives of the College of Physicians and Surgeons.

The provincial election of June 1960 occurred before the Thompson Committee completed its report. I well remember that election. It was my first foray into provincial politics. I had been nominated at a hotly contested nominating convention in April 1960. The election was called for June. As I have noted earlier, almost as soon as the campaign started, it was clear that there was only one issue – the government's proposal to introduce medical care insurance. It was bitterly contested, with the College and the Canadian and American medical associations throwing everything they had at us. But we were re-elected decisively, winning 37 seats out of a total of 55. This convincing election victory was the mandate that we required to move forward with medical care insurance.

The government was not able to move decisively until it had received a report from the Thompson Committee. The interim report arrived on 25 September 1961. It included a recommendation for a plan providing universal coverage and a comprehensive range of benefits to be administered by a public commission.

The Thompson Committee's three representatives of the College of Physicians and Surgeons, supported by the Chamber of Commerce member, argued for a policy of all citizens providing their own medical care insurance from private insurers. The government would subsidize people on low incomes to obtain coverage through existing voluntary agencies. It was clear that no one had changed their position on major issues during the months of hearings of the Thompson Committee.

A special session of the Saskatchewan legislature had already been called to deal with changes in the federal Income Tax Act. The government decided to go ahead and, in effect, legislate the recommendations of the majority of the Thompson Committee. The College took the position that they had a right to be consulted about the terms of the legislation and that this had been promised to them. The government felt that no purpose would be served by hearing the College reiterate the position that it had been taking prior to and during the deliberations of the Thompson Committee. All political parties represented in the legislature supported the bill, in principle, on second reading, although the Opposition opposed some details of the bill in committee deliberations. The bill received royal assent on 17 November 1961.

Meanwhile, Tommy Douglas had been selected as the leader of the newly formed federal New Democratic Party. As soon as the legislative session ended, Tommy resigned as leader of the Saskatchewan CCF, and Woodrow Lloyd was chosen to succeed him. In our system of government, when a prime minister or premier resigns, all of the cabinet resigns as well. A cabinet shuffle, great or small, is almost inevitable, and so it was, as I have noted, that I left my post as minister of education and became provincial treasurer.

The Battle Heats Up

There are a number of very good accounts of the battle which ensued during the period between the passing of The Medical Care Insurance Act in November 1961 and the end of the doctors' strike on 28 July 1962. I'll not try to repeat those narratives, but rather to reflect upon this period from my own perspective as someone who was deeply involved.

Our first task was to set up the commission provided for by the Act. The College of Physicians and Surgeons made it clear in public and in private that they would have nothing to do with the commission. As the College president, Dr Harold Dalgleish, put it, 'We have no intention of negotiating on the bill or any part of it, including the commission.' Faced with the College's refusal to co-operate in making the insurance plan work, the government decided to proceed with setting up the Medical Care Insurance Commission without representatives from the College. It included three physicians: Dr Burns Roth, deputy minister of health, Dr O.K. Hjertaas, a distinguished practitioner from Prince Albert, where he had been chief of surgery at each of the city's hospitals, and Dr Sam Wolfe, a member of the faculty of medicine at the province's only medical school. The College nominated none of these men. Other commission members were: Stuart Robertson, secretary of the Swift Current Health Region, which had been operating a medical care insurance plan for more than a dozen years, A.V. Kipling, chairman of the Melfort Health Region, and G.J.D. Taylor, a distinguished Saskatoon lawyer. The chairperson was Donald Tansley, an experienced public servant who had served as deputy provincial treasurer, and as a board member of the Saskatchewan Power Corporation and of the University Hospital. Don had gained a reputation as 'Mr Unflappable.' In later years he went on to have a brilliant career in Ghana representing the Canadian International Development Agency (CIDA), with the International Red Cross in Geneva, and as a deputy minister in the New Brunswick and federal governments.

In June of 1961 Prime Minister Diefenbaker took another step in his moves to be part of the emerging changes in health care insurance by appointing a Royal Commission on Health Services. It was headed by his old friend Mr Justice Emmett Hall of the Supreme Court of Canada, formerly chief justice of Saskatchewan and, still earlier, a leading lawyer in Saskatoon. This Commission had commenced its hearings and was in Saskatchewan in January 1962. The College had an opportunity in its submission to recognize the new realities created by the passage of The Medical Care Insurance Act. It chose to state again its objection to universal, comprehensive, government-administered medical care insurance. To quote a snippet from that submission, 'We cannot agree to render service under the gun.' They went on to say: 'We would however continue to treat our patients in accordance with our capabilities. We would presume that patients presenting receipts of payment would be able to obtain reimbursement from the insurance program.'[2]

I do not think I picked up the full significance of these last words of

2 Saskatchewan, College of Physicians and Surgeons, and Canadian Medical Assoication, *Brief to the Royal Commission on Health Services* (Regina, Saskatchewan, 22 January 1962), 23, §118.

the submission. I was, however, reaching the conclusion that this was the College's game plan. They would continue to practise, submit their bills to the patients, encourage those patients to believe that they would receive full reimbursement, and would thus put public pressure on the government to come up with the type of arrangement favoured by the College.

My cabinet colleagues and I continued to believe that the College would come around to the idea of public medical care insurance. The College's often repeated position was that those who could afford health care insurance should purchase it from private carriers, such as the doctor-sponsored plans Medical Services Incorporated (MSI) and Group Medical Services (GMS). Patients who could not afford the premium would be assisted with the premiums by the government. It did not seem to us such a stretch to have the doctors paid by a government insurer rather than by MSI or GMS. Each of these insurers paid 85 per cent of the unofficial fee schedule established by the medical profession. The government had indicated that it would make the same payment as MSI and GMS were paying.

You may well ask what the dispute was about. During the election of 1960, and the dispute and strike of 1961 and 1962, the College alleged that they feared that a medicare insurance plan would interfere with the way they treated their patients. Some of the more outrageous claims – for example, that the plan would mean the measles could only be treated on Tuesdays and pneumonia on Thursdays, and that everything you told your doctors would be repeated to government officials – could be readily dismissed. But the College was able to convince some of its members that there would be a substantial change in the way doctors treated their patients. Some doctors may have believed these stories, but I doubted, and still doubt, that the leaders of the College believed that such was the case.

It is, of course, possible that insurance arrangements can affect the way doctors and patients interact. There are persistent reports from the United States that some health maintenance organizations (HMOs) act in a very intrusive way in telling doctors, with respect to individual patients being treated, which procedures will and will not be paid for by the insurer. I am not aware of doctors complaining on this score in Canada during the last forty years, and I don't believe that this was a real fear in 1962. We'd had public health care insurance in the Swift Current Health Region since 1946, and had it for cancer patients and some medical indigents for well over ten years.

As I saw it, the way physicians practised medicine was not a genuine issue. The way physicians were paid for their services was a genuine issue. I will return to this point.

There were only desultory contacts made during February and March of 1961, notwithstanding the efforts of the Medical Care Insurance Commission and Bill Davies, the minister of health, to promote a dialogue. Finally the College agreed to meet, and sessions between its representatives and the cabinet were held on March 28, April 1, and April 11. By then tension was rising. The College had raised objections to provisions of the Act which they said threatened professional independence. The premier offered to make substantial changes. The College countered with a proposal that medical care insurance be made available though existing or new voluntary prepaid health agencies, that the government pay the full premium for the medically indigent, to whom charges would be limited, and for all other citizens, the government would pay a flat subsidy and the insurers would set their own premiums.

It was clear that the College was rejecting the heart of the government proposal – the single payer. The dispute could be expressed in terms of a government-operated insurance plan versus privately operated insurance plans. But that does not catch the core of the disagreement, which was this: Are fees charged by physicians to be set by physicians unilaterally, or by negotiation between the physicians or their representatives and patients or their representatives? It would be hard to find insurers agreeing to insure the cost of services if the providers had an unlimited right to set the charges for their services. One cannot imagine automobile insurers agreeing to insure the cost of automobile repairs without the right to negotiate with the repair shops. And if the repair shops had a monopoly on the legal repair of automobiles, as physicians hold on the legal delivery of physicians' services, automobile insurance would be unattainable.

But the College seemed to take the position that the unfettered right to charge whatever they wished for their services was an essential part of professional independence. That became the nub of the dispute. After the failure of our late March, early April meetings, I became convinced that we could reach no agreement with the College consistent with the basic principles of the Act passed by the legislature. I was also firm in my belief that when an issue is presented in clear terms to the electorate in an election, when as a result of that election a legislature is elected, and when that legislature enacts legislation to put into effect the policy presented to the electorate, the voters have a right to see that legislation put

into effect regardless of the opposition of a small group, however powerful. The College had had many opportunities to present its point of view.
But at no time, either before or after the passage of the Act, did it indicate any willingness to negotiate within the general principles that had
been recommended by the Thompson Committee and incorporated
into the Act.

My colleagues and I considered our position after the failure of the
'summit' talks. It was clear that we had an obligation to preserve the
essence of the Act and to protect the public against unreasonable medical bills. We also wanted to head off the political pressure that would
arise if doctors billed their patients and the patients submitted their bills
for reimbursement. If our reimbursement had to cover whatever was
billed, there would be no limit to the amount of money to be paid to
doctors by taxpayers. If our reimbursement did not cover the whole bill,
patients would be concerned about who would pay the remaining
amount. It would not be what we had hoped for and promised. We
accordingly acted to put the Medical Care Insurance Commission in the
same position as other insurers, and, incidentally, the same as that of
MSI and GMS. Amendments to the Act were introduced to make clear
that the Commission could represent patients in disputes over the fair
value of medical fees. It did not prevent doctors and patients from making agreements on fees. It simply provided that where no agreement was
made, the Commission could represent the patient in arriving at the
fair value of the service rendered. The Workers Compensation Board,
under which physicians in Saskatchewan had rendered services and
been paid for a generation, had a provision to the same effect. The legislation was introduced and passed – over the vehement objection of the
College.

I argued to my colleagues that we should take this step. I think that we
knew that the doctors would be upset. But upset or not, we had not seen
any indication that anything we did would induce the College to co-operate with the public plan as it had been outlined in legislation. The fat was
in the fire. The College called an emergency meeting of all members for
May 3rd in Regina. Premier Lloyd asked for an opportunity to speak to
them. Woodrow knew that the doctors would be hostile, but he was
determined to try to provide a calm, rational statement of the government's position. He wanted an opportunity to show that the plan would
meet the objectives of both the profession and the public. I think that
he wanted to feel that he had done everything possible to avoid a confrontation. Woodrow had a faith, perhaps more admirable than well

founded, that people were essentially decent and fair-minded, and that if
you treated them in a calm and rational way, they would respond in kind.

I had some sense of how he felt. My own family doctor, Boris Mesbur
in Regina, arranged a meeting of the Regina District Medical Society and
asked me to speak. I took the same tack as Woodrow, although I was
probably more argumentative, a legacy of my legal training. I could not
overcome the doctors' suspicion that they were dealing with a mono-
lithic wickedness called government. I tried to explain that there were
different points of view in government and that compromise was the
order of the day. My meeting was polite, cool, and pointless.

Woodrow's task at the meeting of May 3rd was made more difficult by
the actions of our colleague Walter Erb. He had been minister of health
when Tommy Douglas left for Ottawa. There had been grumbling in the
caucus and party about his performance and, in particular, about the
slow progress of the Thompson Committee and the drafting of legislation for medicare insurance. Mr Erb was not forceful in dealing with the
College, although I'm not sure it would have made any difference to
have a minister of a different temperament. When Woodrow became
premier and shuffled his cabinet, Mr Erb was switched to public works,
and Bill Davies became minister of health. He was an old trade union
negotiator, well spoken and suave, and was perhaps better fitted to navigate the troubled waters that seemed to be emerging in our launch of
the medical care plan. At any rate, reports had it that Mr Erb was not
happy with the switch. As I was to learn later, it is not possible to please
everyone when crafting a cabinet.

As the doctors became more militant, we began hearing rumours that
Mr Erb was unhappy with the government's approach. In March, at one
of our many cabinet meetings on the looming medicare crisis, the minister of agriculture, Toby Nollett, and I cornered Mr Erb in the premier's
office next to the cabinet room. There were just the three of us present.
We put directly to him that we had heard rumours that he was thinking
of leaving cabinet and caucus. Was there any truth to the rumours? We
got from him a clear and categorical denial, so that Toby and I were satisfied. We should not have been. A few weeks later, as the tension
mounted between the College and us, the premier was scheduled to
meet and address the assembled doctors on May 3rd. That morning,
without any prior contact with Premier Lloyd, Mr Erb slipped under the
door of the premier's office his written resignation from the cabinet and
caucus. He would sit in the legislature as an independent. Mr Erb immediately gave the news to the media and it was widely broadcast. That

served to boost the spirits of the hundreds of assembled doctors and made the atmosphere much more difficult for Woodrow's speech.

I felt that it was a despicable thing to do and a sharp departure from the minimum courtesy that Walter Erb owed to his colleagues. There are times when you have to part company with your colleagues. But you do it with dignity and not in a way that causes embarrassment. Mr Erb may have felt that he had grounds for taking such an action, but he had no grounds for doing so in a way that was clearly disrespectful and discourteous to his leader and his colleagues and designed to embarrass them. There are standards of decent conduct, and in my view, he transgressed them.

Doctors attending the May 3rd meeting passed resolutions advising the government that if the Act was implemented on July 1st, as had been announced, the doctors would withdraw their services. They advised that only the repeal of the Act would convince them of the government's true intention to meet their concerns. It was widely recognized that the government and the College were on a collision course. From this day in May through to the end of July, the medicare dispute consumed public discourse in the province. The government began to plan in earnest for the eventuality of a doctors' strike. There had never been a full-blown strike of doctors in North America, but that didn't mean it couldn't happen.

Planning for a Strike

We took steps to see if doctors could be recruited in Britain and Ireland. There was good reason for this. Provincial law provided that doctors who were qualified to practise in the United Kingdom and Ireland were entitled to be registered to practise in Saskatchewan upon submitting proof of their standing. The College had no authority to require proof of where they had trained and what courses they had completed. On the other hand, doctors who were qualified to practise in the United States who applied to practise in Saskatchewan could be required to produce details of their education, their experience, and other relevant material so that the College could determine their fitness to practise. We anticipated that even if we could have recruited the top medical staff of the Mayo Clinic in Rochester, Minnesota, the College would have taken a month or two to check their fitness to practise medicine in Saskatchewan.

So we concentrated our efforts in Britain and Ireland. We ran ads in British journals, particularly the medical publication *Lancet*. We conducted interviews at Saskatchewan House, the province's diplomatic headquarters on Chester Street in London. A number of doctors expressed a willingness to come to help if there was a strike. Clearly many felt that this would not happen – full-blown doctors' strikes just did not happen.

We went further. We arranged for teams of doctors who practised at the Steelworkers union clinic in Pittsburgh and the Auto Workers union clinic in Detroit to come to Saskatchewan should there be a total withdrawal of services. They would not be legally qualified to practise in the province, but if there was a total withdrawal of services by our local doctors, we didn't think there would be many quibbles about whether these highly trained and experienced doctors could practise, even if they had not been cleared with the College. But this was a back-up position. As it turned out, we did not need to use their services. Meanwhile the storm clouds were gathering. It was beginning to seep into the consciousness of the government, the doctors, the media, and the public that there could be a doctors' strike. Hospitals and the hospital association became alarmed. Local governments, heavily involved as they were with hospitals, also showed great concern. Traditional political opponents of the government, headed by the Opposition Liberals, began to see public concern as a way to embarrass the government.

The cabinet and cabinet committees met with groups on an almost daily basis. We adopted a war-cabinet mode. Bill Davies, the minister of health, along with the Medical Care Insurance Commission, was responsible for keeping the system operating and for recruiting overseas doctors. The premier and most of the rest of us met with the many delegations, exploring all the avenues, however unpromising, for a possible compromise.

My role was to devise defences against possible attacks on the legal front. This was not so fanciful a role as it might now seem. Saskatchewan had a lieutenant-governor, Mr F.L. Bastedo, who had less than a full understanding of his constitutional role. He had been appointed in 1958, and on more than one occasion he declined to sign an order-in-council because he did not agree with the policy set out in it. Rather than make an issue of this surprising conduct, we would try to find a time when he was not available. We would then take the order (and others) to the administrator, a person who acts as a sort of deputy lieutenant-governor. That administrator was Chief Justice Ted Culliton. He had a full appreciation of his role, having been a cabinet minister in the Liberal government of Premier William Patterson. Mr Bastedo declined in 1961 to give royal assent to a bill passed by the legislature, The Mineral Contracts Alterations Act, because he did not like the terms of the bill. We speculated that he felt it was unfair to major oil companies, some of whom had been his clients when he was in private practice in Regina. He reserved the bill for the consideration of Canada's governor general, and he did so without any instructions from Ottawa. It was wholly improper, in a constitutional sense, for the lieutenant-governor, acting on his own initiative, to so reserve the bill. It would probably have been improper for the federal government to have purported to provide any such instructions, since the power of disallowance has fallen into disuse. We responded as if the lieutenant-governor was acting on instructions from Ottawa, and we hoped to make an issue of it. We were clearly on the side of the angels. The Ottawa government saw the issue the same way. They moved with unaccustomed alacrity in giving assent to the bill, thus nullifying Mr Bastedo's action.

With this background, the cabinet considered the possibility that the lieutenant-governor might attempt to dismiss the government and call an election. There was clearly no basis for such an action, and it would have been grossly improper for the lieutenant-governor to attempt to do so, but we were not at all sure that this would stop him from proceeding in an unconstitutional manner.

We wondered whether the rising paranoia was beginning to get to us. However, that our fears were not wholly fanciful was underlined a year later. When The Medical Care Insurance Act was passed and a premium was payable by all residents, the lieutenant-governor declined to pay his premium. C.S. Davis, a judge of the Court of Queen's Bench, similarly declined. Their argument, as I understood it, was that they were employees of the federal government and therefore not required to pay the medicare premium. This argument had no merit, and our attorney general felt that he should prosecute one or both to establish the point. He was persuaded to speak first to the federal minister of justice, then the Honourable E. Davie Fulton. Matters proceeded apace in Ottawa, and each of the delinquents paid the premium in short order.

We suspected that some of the judges were strongly opposed to the Act. We feared that some group would apply to the courts to strike it down or delay its implementation. We were confident that the Act was valid in all respects, but with a little judge shopping, a group could have initial success. To deal with this possibility, we drafted, but did not pass, an Order-in-Council under the authority of The Health Services Act which would have put back into law the basic structure of the insurance plan. I don't know whether it would have worked long enough for us to appeal a rogue decision by a Queen's Bench judge, but it might have. Fortunately we never had to find out.

The public was being mobilized to support the doctors and oppose the government. People who were prominent supporters of the Liberal Party created an organization called the Keep Our Doctors Committee – the KOD. A smaller group, primarily Conservatives, founded a Save Our Saskatchewan Committee, the SOS. There were public meetings, radio, TV, and newspaper ads, and letter writing campaigns – the whole bag of tools of a well-organized and well-financed public relations campaign. The focus of the campaign was that the doctors would stop practising if the Act came into effect on July 1st, and that then doctors would leave the province. The slogan was, 'You are going to lose your doctor,' and many people became alarmed. Premier Lloyd discouraged the organization of counter meetings and rallies to support medicare. He felt, I think rightly, that this would only inflame the already poisoned atmosphere. In any case, we could not have put our position through the press. No daily paper supported the government. Of the several dozen weeklies, I recall only two that supported medicare, the *Wakaw Recorder* and the *Prairie Messenger*, a publication of the Benedictine monks at St Peter's Abbey near Humboldt.

The tension rose. At this point there was a federal election on June 18th. In Saskatchewan the unarticulated election issue was 'Do you support the CCF-NDP and their medicare plan or not?' Tommy Douglas, the new leader of the federal NDP, was our party's candidate in Regina. The Conservatives under John Diefenbaker had the best chance to defeat Douglas. So lifelong Liberals were active in the support of the Tory candidate, Ken More, a decent man of no particular distinction. A well-established campaign practice at the time was to have a parade of vehicles, replete with banners and signs, through the downtown of Regina. I have watched many and ridden in many. As a sitting Regina cabinet minister, I rode in Tommy's June 1962 parade. The weather was sunny and warm, but everything else was very cool, when it wasn't hostile. There were long stretches of total silence. It was eerie, and all but shouted, 'Tommy we love you, but we can't support you this time.' And they did not support him. He received less than 29 per cent of the vote.

I remember well the rally after the polls closed and the results became known at the Tommy Douglas 'victory' headquarters. It was a small and subdued affair. I've never seen Tommy more magnificent when, after thanking his supporters for their work under difficult circumstances, he closed with his now oft-quoted words: "'Fight on my men," said Sir Andrew Barton. "I am hurt but I am not slain, I'll lay me down and bleed awhile and then I'll rise, and fight again."'

Tommy Douglas, partly by skilled artifice and partly because of the essential spirit of the man, never failed to inspire.

The federal election confirmed that our medicare plan was in deep trouble with the public. And this is hardly surprising, considering the way the media was operating. The *Regina Leader Post* and the *Saskatoon Star Phoenix* abandoned all semblance of reporting the news impartially and campaigned in editorials and in news columns against the medicare plan. After the crisis was over, I wrote an article on this press coverage, which was published in a 1964 issue of *Queen's Quarterly*, the quarterly put out by Queen's University in Kingston, Ontario.

The public was becoming increasingly alarmed, and we were losing the public relations war. The government made a major concession. We passed an Order-in-Council providing that the doctors could practise in the ordinary way and bill their patients privately (which was true in any case), and that the patient could be reimbursed from the plan the amount provided in the plan's payment schedule for doctors. This would have allowed practice to continue uninterrupted, allowed doctors to charge any fees they wanted, and effectively allowed them to collect scheduled amounts from the plan without agreeing that such payments would be payments in full. The government would then be under continued public pressure to meet any increases in fees that doctors might care to impose.

It was a last-ditch attempt to avoid a strike, and an unusual one. Fortunately for the government and, I would say, for the people of Canada, the doctors were so confident of complete victory that they failed to take up the new offer. They decided to stay the course.

5

The Doctors' Strike, Its Aftermath, and Some Current Issues

July 1st dawned warm and sunny. By July 2nd it was clear that the great majority of doctors had stopped practising. Perhaps 150 doctors in private practice remained on duty, and they were practising without fees as an emergency service operated by the College. A handful of hospitals remained in operation. The other hospitals sent their patients home or transferred them to the hospitals remaining open. Stories of people travelling long distances for care began to emerge. The death of a child was (questionably) attributed to the strike. Tensions continued to rise. There was an expectation among many that the strike would be a three-day wonder. I was not among them. I couldn't see the basis of a quick settlement. The doctors were very confident that they had the public's support. They were right. We felt very strongly that the government had a mandate to bring in the plan, that it was a good plan, that it would work and work well, and that we were not about to concede defeat to a small group, however well meaning some of them may have been. Premier Lloyd was a very reasonable but very determined man, and so were most of his colleagues.

The KOD swung into action, holding rallies throughout the province. In Regina, a campaign was mounted to telephone cabinet ministers. The calls were made at all hours of the day and night. The KOD published our telephone numbers in the press, which ran them prominently. Each morning we turned on the radio to see what horror story we would have to deal with when we got to the office. It was an exhilarating time but a stressful one.

The strike soon became an international news phenomenon. Reporters poured into Regina from all over the world. There were skilled reporters from major London, New York, Washington, Los Angeles, and

Boston dailies, as well as reporters for electronic media and all major Canadian news outlets. We had two press conferences a day to feed the voracious demand for news. As I've noted, after the crisis was over, I wrote an article on the press coverage, published in the *Queen's Quarterly*. During the period commencing 30 June 1962 and ending on July 26th, when the strike was effectively over, the *Toronto Star* provided blanket coverage. They began with a story on June 30 titled 'Fear and Hate Fill Saskatchewan on the Eve of Doctors' Strike.' Up to July 26th, they published over 175 items. Other papers gave the story heavy coverage as well. The *New York Times* published about 25 items, the Australian *Melbourne Herald*, 11, the *London Times*, 18, while British television ran 38 items, all within twenty-six days.

A few days into July, two subtle changes began to take place. The first was that the outside media noted there were two strikes taking place – the one they were covering and the one being reported by the Saskatchewan media. Outside media began to report, in particular, on the performance of the *Regina Leader Post* and the *Saskatoon Star Phoenix*, and these two papers became defensive. They began to contend that a specialized health reporter from, say, the *Washington Post* did not understand the underlying issues involved. For the *Leader Post*, hardly recognized as a world leader in journalism, to chide the reporters from the *Washington Post* or the *New York Times* as unable to grasp the issues and report effectively was not a promising line of argument. And so the *Leader Post* and *Star Phoenix* were forced to rein in their worst excesses.

The second change was a shift from talking about the medical care insurance plan to talking about the legitimacy of a strike by doctors as a means of opposing a law passed by a legislature after an election in which the plan was the major issue. Such prominent medical journals as the *Lancet* in Britain questioned the ethics of a doctors' strike in these circumstances. Saskatchewan striking doctors began to feel the heat. I always suspected that a good number of them were uncomfortable with the strike, particularly when the days grew into weeks. The city specialists were still resolute. The rural general practitioners were much less so.

It is not easy to pinpoint when the tide turned. I believe the change came with one of the many speeches given by the Reverend Athol Murray, a fierce opponent of the plan. He called on the government to withdraw the Act, and if they did not, he thundered, 'There will be blood running in the streets, and God help us if it doesn't.'

When I heard these words repeated on the radio, I remember thinking, 'That does it. People are angry about the medicare plan, but they're

not calling for blood to run in the streets. The KOD has overreached.'
And so it proved to be. The great KOD rally on July 11th in front of the
Legislative Building was a relatively sedate affair, with fewer than five
thousand people. Predictions had been for several times that number.

British doctors began to flow in and set up practices where doctors
were on strike. In many communities, including Saskatoon, Regina, and
Prince Albert, patient-sponsored community clinics were organized and
began to attract large patient lists. In Prince Albert, Orville Hjertaas was
a prominent doctor who had been chief of surgery at each of the city's
two hospitals. He supported the medical care plan, but after July 1st Dr
Hjertaas could perform no surgery since no doctor in the city would
agree to assist him. He lost no time in heading up a community clinic
and getting doctors from outside Saskatchewan to assist him. It was not
many years before the number of doctors practising at the Hjertaas clinic
was equal to all other doctors in private practice in Prince Albert. So far
as the strike was concerned, it was clear in Prince Albert that there would
be medical services available, and there was soon a group of doctors
ready to serve their patients.

It is also fair to say that the emergency services provided by physicians
organized by the College at major hospitals throughout the province
were seen to be reasonably adequate.

The panic among the public seemed to be subsiding. And the pressure on the profession seemed to be increasing. In retrospect, I believe
that the College was concluding that it could not keep its troops in line.
For whatever reason, the College made a crucial move. In mid-July, the
CCF was holding its annual convention in Saskatoon, with hundreds of
delegates in attendance. Dr Harold Dalgleish, the president of the College, asked if he could address the delegates. Shorn of the verbiage in
which it was wrapped, Dr Dalgleish's speech was a call for the reopening
of negotiations, without any requirement that the Act be withdrawn.
Unless there was a trap, which we suspected but could not detect, the
College was suing for peace. We were, of course, delighted, but reluctant
to accept what we thought we were hearing.

And then a curious thing happened.

A new player emerged: Stephen, Lord Taylor. He was a British physician and life peer appointed to the House of Lords in Britain by the
Labour government of Clement Attlee. Taylor had spent a brief time in
Saskatchewan in 1946 and was known to Graham Spry, Saskatchewan's
astute agent general in London. At the suggestion of national leaders of
the freshly minted New Democratic Party, Premier Lloyd contacted Lord

Taylor and asked him to become a special adviser to the government on the medicare dispute. He agreed to come but was unable to leave London until July 16th. So he arrived in Saskatchewan at just about the time that Premier Lloyd was addressing the provincial convention on the morning of July 18th. Dr Dalgleish spoke on the afternoon of the same day.

Much to the surprise of both the government and the College, Lord Taylor made it clear that he was going to act as a mediator between the two sides. As he moved into the centre of negotiations, it is hard to know whether the musical fanfare should have been 'Hail the Conquering Hero' or 'Send in the Clowns.' He was at the convention to hear Dr Dalgleish speak and then went over to the College's headquarters in the Medical Arts Clinic to meet with their council. He was very skilful in getting the College to consider what it could salvage out of the dispute, and in having it focus on issues that the government could concede. The College had been steadfast in pushing for an insurance system in which the government would subsidize, for low income families, premiums charged by two doctor-sponsored private insurers – MSI and GMS. All others would pay their own way. I believe that the College harboured the hope that a future government could be persuaded to go their route, and accordingly the College was anxious for MSI and GMS to have a role, however nominal, so long as it kept the organizations intact. We saw no useful role for MSI or GMS but were willing to consider a role as a concession to work toward a settlement. Taylor convinced the College that he could wring this concession out of the government.

Lord Taylor shuttled back and forth between the Medical Arts Clinic (the College's headquarters) and the Bessborough Hotel, where the convention was occurring and where members of the cabinet were staying. With appropriate fanfare, Taylor had himself driven the two blocks between the clinic and the hotel and had his car parked in the 'No Parking' zone at the hotel's entrance, with a blank piece of House of Lords stationery tucked under the windshield wiper.

Lord Taylor's negotiation tactics involved histrionics worthy of a Shakespearian actor playing Mark Antony. But they were effective at a time when it is not clear what else would have worked. Perhaps the best reflection of Taylor's role can be found in a brief comment by College president Dr Dalgleish to Al Johnson, deputy provincial treasurer and a key government player. In his book *Dream No Little Dreams*, Johnson reports Dalgleish as saying to him, 'Al, what is it with this man Taylor? You guys didn't invite him as a mediator and we certainly didn't. Yet now when we won't agree with him on a particular proposal he threatens to go home and we find ourselves begging him to stay on.'

Taylor worked his magic, and an agreement was reached and signed on July 23rd. Some changes were made in the legislation, changes which we regarded as cosmetic. We agreed to remove the provisions we had inserted in April giving the Commission the right to bargain for patients. They had served their purpose since the Act provided that, in general, fees would be bargained and that the agreed fees had to be accepted as payment in full. We agreed to a role for MSI and GMS. I regarded the settlement as a substantial victory, except for the provisions that allowed doctors to bill patients directly, with patients having the right to claim reimbursement. That never proved to be a problem. Perhaps I had overestimated the danger of this provision.

The Aftermath

The Saskatoon agreement of 23 July 1962 ended the immediate medicare dispute, and a subsequent session of the legislature made minor changes to the Act. The amendments received royal assent on 2 August 1962. After a brief respite to catch our breath, the government reorganized to tackle the unresolved problems from the dispute, and other business that had been set aside while the government and much of the province were consumed by the dispute and the strike during May, June, and July. Premier Lloyd reorganized the cabinet and I became minister of health on 7 September 1962, my thirty-seventh birthday.

My work in this portfolio was to deal with the bitterness and, as I would contend, the obstruction of many in the medical profession who had not yet adjusted to the fact that a government-administered medical care insurance plan was a fact they had to live with.

Two major matters left unresolved by the Saskatoon agreement were the treatment of insured services in radiology and pathology (X-ray and laboratory services). The other problems were those of harassment surrounding hospital privileges. The Saskatoon agreement made clear that there was to be no retaliation either way against doctors who had a position for or against the introduction of the medical care plan.

During the strike such retaliation had been obvious and severe. It occurred in the case of Dr Hjertaas in Prince Albert, but in other centres as well. A classic case surrounded the Regina General Hospital. Highly competent doctors who had come to Regina to assist during the strike were unable to obtain hospital privileges. The government appointed a royal commission headed by Mr Justice Mervyn Woods to examine various allegations of discrimination. His report left no doubt that doctors were taking retaliatory measures against physicians who had supported the introduction of the medical care plan.

Uglier manifestations were allegations of improper practice levelled against some of the doctors who had come to Saskatchewan during the strike and who had remained. None of these allegations was ever substantiated, but the fact that the College proceeded to investigate and in some cases prosecute them placed a great stress on doctors who had supported the introduction of the plan.

Time proved to be the only medicine that brought a cure for these unprofessional activities by some members of the medical profession.

We in the government in 1962 believed that we had won a huge victory. We had introduced as law, publicly administered, comprehensive, universal medical care on a single-payer model over the determined objection of the organized medical profession. It was a great tribute to Tommy Douglas, who had pioneered its legislation, and Woodrow Lloyd, who had brought it to reality against tough opposition. Once established in Saskatchewan, it quickly spread across Canada. For Canadians, medicare, pioneered in Saskatchewan, has become a badge of our common citizenship.

In recent years Canadian political discourse is often about the 'crisis' in medicare. I don't accept this description of the issue. I can hardly recall a time when the media did not assert that medicare was in crisis. Yet by almost any standard, health care has slowly (and sometimes not so slowly) improved over the last forty years. We do well. A large group of people have a substantial interest in having more money spent on health care. So we may confidently expect that 'crises' will continue to be reported. A healthy scepticism is indicated.

I do not wish to downplay the real issues faced by our provincial health plans in providing high-quality timely care. There are problems and real problems. In any country where health care is provided without cost, or at nominal cost, to the patient at the time of delivery of the service, there is a problem of limiting the demand for service. To use the language of the economists, when health care is a 'free good,' and when demand can be initiated by both the health care provider and by the patient, the demand for services can be very great. It can be very nearly infinite. Clearly, demand must be limited.

Demand for health care services can be limited the same way as the demand for, say, potatoes is limited – by putting a price on the service. Those who are unwilling or unable to pay will not demand the service. Demand can be reduced to match supply. This is rationing by price – by using the same market forces that govern the price of potatoes.

Demand for services can also be limited by limiting the supply. If the number of hospital beds is limited, clearly the demand will be limited or, at least, not satisfied. If there are a limited number of doctors, the use of doctors' services will be restricted. The belief is that if the supply is limited, the people who operate the health care system will restrict access by serving only those with the greatest medical need. This is rationing by limiting supply and by using the resources to meet the most pressing medical need.

Some countries combine these two systems. They operate a general system for all people by using a limited supply of hospitals, doctors, nurses, and other providers. People of means who are unwilling to accept the inevitable delays in getting services, and sometimes the denial of services inherent in any system of rationing by limiting supply, are permitted to purchase services outside the public system on the basis of rationing by price. This two-tier, safety-valve system can be made to work with the goodwill of the providers and the patients.

But there are significant dangers in this two-tier approach. Very often the advocates of a private system want, not a separate private system, but rather a gloss on the basic public system. They wish to use hospitals paid for by the public and being fully used in the public system. They wish to use doctors, nurses, and other health care providers trained in public universities and used in the public system. The separate private system, so described, does not increase resources. It simply allows people willing and able to pay for services to receive services ahead of other people with greater medical need. This means that there are fewer resources for the public system and supply becomes less adequate.

In many parts of Canada, people can access a private system by going to the United States and obtaining private care. Comparatively few people do so because of cost and perhaps inconvenience, although in many parts of Canada going to the United States for health services is no more difficult than the trip to the next major centre that is the lot of millions of Canadians. This seems to suggest that many of the people who call for a private health system in fact seek a public health system with some private attributes that allow them to get priority treatment largely paid for from the public purse.

Another method of rationing is appearing in the United States. This is a method used by the health maintenance organizations (HMOs), which typically provide medical and hospital care at prices bargained with employers. The HMOs appoint adjusters, who must approve in advance major surgical and medical procedures proposed by attending physicians and surgeons. The adjusters are cost-conscious, accountant-type persons, and medical people frequently resent their interventions.

Yet there is the germ of an idea here. Our system, which pits virtually unlimited demand against limited supply, generates its own resentments among patients and providers alike. It would be helped if providers, particularly physicians, could be persuaded that the long-term interests of health care would best be served by physicians consciously developing a dual loyalty – first to their patients and secondly to the health insurance system, to protect it from demands of marginal utility. But I don't underestimate the difficulties of such a proposal. The training of physicians is heavily oriented to the idea that their overarching duty is to their patient. If a patient might, on balance, benefit from another test or another procedure, physicians may well feel that they should proceed in that direction and let the politicians and public servants figure out how to pay for it. And that is not all bad. As an individual, if I need medical attention, there is much to be said for having a physician who is my unquestioned champion and advocate, with no divided loyalties.

So some difficult, indeed sometimes nasty, choices must be made.

The easy course of action is simply to call for more public money to be spent. And certainly that can be done. As a percentage of our total incomes – or gross national product, to use the language of economists – our spending is high, but by no means the highest in the world. But I cannot feel that simply spending more will deal with the issue of controlling demand of a free good. Nor do I think that we as a society should spend very much more on health care. The money would be better spent on other determinants of health: things like affordable housing; the difficult task of dealing more effectively with preventable conditions such as fetal alcohol syndrome, addictions, and the like.

The more difficult course of action is to seek other ways to control demand. The Canada Health Council offers some prospects in certain areas.

I have sometimes suggested facetiously that the Canadian government should acquire a few hospitals in communities in the United States close to the Canadian border. Transport arrangements might even be added.

The hospitals would operate with professional and non-professional staff trained elsewhere than in Canada and would operate on a cost-recovery basis to cover both capital and operating costs. This would be clearly identifiable as health care without a substantial public component – private health care – and should satisfy the frequent calls for this service. I'm not sure it would do so.

There are sometimes calls for health care premiums. I believe this to be largely irrelevant. Public health care must be paid for by taxes. Health care premiums are nothing more than a specific tax. Which tax is chosen to finance health care raises considerations of over-all tax fairness that cannot be sensibly considered by discussing one tax only. Nor is there any evidence that the demands for health services are in any way affected by whether or not a specific health care premium or tax is levied.

It is sometimes suggested that there should be premiums of varying amounts based upon ability to pay. We already have an income tax system based upon ability to pay. It is not easy to understand the benefit of another parallel system based upon some other test of ability to pay. There are almost endless variations on the theme that we can find another label for a tax so as to make it more acceptable. One variation is to adjust the amount of premium or tax depending upon the amount of insured services used – an after-the-event user fee. A plan to levy higher taxes on the sick does not, at first glance, appear promising. More details would need to be known to make any rational judgment on such a proposal.

When services such as health care are paid for out of general revenues, taxes paid by corporations, either as income taxes or sales taxes, are usually thought of as a source of money. When services are paid for out of health care premiums, there is usually little consideration given to levying premiums on corporations.

In general I have found that in matters of tax, tax incidence (that is, who really pays), and tax fairness, the devil is in the details. A specific proposal needs to be examined. But as I suggested earlier, the question of what tax should be used to pay for health care is a very much less pressing matter than the question of limiting the demand for health care and making sure that we do not spend large amounts on health care of only marginal value. This money is needed for much more important spending: to improve overall health and spending outside the health care system, to improve our overall well-being, and to make sure that governments spend our money in pursuit of the objective of fair shares for all in a free society.

6

Politics 1964 to 1971

We went into the 1964 election expecting that we would win. We simply had not appreciated the extent to which the medicare dispute had polarized opinion in Saskatchewan. We had won the medicare battle; the medicare plan was working and working well. The Opposition would not have dared to suggest that they would dismantle the Medical Care Insurance Plan. Nonetheless, there were many people who had been bruised by the battle. A further factor was that the medical care dispute had consumed an enormous amount of the energy and creativity of the government and its members. We were simply not up to our normal and needed fighting trim.

In addition to this, Ross Thatcher had done an efficient job of gathering support for the Liberal Party from many who had supported the Social Credit Party in the 1960 election. Between 1960 and 1964, in percentage of the total vote, the Conservative vote increased only modestly from 13.9 per cent to 18.9 per cent, the Social Credit declined sharply from 12.3 per cent to .39 per cent. The Liberal vote went up from 32.7 per cent to 40.4 per cent, and the CCF vote went down slightly from 40.8 per cent to 40.3 per cent. Popular vote aside, the Liberals got 32 seats to 25 for the CCF; one Conservative was elected.

The new government of Ross Thatcher was sworn in on 22 May 1964. I had served my first term in the legislature and had retained my seat in Regina, but I asked myself: 'Is this it or do I move on to another province and pursue a career in law?' But I don't remember being much troubled. I recognized that I was hooked and that politics was a fulfilling way to spend my life. I had retained my seat in Regina, the two-member seat of Regina West, but needless to say I was no longer a minister. The pay as an MLA was modest, indeed meagre, and this had to be supplemented. I needed to find some additional employment, and I chose to go into legal practice. Within three or four months, I had formed a partnership with Jim Griffin and John Beke under the firm name of Griffin Blakeney Beke. Griffin was an experienced trial lawyer, and Beke was just back from earning his doctor of jurisprudence degree at the University of Michigan. We were congenial partners. We did not prosper greatly, but we had lots of business and made a comfortable living.

In the 1960s, Regina was a pleasant place to practise law. The lawyers wanted to represent their clients effectively but did not wish to take advantage of every slip by a fellow practitioner. At an early stage, I was taken aside and advised of the small number of lawyers who would, as the phrase went, 'pull the rules.' Others would tactfully let you know when you had made a procedural error and expected you to do the same. As an example, if my pleadings were defective and another lawyer could move to have a particular paragraph struck out, and if he knew that I would almost certainly get leave to amend, he would simply call me on the phone. He would advise that he thought my pleading was defective, that he could not let this pass, and that if I did not amend the pleadings, he would launch a motion. I would then, of course, look at the pleadings, and if I thought he was right, I would put in amended pleadings and we were both saved a trip to a judge sitting in chambers (an informal procedure) and the time and costs that went with it. On matters of substance there were, of course, vigorous disputes, although even here lawyers generally tried to discourage their clients from pursuing actions driven by motives of malice or spite or pride. Settlements could usually be worked out, unless there was a clear disagreement on the facts. Relations with one's fellow practitioners were of a high order. Perhaps I look back on those years through a rose-coloured rear-view mirror, but I think what I remember is largely true. I can think of practically no instance when I said to myself of a fellow practitioner, 'That son of a bitch.'

Law Practice

My law practice was a general one that concentrated on commercial law as it relates to small businesses. I did virtually no criminal law, except for a small number of essentially pro bono cases in which people had fallen afoul of the law. My conclusion was that for many of them, the chief offence committed by the accused was being not too bright. I recall one case of a young man being brought in by his father or his uncle because he was charged with some minor offence. I became annoyed with the young man when he could not remember where events happened, until the older man explained that the young man did not know the names of streets because he could not read the street signs. After some heavy sledding to get the facts, we were able to establish his innocence. It was clear to me that he had been charged because he could not give an intelligible account of his movements. He simply did not understand the questions, and gave evasive and incoherent answers. It seems to me that the law levies a heavy penalty on stupidity.

I did very little work in the field of domestic relations. This can be a very difficult field of legal practice. I recall one divorce action in which I acted for the husband. He was as rational, analytical, and hard-headed a man as I have known. A favourable settlement had been negotiated. He declined to accept the settlement because he wanted possession of the dining-room suite. This furniture had no sentimental value for anyone, but for some reason unknown to me, he did not wish his wife to have the dining-room suite. In the circumstances this was totally irrational, but I had great difficulty in finally getting him to forget about the table and chairs and accept what was clearly a good settlement. Not all or most, but quite a few, clients involved in divorce actions become obsessed with gaining some small advantage, or more often, preventing the departing spouse from gaining some small advantage. Lawyers find themselves acting as mediators and sometimes psychiatrists, dealing with tensions which have developed over many years and which have exploded during the divorce proceedings.

I spent most of my time incorporating companies, drafting construction contracts, dealing with mechanics' liens (as they then were known), and other duties falling to lawyers when they're acting as the scribes of business entrepreneurs. I continued in the partnership until I became a full-time politician again as leader of the Opposition in 1970.

Meanwhile life at home was hectic. Anne and I had a son, David, in February 1964. In July 1962, we had joined a community clinic in Regina as it was being organized. The clinic was a group of citizens working with a group of doctors who opposed the strike and who were willing to practise under the medicare plan. Dr David Road was a highly competent general practitioner from England, who became our family doctor and in whom we had a great deal of confidence. A dispute like the medicare dispute forces difficult decisions upon many people affected by it. Our family doctor had been Dr Boris Mesbur, whom we liked and whom we thought was a thoroughly competent and decent man. We felt that he did not fully support the doctors' strike but was in no position to continue to practise in opposition to the overwhelming decision of his colleagues in the College of Physicians and Surgeons. As I've noted earlier, Dr Mesbur had arranged for me to speak to the Regina District Medical Society just before the strike occurred, to see if I could hold out any basis for reaching an agreement. They had little understanding of how governments work, and I probably had little understanding of the psyche of doctors who practise under the stress of making difficult decisions in the course of their work. At any rate, I was not successful in finding a way to a settlement.

When the strike occurred in July 1962, Anne and I had to make a decision about a family doctor for ourselves and our two children, aged nine and seven. We became patients of Dr Road, and when Anne became pregnant, he was her doctor. Although Dr Road was clearly highly competent, neither of the Regina hospitals would give him hospital privileges. The medical staffs of the two organizations were effectively controlled by the College of Physicians and Surgeons, and they were finding ways to refuse hospital privileges for any doctor who did not support the strike. As I have noted, the Saskatoon agreement of July 1962 specifically prohibited the doctors from discriminating against pro-medicare doctors in awarding of hospital privileges. This, however, did not prevent rampant discrimination.

As a private issue, it meant that Dr Road could not deliver our baby in a Regina hospital. The choices were to change doctors to one who had hospital privileges, to go to Saskatoon, where the University Hospital staff would deliver the baby, or to have the baby delivered by Dr Road in our home in Regina. Dr Road was skilled at home deliveries, as were a number of English doctors. But it was not an easy decision. Anne was thirty-six years old and this was her first child. There appeared to be no complications, and, accordingly, we decided on the baby being delivered at home. Dr Road and his associate, Dr Powers, arrived at the house complete with all their kit, including an oxygen tank, in cardboard boxes, and at about eight o'clock in the morning on 7 February 1964, David was delivered at 3135 Montague Street in Regina without incident. It was a minor story in the press since I was minister of health and my doctor could not get hospital privileges.

Anne and David were fine.

In Regina we attended the Argyle Road Baptist Church, where our children went to Sunday school and where I taught Sunday school for young teenagers for several years. In 1968, Margaret was born. She was delivered more conventionally in the Pasqua Hospital in Regina. We were just in the midst of having a house built for ourselves in the area of Regina which I represented after the 1964 and later elections. We moved our church affiliation to the nearby St John's United Church. Soon Anne was singing in the choir, and we had some warm friends there.

We acquired a series of station wagons into which we packed the smalls for trips to Florida, where my mother lived, to Ontario and Nova Scotia to visit relatives, and to Vancouver, Victoria, and the Oregon Coast. We went to Nova Scotia to see friends and to show the children and the new baby to the Schwartz and Gorham relatives.

At Christmas 1964 we headed to Florida to visit my mother, who lived in St Petersburg. I remember how bitterly cold it was when we left Regina. I recall arriving at St Joseph, Missouri, which is near Kansas City. We had stayed the night in Nebraska and noted in St Joseph that fresh fruit was displayed for sale outdoors. We looked around and realized that we were the only ones who were wearing snow boots and winter hats. We took off our winter clothes there in the street and stowed them in the car-top carrier with that wonderful feeling that Prairie people get when they have escaped the rigours of winter even if only for a brief time. We crossed the Mississippi and called at a service station in Memphis, Tennessee, to get some gasoline. The young man who was checking my oil noticed the electrical cord coming out of the engine. He asked me what it was, and I explained that it was a block heater, which we needed in order to keep the engine and the engine oil warm to allow the car to operate up north in Saskatchewan – the jaw-breaking name that he saw on our licence plate. His look made it clear that I must have thought he was a real rube to believe a yarn like that. We felt we were even further away from the grip of winter when we ran into service-station workers who had never heard of a block heater. And so we arrived at my mother's place in St Petersburg, where, in her backyard, there was a tree from which we could pick oranges.

Car trips of several days developed a pace and a rhythm of periods of activity and inactivity which were difficult to duplicate in the more frenetic holidays based upon air travel and a sense that one had to fill each unforgiving minute with things that the children should see and experience. In the car the children could often look out and see the passing scene and as often look inward and find some way to amuse themselves, as they seemed to be able to do with such skill and ingenuity.

We had a small and very minimal cottage at a lake near Regina. Our next-door neighbours at the beach, the Surjiks, had a husband and a son

named David, not to mention other children, and we had a son David. As
Anne and Myrtle Surjik sat in their chairs on the beach and supervised
the horde, they quickly learned that to shout 'David' was not helpful.
They renamed them for beach purposes D-1, D-2, and D-3.

By today's standards I was not a very good dad. I worked hard at my
jobs and worked most evenings. The only break from that was when I
practised law in the 1960s. I worked forty or perhaps fifty hours a week
then and came to regard that as a rest cure. I probably didn't have to
work as much as I did in government. But I liked the work and wanted to
do a good job. We did take holiday trips. I greatly enjoyed them and I
think the children did as well. But I didn't spend much time with the
children at home. Neither Anne nor I regarded this as unusual. Aside
from a few essentially volunteer jobs, she was a full-time homemaker, as
each of our mothers had been. And each of our fathers had been small
businessmen in difficult times and had not spent much time with the
children. My family used to go on car trips which I greatly enjoyed. Other
than these, I cannot remember my father ever taking me to hockey or
skating or anywhere else, except for one or two fishing trips, and my children would tell somewhat the same tale. It seemed the norm. Indeed, I
can recall cabinet ministers and senior public servants working on final-
izing the provincial budget on the afternoon of Christmas Day. That was
a bit much and I think was not repeated. But I did not feel hard done by
and I didn't think our wives did either. It was just the way things were.

I can recall Margaret as a young girl going to a friend's house for sup-
per. When the meal was over, the husband went into the living room,
turned on the television, and just sat. She was totally conditioned to me
rising from the table and going into my little home office or back to the
Legislative Building; she'd not seen a stay-home-in-the-evening dad
before and remarked to us on this strange phenomenon.

Being a party leader or a cabinet minister living in your constituency is
really a full-time job. During the day I worked in my office dealing with
public servants and the public for the normal 8:30–5:00, Monday to Friday week. But I also had many public functions and duties with the party.
The party workers were volunteers. Since they worked at regular jobs,
party work was done in the evenings and on weekends. That meant that
on many nights and many weekends I had to go to meetings, rallies, and
picnics, often far away from home. Sometimes the children went with me
when I went off to a picnic, which was an adventure for them. But this life
meant that other people were setting my agenda most of the time.

As I have noted, the 1964 election saw me elected in the new two-member constituency of Regina West but saw our party lose the government. The defeat meant that Premier Lloyd became leader of the Opposition. J.H. Brockelbank, a veteran member who had served in the legislature continuously since 1938, became deputy leader. 'Brock' was one of the most able, principled, and selfless people I have met in my lifetime. I served as financial critic and soon had my baptism of fire in that role in replying to the Liberal budget of 1965. The Liberal government of Ross Thatcher was clearly a more conservative government than had been the Douglas and Lloyd governments. They placed considerable reliance on the private sector and launched a development program under the slogan 'Open for Business.' They set about to lower taxes and to restrict the areas in which government operated.

They disposed of some of the Crown enterprises – a brick plant at Estevan and Saskatchewan Government Airways, which operated across northern Saskatchewan. But there was no wholesale dismantling of the utilities. They set about to get a pulp mill in northern Saskatchewan and succeeded in getting the Landegger organization of Austria and New York to set up a pulp mill in Prince Albert with massive government support. We were somewhat critical of the level of government support and the nature of the undertakings given to the government by the sponsors, but we had no reason to doubt that the Landegger people were competent and hoped to make their profits by operating the mill as a successful commercial enterprise.

1967 Election

The 1967 election was vigorously fought. The Liberals had, I believe, some hopes of, as they would have phrased it, 'eradicating socialism.' We failed to gain government but we by no means did badly. The popular vote was Liberals 45.6 per cent, NDP 44.4 per cent, and the seat count was Liberals 35 and NDP 24.

Our 1967 showing was strong. Not only did we have 24 seats but we had a core of new members who were obviously very able. These included Adolph Matsalla, Miro Kwasnica, John Messer, John Kowalchuk, Roy Romanow, and Ted Bowerman. Of those six, five served as cabinet ministers in our government between 1971 and 1982, and Romanow was a future premier. With this new infusion of youth and talent and with our victory in the Kelvington by-election in June of 1969, we were able to project ourselves as the voice of the future.

J.H. Brockelbank did not contest the 1967 election, and I was named deputy leader (an informal designation) as well as finance critic.

The years from 1967 to 1971 were difficult ones for the Saskatchewan economy. The Thatcher government responded by attempting to cut expenses or at least to keep them from rising sharply. They hit upon the idea of charging user fees for people who used hospital and medical services insured under the insurance plans. The government called them utilization fees. We immediately labelled them deterrent fees. To use today's language, we kept on message and never referred to them as anything but deterrent fees. We staged what amounted to a filibuster against the fees. I recall speaking in the legislature for well over four hours, using reams of statistics on the impact of the deterrent fees. It is very easy to show that such fees would bear particularly heavily on older people and on young couples with families. Our argument was simple: 'Deterrent fees are a tax. They are a tax to pay for the cost of the medical and hospital plans. The government by its actions is saying that older people in their seventies and eighties and young couples with families are best able to pay these new taxes. We disagree.'

As I recall, some of the figures garnered from the annual reports of the medical care insurance plans showed that a couple, each age seventy-five, with no dependants, used hospital care seven times as much as a couple, each age thirty-five, with no dependants. We doubted that they had seven times the capacity to pay the tax. This was a major plank in our election platform for the 1971 election. Following our election in June of 1971, one of our first acts was to convene a special session of the new legislature to, among one or two other things, abolish deterrent fees.

The Thatcher government was a formidable opponent. We were assisted by the fact that Mr Thatcher was not well. We knew that he had diabetes, but we did not know that this disease was putting a considerable strain upon him, which caused him sometimes to act in a brusque and arbitrary way. His deputy premier was Davie Steuart, the former mayor of Prince Albert. Davie was shrewd and irrepressible. Referring to Mr Thatcher's irritability, he once said, 'If there is any major group in the province which we have not offended, it is because we haven't met them yet.'

Steuart used humour in a positively lethal way in the legislature. I remember in 1971 I was waxing eloquent in the Throne Speech debate in the legislature. The oratorical style of the day allowed a level of hyperbole which would seem over the top today. I was referring to the seven years of Liberal government – the seven long years, the seven lean years, the seven gaunt years. I was comparing these seven long, lean, gaunt years with the seven years of plague of ancient Egypt. Davie was heckling, as was his wont. I was using the biblical quote, '... and out of the depths of the Nile came the seven lean kine.' Steuart interjected. 'That's the NDP.' I continued the quote without a pause. 'And the seven lean kine ate up the seven fat kine' (Genesis 41:2-3). The house broke out in laughter. Davie Steuart's seatmate Dave Boldt – a good Mennonite – whispered very audibly to Davie Steuart, 'Dave, you should know your Bible better.' Steuart (a Roman Catholic), without allowing a nanosecond to intervene, said, 'That damned Protestant Bible.' By this time everybody was laughing, including me. And I found it impossible to recreate the level of indignation with which I had started in commenting on the seven long years of Liberal mismanagement. Steuart's interjections were definitely entertaining, but not helpful to an Opposition that was on the attack.

Dave Steuart, as well as being deputy premier, was also provincial treasurer, or the minister of finance, as we would now term it. After the election of 1967, the budget introduced in the spring of 1968 called for new taxes, utilization fees, and the closing of small hospitals. It was not a good news budget. As Steuart put it, 'This is probably the first time in the history of the legislature that the provincial treasurer delivered the budget, not from his desk but from under his desk.'

The University of Saskatchewan

Since the founding of the University of Saskatchewan there had been a strong tradition that the government would not try to interfere with its internal workings. A policy of non-interference is not nearly as straightforward as it sounds. A university like the University of Saskatchewan is really a multiversity. It has the job of teaching the wisdom of the ages and adding to that wisdom, and so performing the role of the traditional liberal arts university associated with the name of Cardinal John Henry Newman. But it also performs the role of a social service agency on behalf of its constituent community. It teaches about moral philosophy but also about how to grow better wheat. It trains English scholars but also dentists and pharmacists.

Governments have always involved themselves in questions of the number of people trained in the professional and occupational faculties and have always refrained from becoming involved in what was taught, particularly in the fields of liberal arts and the pure sciences. The relationship which developed over the years was one in which the senior people of the university, the president, the chancellor, and the chairman of the board, met annually with the cabinet to outline what the university proposed to do and what resources it needed from government. The government appointed some members to the board of governors. For a good number of years, it was customary to have a senior person from the department responsible for university education and another from the finance department serve on the board to provide a channel of information to the government. The information flowed both ways. With these structures in place, the provincial budget contained a global sum for the university, which was distributed among the faculties as the board determined. This seemed to establish an appropriate balance between the government's need to be responsible for the large sums of public money spent by the university and the university's need to protect the academic freedom required for its proper functioning as an institution of higher education.

Mr Thatcher became exasperated with this admittedly imprecise level of financial accountability. He proposed a detailed review by the government of the way the university spent its money. He proposed what he called a line-by-line review of the budget. The university reacted angrily. We, as an Opposition, fully supported the university in their concern. It is not easy to strike the right relationship between the proper desire of the government to see that large sums of money spent by a university are spent in the public interest, as seen by the government and the public, and the need to protect the university from inappropriate pressure by politicians – pressure which might well inhibit the role of the university as a commentator on public issues and as a seeker after new and perhaps uncomfortable truths. In any event, Mr Thatcher relented and reverted to the old arrangements, but not before stirring up a storm in the university circles and more than a ripple among the public and press.

Labour Legislation

Another area of social controversy during these years (1967 to 1971) was the matter of strikes and, particularly, strikes in public services. Compared with other provinces, Saskatchewan had interesting positions with respect to collective bargaining. The modern era of collective bargaining for all employees in North America, except tradesmen, began in the

1930s in the United States in the days of President Franklin Roosevelt. There the Wagner Act set out a pattern for collective bargaining, primarily for the private sector. The Canadian experience comes mostly from regulations made during the Second World War under an Order-in-Council, PC1003. At the end of the war, provincial governments moved into the field. Saskatchewan was first in with an overall approach. The Trade Union Act of 1944 (assented to in 1945) was broadly patterned off the Wagner Act. The Trade Union Act gave collective bargaining rights to all employees in Saskatchewan, whether employed in the private or the public sector and whether employed in so-called essential services or not. This structure proved satisfactory from 1945 onwards. If there was a threatened strike in an essential service, the possibility of the legislature passing special legislation deterred irresponsible action on either side of the dispute. Most (I believe, all) other provinces had legislation that restricted the right of employees providing essential services to go on strike. The Douglas-Lloyd government felt that this was open to abuse by governments and preferred the freedom-to-strike model.

The Thatcher government introduced legislation that gave the cabinet the right to terminate work stoppages in essential undertakings, and to submit the matters in dispute to arbitration by an arbitrator selected by cabinet. Amendments widened the definition of what constituted an emergency to permit compulsory arbitration to be invoked. The 1966 Act referred to utilities, broadly defined, and health services. Later, construction activities were added. By 1971 the definition had been broadened to include labour disputes in which, in the opinion of the cabinet, 'a state of emergency exists in the province or any area of the province by reason of a labour dispute in such circumstances that the public interest or welfare may be in jeopardy.'

The labour movement interpreted this as authority for the cabinet to impose arbitration with respect to almost any dispute for which a strike was proving effective. The right to strike was, to them, a precious right, and they bitterly resented the Act. These pieces of legislation were called Bill 2, being the number of the bill by which the original legislation was introduced into the legislature in 1966.

Mr Thatcher also talked in imprecise terms about something he called labour courts. The idea was that when there were industrial disputes, the matter could and should be settled in the way that many other disputes in society are settled – by referring the matter to a court which can give a final decision. The public discussion of that idea revealed some gaping holes in the concept.

Courts enforce laws which are passed by Parliament and legislatures, or which have come down to us over many decades and centuries as common law. Parliament and legislatures have not set out the basis upon which industrial disputes should be settled; nor is there a body of common law on the subject. There is no general agreement in society on what are fair wages and working conditions. Accordingly, there is no law for the courts to apply. Courts in civil matters do not ordinarily decide what is fair or what is reasonable, but rather what the law provides for. And in matters of industrial relations, the law has not made rules. So the proposal that labour courts could operate like ordinary civil courts could not work unless Parliament and legislatures first set out the rules that should apply. The idea of labour courts never moved beyond the realm of rhetoric.

Agriculture

The years of 1968 to 1971 were difficult years for Saskatchewan farmers. Markets for Canadian grains simply could not absorb all of the production. Prices plummeted. The price offered by the Canadian Wheat Board for wheat in 1970 was $1.28 a bushel. But that was only for wheat which the farmer was lucky enough to be able to deliver to the Canadian Wheat Board. Elevators across the Prairies were full – 'plugged,' to use the jargon of the day. Wheat that could not be sold to the Canadian Wheat Board could be readily bought in the local gray market for, say, two bushels for a dollar. In this situation, the federal government mounted a program to persuade farmers not to grow grain. Payments were available if a farmer did not grow grain for regular markets. This program was labelled LIFT – Lower Inventories for Tomorrow. The program became identified with Otto Lang, the federal Liberal minister in charge of the Canadian Wheat Board. Prior to the election of 1971, the NDP, as the official Opposition in the provincial legislature, launched a campaign against the LIFT program. We felt that the federal government would be better advised to purchase more grain and make it available to countries, particularly in Africa, that were in need of food aid rather than to pay farmers not to grow grain. Clearly there were arguments both ways. But this was our position, and we ascribed some responsibility for the federal government's actions to the provincial government. In the campaign words of my colleague Roy Romanow, 'A Liberal is a Liberal is a Liberal.'

As it turned out, if farmers had continued to grow grain and kept the grain long enough, they would have done very well indeed. By 1974, Canada could sell all of the grain it could grow, and prices had moved from $1.28 to $4.50 or $5.00 a bushel.

The New Democrats were not alone in being critical of Otto Lang. Former Prime Minister John Diefenbaker, one of the best stump speakers that Canada has ever produced, was both scathing and amusing in his attacks on Lang. Otto Lang is a son of Saskatchewan. His father was an educator in Humboldt, Saskatchewan, and Otto grew up there. He excelled as an A student. He graduated in law from the University of Saskatchewan, was awarded a Rhodes Scholarship, and following his studies at Oxford, returned to teach law at the University of Saskatchewan. He became dean of law at the young age of thirty in 1962. In 1968 he was elected to the House of Commons and served in the cabinet of Prime Minister Trudeau from 1970 to 1979 in key portfolios such as justice, transport, and minister in charge of the Canadian Wheat Board.

John G. Diefenbaker served as prime minister from 1957 to 1963 and continued as a Member of Parliament until his death in 1979. It would be difficult to find two more different personalities than John Diefenbaker and Otto Lang. Diefenbaker was a tribune of the people, an outstanding platform speaker and reader of crowds. I've seen him speak for twenty minutes, holding the audience in the palm of his hand, while hardly completing a thought. By the use of gesture, code words, and pauses, he conveyed his meaning, or, perhaps more accurately, the meaning that each of his listeners wanted to take from his words. That is no mean skill. Diefenbaker used humour, subtle suggestions, changes of voice and cadence – all the tools of a great orator. When on the stump, he rarely indulged in any careful analysis of issues – his appeal was emotional rather than cerebral.

Otto Lang, on the other hand, was almost clinical in his presentation. He lined up his facts, made a logical argument, and invited his audience to embrace his analysis of the issues under discussion. Levity was rarely part of his presentation.

Diefenbaker, in his later years, became even more irrepressible and even more entertaining. Otto Lang was the butt of many of Dief's sallies. Diefenbaker set out to make merry with the LIFT plan and with its putative parent, Otto Lang. Otto's name was Otto Emil Lang. Diefenbaker launched forth, excoriating the LIFT plan, and Lang, by referring to 'Lang' as a four-letter word, then going on to refer to 'Otto Lang,' two four-letter words, and then to refer to 'Otto Emil Lang,' three four-letter words. This could take up to five minutes with appropriate repetition.

Another line of attack was based upon the baseball caps widely worn in rural Saskatchewan. The caps frequently bear an emblem, perhaps Deere, representing the John Deere farm machine company, or UGG, representing the United Grain Growers (as they then were), a well-known grain company, or POOL, representing the Saskatchewan Wheat Pool, then the province's largest grain company. Dief would profess ignorance about what the cap badges meant. He would opine that UGG perhaps stood for 'Us Good Guys.' He didn't know what POOL stood for, but he understood that the last three letters stood for 'on Otto Lang.'

Such was the nature of Saskatchewan politics in the 1960s and 1970s.

I got in Mr Diefenbaker's bad books quite accidentally, if quite carelessly. It was in the 1970s, shortly before Diefenbaker's death in 1979. I was speaking at a function associated with a meeting of the Learned Societies, as it was then called, a conclave of academics at the University of Saskatchewan. Mr Diefenbaker was chancellor of the university at the time and seated behind me on the platform. I was holding forth about Canadian political history. I departed from my script, why, I don't know. Out came a line – 'The history of Canadian public life is filled with political dinosaurs – and they're not all dead.' I was not thinking of Mr Diefenbaker. I should have been. Mistakenly, but understandably, he felt that I had taken a shot at him. He was not amused.

Party Leader

Woodrow Lloyd gave outstanding policy leadership and engaged the party province-wide to consider the challenges confronting Saskatchewan. His work led to the party developing a comprehensive election program for the 1971 election. Every political party needs a steady flow of ideas on how to deal with the problems of today and tomorrow. There are many sources of ideas. Most come to the politicians in raw form and often take too much checking and honing to be very useful. The trick is to get people who will put forward some reasonably well developed proposals, ones for which the pros and cons have been at least considered. The NDP, and the CCF before it, had some reliable sources. Each was not reliable all the time, because inspiration seemed to come in waves. But some proposals would flow from farm groups, from academics at the university, from the teacher's federation and some groups of teachers, from trade union groups, and from co-operative organizations.

·When our party was in office, the public service was a fruitful source of progressive proposals, and on occasion business groups would put forward ideas. But it seems that when our party was in opposition, ideas flowed concerning what grand designs should be considered and how the province should look ten or fifteen years hence. In office, the external groups lowered their sights to what the government should do – and often do for them – in the next twelve months. In these circumstances, the government found itself increasingly relying on the public service for proposals for longer-term projects. This is not healthy. No social democratic party can prosper for long unless it has before it a vision of a better society and unless it holds out such a vision to the public. And, in office, this becomes increasingly difficult.

Woodrow stepped down as party leader in 1970. His resignation launched a spirited leadership contest. I was first in the ring. I had been an MLA for ten years, a cabinet minister, and deputy leader of the Opposition. I was regarded as the choice of the establishment. Roy Romanow had been an MLA for three years, was very able and charismatic, and represented the new wave in the party. George Taylor was a distinguished labour lawyer, had been active in civic politics, and was highly regarded by labour and other groups in the party. George went on to be the province's pre-eminent labour lawyer. Don Mitchell was an able young man who represented the Waffle group, which wished to steer the party on a more left-leaning course, as then understood. Don went on to serve a period as mayor of Moose Jaw.

I thought I would win without too much difficulty. Such was not to be. Roy Romanow mounted a spirited campaign, and there was action on behalf of Taylor and Mitchell. On a hot Saturday afternoon in July of 1970 in the Regina Armouries, delegates voted and voted again, and again. I trailed Roy narrowly on the first ballot, which dropped Taylor. I picked up some ground in the second, which dropped Mitchell, but was still trailing Romanow. And finally, on the third ballot, I was selected. I do not recommend this type of contest as a way to spend a relaxing Saturday afternoon. But truth, beauty, and justice ultimately prevailed, and I was once again a full-time politician. I became leader of the Opposition and set about to organize for the provincial election expected in June of 1971. This transition marked the end of what I look back upon as six years of relatively tranquil living, largely unaffected by the many crises created by the world of politics.

7

In Office

We convened a special session of the legislature on 28 July 1971, just four weeks after we assumed office. There were a number of things that we wanted to get done as soon as possible. We had campaigned vigorously against the user fees imposed by the Thatcher government in 1968 on people who visited a doctor's office or were in hospital – what we called deterrent fees. We set about to abolish those fees forthwith. The recorded vote in the legislature was unanimous. The members of the Liberal Party who had defended these fees so vigorously for three years voted for their removal.

We also set about to repeal The Essential Services Emergency Act, Bill 2. It was an early part of the business at the special session. The Opposition agreed to the repeal of the Act without a recorded vote or without any record of the vote being 'on division.'

Our approach was that employees had the right to strike. Equally, society had the right to protect itself against any strike that generally imperilled public welfare. We felt that the fairest course of action was to allow an unrestricted right to strike and to summon the legislature to pass special legislation to provide for an arbitrated settlement when a strike imperils public welfare. Later we passed legislation to permit cabinet to postpone a strike during those few days every four years or so when there is no legislature – the period after an election is called and before newly elected members of the legislature are officially declared elected. During our years in office between 1971 and 1982, the legislature was summoned to deal with a few work stoppages – at the Saskatchewan Power Corporation in about mid-winter, at a large group of hospitals, and on a couple of other occasions.

We were able to do a few other things at this special session. We removed the medicare family tax for people over sixty-five; we reduced hours of work before overtime provisions kicked in; we gave extra protection to farmers against the seizure of their land and machinery by creditors; and we removed charges against the estates of patients who had received treatment for mental illness. In 1968 the government had enacted legislation which provided that if a person died who had received treatment in a mental hospital, the costs of his or her care could be recovered from his or her estate, except for a modest exemption for widows. We thought that this was a retrograde step – drawing a sharp distinction between the way we dealt with physical illness and with mental illness and victimized families of the mentally ill, who were often among the neediest in the province. We had made all these arguments and more, as forcefully as we could, in 1968 when the issue was before the legislature, but to no avail. So we lost no time in repealing the changes made. Once again the Opposition members voted for the repeal of the changes they had so stoutly defended three years before.

We wound up the work of the special session on August 11 after two productive weeks.

One of the great satisfactions of public life is being able, sometimes, to bring about some changes that are desirable and important. We ended this short session satisfied that we had made a good start on our agenda for change. We were very fortunate to have our election program, 'New Deal for People,' as a road map. Some ministers simply handed the program booklet to their senior public servants and asked what we needed to do to make these things happen. Many of the proposals could not be accomplished in a month or a year, and we needed to have some concrete results by the next election, which we assumed would be in June 1975.

We set out to be an activist government and to make the changes we had outlined in our platform. We believed, profoundly, that much could be done and should be done. Some indication of our frenetic pace can be found in the sheer number and size of new laws passed. In its 1972 session, the legislature passed fully 150 laws, totalling 890 pages. In 1973 the number was 124, covering 641 pages. Each was greater than produced in any previous session in the history of the province.

Federal-Provincial Issues

My first federal-provincial conference was in the early fall of 1971. The group who gathered at 24 Sussex Drive with the prime minister for the traditional dinner were in some sense a new generation of political leaders. We had two venerable and seasoned veterans, Joey Smallwood of Newfoundland, who had been premier since 1949, and W.A.C. (Wacky) Bennett, premier of British Columbia since 1952. Both would be gone in 1972. Alex Campbell of Prince Edward Island, although only thirty-eight years old, had been premier since 1966 and was in his second term. All the others were serving their first term in office, and Peter Lougheed of Alberta and I had hardly found the washrooms in our respective offices.

It was a new group and in some sense a new breed of politician. I had taken office in 1971. Besides myself there was Pierre Trudeau, prime minister since 1968, Gerald Regan of Nova Scotia (premier in 1970), Richard Hatfield of New Brunswick (1970), Robert Bourassa of Quebec (1970), Bill Davis of Ontario (1971), Ed Schreyer of Manitoba (1969), and Peter Lougheed of Alberta (1971). Trudeau continued in office (with the brief Joe Clark interregnum) until the 1980s and the patriation of the Constitution in 1982, as did Hatfield, Davis, Lougheed, and I.

Other faces appeared – Frank Moores and Brian Peckford in Newfoundland, Bennett Campbell, Angus MacLean, and Jim Lee in Prince Edward Island, John Buchanan in Nova Scotia, René Lévesque (a key new face) in Quebec, Sterling Lyon and Howard Pawley (November 1981) in Manitoba, and Dave Barrett and Bill Bennett (son of W.A.C.) in British Columbia. But a core of first ministers remained remarkably stable and served to shape the agenda of key federal-provincial issues, particularly the patriation of the Constitution, Quebec's place in Canada, and energy matters, all issues which dominated national politics in the dozen years following 1971.

The interaction among the ideas and the personalities of this core – Trudeau, Hatfield, Davis, Lougheed, and I – together, of course, with René Lévesque, played a major role in the dynamics of federal-provincial relations in Canada during the decade ending in 1982. I believe it was Lord Palmerston who said that England had no friends, only interests. And it is sometimes said that in tough negotiations the matter is always one of issues and interests, and not one of friends or personalities. That is not true, or, at least, only partially true. The personalities, skills, and egos of negotiators are almost always factors. They certainly were during the negotiations of the 1970s.

During the period commencing with the Victoria Charter – the aborted agreement covering constitutional change arrived at in June of 1971 – and ending with the formal patriation of the Constitution in April 1982, there were four major issues in federal-provincial relations, from a

Saskatchewan point of view. The first was oil pricing – the controversy surrounding the price for oil and natural gas and what the producing provinces should receive both for products sold domestically and for products exported, culminating in the controversy surrounding the National Energy Program. This general issue involved other minerals as well. Secondly, there were issues surrounding the place of Quebec in Confederation, culminating in the referendum held in Quebec in May 1980. Thirdly, there was the issue and controversy surrounding the patriation of the Constitution, culminating in its formal patriation in April of 1982 without the agreement of the government of Quebec. The fourth was a range of agricultural issues, which are always near the top of political issues in Saskatchewan.

It was not all a question of grappling with major issues. New boys like me had to learn about the customs and mores elsewhere in Canada. I recall that when we had that first dinner at the prime minister's residence, discussion turned to the Constitution (in those days it went with the dessert at 24 Sussex). The government of Quebec in July had rejected the Victoria Charter of June. At our dinner, Mr Trudeau and Mr Bourassa got into a heated discussion about it. Mr Trudeau berated Mr Bourassa in no uncertain terms. Words like 'If you had any guts, this problem would be over' were exchanged. I was really shocked but said nothing. Later, Peter Lougheed and I were walking out together. One of us said, 'Well, what did you think of that?' The other replied, 'If he had talked like that to me I know what I would have done. I would have said, "Thank you Mr Prime Minister. I don't think I can be of any further help in this discussion. Good evening to you all," and I would have been out of there like a shot.'

Later we saw the same style of discourse between Mr Trudeau and René Lévesque after Mr Lévesque became premier of Quebec on 25 November 1976. But this time it was a duel. Mr Trudeau addressed unflattering remarks to Mr Lévesque. Mr Lévesque answered in kind. They continued in increasingly rapid and vituperative French. Then they looked around the table and noticed that the French was too fast for the rest of us. We were not getting the full benefit of their remarks. So each switched to English and continued the pleasantries. By this time we had become a little more familiar with the Quebec style of political address, at least in the 1970s.

Back on the home front, after the July session of the legislature, we turned our minds to charting our next steps. I'll try to touch on some of the major issues that we wrestled with over the next eleven years.

8

Drills, Pills, Skills, Pancakes, and Parks

Any NDP government coming to office in Saskatchewan would seek to protect and expand medicare. Our goal during our eleven-year term was to secure hospital and medical care insurance and to build toward the dream of a universal comprehensive health care insurance plan for all the people of Saskatchewan.

We were conscious of the fact that we were breaking some new ground. In the 1950s and 1960s, we in Saskatchewan were greatly helped by the decision of the Diefenbaker government to share the cost of hospital care insurance and the decision of the Pearson government in 1966 to share the cost of medical care insurance. But we were unsure how strong the commitment of the federal government was to continue to be a 50/50 partner in sharing the costs. And we were mindful of the fact that public health care insurance was strongly opposed in the United States and that there would probably be a continuing drumbeat of opposition heard and felt in Canada, as has proved to be the case. In the United States the drug companies and many in the medical establishment opposed the very principles of hospital and medical care insurance. Some of these views are echoed in Canada, and the persistent calls for private medical care insurance continue to be heard. We should not let down our guard in defending medicare.

We were wary of any moves to dilute the universal, comprehensive, accessible principles. We saw user fees – deterrent fees, as we called them – as an attack on accessibility that might grow to be a real threat. We did not see family medical care taxes as an attack on the insurance plans so long as the taxes or premiums were reasonable and so long as access to care did not depend on paying the tax. Rather, we saw those taxes as regressive and less desirable than financing medical care from taxes based on ability to pay.

So our policy was to eliminate deterrent fees and premium-like taxes.

We were wary of any attempt by the federal government to back away from its role as a 50/50 partner in sharing costs. We were unhappy about moves taken in the 1970s by the federal government to convert the sharing agreements (roughly 50/50 sharing) to block grants. We liked the flexibility of block grants, but we feared that formulas for the grants would be tinkered with in order to cut down the cost to the federal treasury. Perhaps more dangerous was that federal politicians would lose their interest in the quality of health care when from their point of view it became simply a matter of a block-grant formula, something the ordinary citizen would care nothing about. As I said at the time, it was going to be hard for federal candidates to quicken the pulse of the voters, not by talking about paying half the cost of operating their fine local hospital, but by a rousing speech on block grants and equalized tax points.

Children's Dental Program

In our election program, 'New Deal for People,' we had spoken of our wish to expand the scope of medial care insurance to include dentistry and prescription drugs. In dentistry we saw the major problem as the relatively poor state of dental health among children, especially rural children. There was a real shortage of dentists in Saskatchewan, especially in rural areas. In 1971 there were just 185 dentists in Saskatchewan – a ratio of one dentist for 5,000 people. This was the lowest of any province in Canada. As might be expected, a disproportionate number of the dentists were in Regina and Saskatoon.

There were wide areas of the province where the nearest dentists were fifty miles away. So we decided to tackle the children's dental health issue first. The problem had been considered for some time, and a pilot project had operated in the Oxbow area of southeast Saskatchewan for a few years, using not dentists but para-professionals to deliver routine services. These para-professionals were sometimes called dental nurses and at other times dental therapists.

We were anxious to get going as rapidly as possible. The first job was to train the therapists. We established a school in 1972 to give a two-year course of instruction. Students began graduating in 1974, and they fanned out across the province offering services to the youngest primary school students. With each graduating class, we were able to add two more school years. For example, if grades one and two were covered in year one of the program, grades one to six were covered by year three.

Dental offices were set up in schools throughout the province. There was a heavy emphasis on preventive dental health.

The program was a resounding success. When I went about rural areas of the province in the late 1970s, I asked people what they thought of it. The parents, particularly the women, were lavish in their praise. Many of these people were doing well financially. It wasn't the savings on dentist bills that was earning the kudos. It became clear that the program was well received for at least two other reasons. When the dentist is fifty miles away and the children are not reporting any trouble with their teeth, parents tended to put off taking them for a check-up. They felt guilty about the neglect. Now this was all done for them. No more guilt. And, secondly, miracle of miracles, a child would come home with stories of the nice lady 'finding a hole in my tooth and filling it' and proudly display the filling. Asked if it hurt, the child denied any suggestion of the process being an ordeal. To parents who still had memories of the terror and agony of the dentistry of their youth, this was indeed a plus.

The hygienists sitting on the schoolroom floor with children gathered around them talking about toothbrushes and showing white teeth ushered in a new era in the relationship between the child patient and the practitioner.

The program was discontinued in 1987 pursuant to a deal made between the Progressive Conservative government and the College of Dental Surgeons. About four hundred employees of the plan were called to locations around the province and summarily terminated. An arrangement was made to have the patients served by private clinics. This was not the finest hour for either the government or the College of Dental Surgeons.

Prescription Drug Program

The other major initiative in health care was the introduction of a prescription drug program. There had been a program for people on social assistance for many years. Our 'New Deal for People' document in 1971 had promised a comprehensive prescription drug insurance program. Walter Smishek, the minister of health in 1971, set up planning units in the department to plan the new drug program. Its most distinctive features were the idea of comprehensive standing offer contracts with drug companies and of a formulary to cover most of the drugs that would be included.

Turning first to the formulary, we found that a list of 200 to 250 drugs would cover 95 per cent of the prescriptions used by Saskatchewan people. This list was compiled from similar lists used by several other organizations. One came from the Saskatoon community clinic, and another had been drawn up by people from the College of Medicine and the College of Pharmacy at the University of Saskatchewan. We received still others from the hospital association and the medical and pharmaceutical associations. The first chairman of the formulary committee was Dr Graham Clarkson, who had been medical director of the Medical Care Insurance Commission during the doctors' strike of 1962. The formulary committee also included Dr David Penman and Dr John Bury of the Department of Health.

The formulary and the permanent committee worked well. It provided a place where the drug companies and others who wished to add drugs to the formulary could go if they could establish that the new drug had particular therapeutic qualities, and did not simply substitute for or combine existing drugs in a way which added little or nothing to therapeutic results.

Perhaps the most substantial change was the idea of standing offer contracts. All the formulary drugs for Saskatchewan hospitals and other public institutions and for use by patients who obtained their formulary drugs from drugstores were to be purchased from drug manufacturers on the basis of standard contracts. For any particular drug, a tender would be called for the total supply of that drug for all these markets for a period of, say, six months. When generic drugs were available on a competitive basis, the savings in drug costs were spectacular. Sometimes the cost of a drug was a tenth of its previous price. When drugs were still under patent in such a way as to prevent generic drug companies from manufacturing and marketing them, savings were less dramatic. Nonetheless, the idea of using standing offer contracts was clearly a good one.

The drug retailers had their drugs supplied under standing offer contracts through wholesalers, who were paid a negotiated margin or handling fee. The pharmacy dispensed the drug and charged a dispensing fee that was negotiated with the drug plan. The patient paid all or the major part of the dispensing fee. The plan paid the full cost of the drug, plus any part of the dispensing fee that was not to be paid by the patient.

The plan was by most measures a clear success. Quite a few doctors continued to give prescriptions for drugs that required the use of the brand-name product rather than the generic drug. We felt that this was doubtless due to the vigorous efforts by representatives of the brand-name drug companies to convince doctors that the generic product was inferior, even though quality-control measures taken by both the federal and provincial governments indicated clearly that this was not the case.

Our plan covered well over 90 per cent of the people using prescription drugs in Saskatchewan. The plan was later greatly modified by the Progressive Conservative government of Grant Devine, which introduced financial barriers, with the result that fewer than 20 per cent of the potential beneficiaries received financial support for the plan. All others, except those covered by social assistance programs, would pay the full cost of their prescriptions, either directly or through private insurance plans. The standing offer contracts fell by the wayside.

It seems to me that in the Saskatchewan prescription drug program of the 1970s there is the germ of a program that would work well for all of Canada. The federal government could organize a formulary committee of pharmacists, physicians, and care directors of hospitals and nursing homes to compile a list of widely used drugs. It could then solicit standing offer contracts for these drugs. Provincial pharmacare plans could adhere to the federal plan and thereby have the most frequently used drugs provided and paid for. The provincial plans could arrange for the wholesale and retail distribution of these drugs and the payment of the distribution costs by either the plans or the patients. The provincial plans might decide to cover infrequently used or experimental drugs. Such a framework would provide massive savings for Canadians, either as taxpayers or patients or both.

The federal government would be aware of the issues of drug supply and drug pricing and how these might be affected by any changes in drug patent legislation. Certainly the plan operated by Saskatchewan in the 1970s received advantages in supply and pricing that did not seem to be available after the changes in drug patent legislation that were introduced in 1988. The cost of providing comprehensive health care to Canadians is rising. By far the sharpest increase is in the cost of prescription drugs. By using its buying power and its law-making power, the federal government could bring about a huge reduction in drug costs. It should not hesitate to do so.

There are disadvantages in being in government in a small province, as opposed to a large and wealthy province like Ontario. But there are advantages too. One of them is that the smaller scale allows one to plan and bring about many changes in a short time. This was particularly true of Saskatchewan in the 1970s. The public were willing to see Saskatchewan resume its role as a social laboratory for Canada after seven years of less activist government while Ross Thatcher's Liberal government was in office.

Healing Labour Relations

We had an agenda for change that had been set out in our 1971 election manifesto, 'New Deal for People.' One of the areas crying for change was the field of labour relations. We had a caucus of forty-five members, but only three or four had close links with the trade union movement. Fortunately, at least two of them were strong, experienced members and served as cabinet ministers throughout our time in office. Walter Smishek became our first minister of health. The other was Gordon Snyder, a railroader with a wry sense of humour. Gordon became minister of labour. I would not ordinarily leave a minister in the same portfolio for eleven years, but Gordon gained the respect of employers and got along so well with the labour movement, that each time I considered a cabinet shuffle I decided that at the Department of Labour, if I made a change, I had nowhere to go but down.

A few years ago, I was in the Legislative Building in Regina at a time when some new ministers were being sworn in. A small group, including Gordon Snyder and I, were standing about chatting. Among the group were Bob Mitchell and Don Ching, each of whom had at one time been a deputy minister of labour when Gordon was minister. Bob Mitchell went on to become an international public servant, and then an MLA and minister of justice, and in retirement he chairs a commission dealing with public complaints against police conduct. Don Ching went on to become CEO of the telephone utility, SaskTel, and later CEO of Areva Canada – the Canadian arm of the giant French nuclear company. Areva operates uranium mines and refining capacity in Canada. We were talking about the new ministers and their challenges. Gordon was asked what advice he would give to a new minister, and his answer was, 'I don't know, I'd probably advise him to do something I was never able to do myself.' To the question 'What would that be?' he replied: 'I'd say to him – get yourself a good deputy.'

Gordon set out to get on with realizing some of our plans, hopes, and dreams for working people. Mr Thatcher's government had, in the eyes of the trade union movement, gutted the right to strike with several pieces of legislation collectively referred to as Bill 2. As noted earlier, we repealed those bills in the special legislative session of July 1971.

   Gordon first strengthened the Department of Labour by adding
research people and enforcement staff. Our first moves in changing the
law were in the broad field of labour standards. In 1971 we established a
universal forty-hour work week, the first province to do so. In 1972 it was
provided that an employee could have a leave of absence to run as a candidate and serve in public office. In 1973 we introduced provisions for
equal pay for similar work, which primarily helped women to get fairer
wages. We also provided for longer annual vacations, four weeks after
twenty years with an employer, and three weeks after one year. These
were firsts in Canada. In 1974 we brought in laws to protect employees
when an employer fails financially. Saskatchewan became the first province to provide for maternity leave and later bereavement leave. We provided for eighteen weeks unpaid maternity leave, and later some
paternity leave. Today our efforts appear to be modest beginnings.
   We tackled minimum wages. In 1971 Saskatchewan had the seventh
highest minimum wages among Canadian provinces. By 1982, when we
left office, we were either first or second. There was some uncertainty
here because Quebec has several different minimums for different sectors, and it was not always easy to compare. Each time there was an
increase, employers complained, sometimes bitterly, and each year
employers as a group made greater profits than the previous year –
almost without exception. Some retailers seem to hope that employees
who worked for other employers would receive high wages, so that they
could spend lots of money in their shops, but that their own employees
would continue to get low wages, to keep costs down. It doesn't work that
way. It seems to me that in times of rising prosperity, employees who get
good wages spend their money and – big surprise – employers do well. As
I look back, I can remember very few times when working people were
being well paid and businesses were losing money. I can remember more
times when business people were doing well, but working people were
struggling. Indeed, that has been too often the case in the last decade.
   Another of our major initiatives was in the field of occupational health
and safety. Too many people are killed or injured on the job. That was certainly true in 1971. And dangers were rising with the introduction of new
technologies and new and largely unknown chemicals. The new law provided for health and safety committees in all workplaces with ten employees or more, and gave these committees power to investigate unsafe
working conditions without the consent of the employer. The committees were made up half of workers and half management, and in case of
a deadlock the Department of Labour people would mediate. The next
step was to provide that workers could refuse to work, if in the opinion of

the worker, the job was unusually dangerous. Employers resisted, some mildly, others strongly. I remember speaking with the union leaders, telling them that we would try this law, but if it was used to harass management as part of collective bargaining, we would repeal it. The law was purely for safety purposes and not to be used as a tactical weapon in larger disputes with employers. The workers respected this. The scheme began to work. The rate of accidents dropped. Employers don't like accidents, and so they gradually accepted the idea, and as their workers' compensation assessments began to drop, many became converts.

It was a pioneering approach – the first in North America. It has now spread widely. Most employers want a safe workplace, but they don't want unions or worker committees running their workplace. Finding the line where all parties accept the management function as an employer concern, and where all parties accept worker health and safety as a joint concern, is sometimes not easy to do. But I feel that we did this to the satisfaction, after some early angst, of both management and workers.

We tried to get a higher level of worker participation in management, both of Crown corporations and private corporations, but with limited success. Management was wary of this departure from long-established norms. But so were the unions. They were darkly suspicious of our motives, and we were suspected of trying to co-opt them, so that they would see problems from a management as well as a worker perspective, and in so doing weaken their militant advocacy on behalf of workers. In a sense, that was true. We felt that it was time for both management and labour to acknowledge that the other side had some merit and that a little reduction in this tendency to demonize the opponent would be no bad thing. We felt that way, but nobody else did. And aside from modest steps in things like work scheduling, little was achieved.

A major step forward was in workers' compensation. The scheme that existed was based on the idea of physical impairment. Thus if two men were in an accident and each permanently lost the use of his left arm, each received the same pension for life because each suffered the same physical impairment. We came to believe that this was wrong-headed. We should not be paying for lost limbs, but rather paying for lost income. If one of our two men was a chartered accountant, his loss of income would be relatively modest. His years of education and training would be largely intact, helping him to earn a living. If the other man was a professional concert pianist, his loss of income would be catastrophic. His years of education and training would be hugely diminished as tools in helping him find a job and working at it.

What was needed was a scheme that stressed income replacement, rehabilitation, and retraining. Perhaps there was another career in music for the concert pianist. The plan should help this come about. We put in place this new plan. It arose from recommendations of a review committee that we set up, which had representatives of trade unions and employers and was headed by Judge Muir of the provincial court at Moose Jaw. Muir was able to get a plan with which both employer and employee representatives agreed. In the field of labour relations, this is in the realm of the miraculous. I felt that Judge Muir had open to him a second career as a magician.

There was a little resistance to the rehabilitation aspect. A few workers felt that if they had a dismemberment injury, they should get a pension for life without being hounded to train for other work. But this pushback was not widespread. Another key part of the new plan was that the income replacement (75 per cent of wages at the time of injury) was indexed annually to the industrial wage scale. This served to keep payments up to a level comparable to the money the worker would have earned if he/she had not been hurt. Both the theory and the working of the new plan were widely accepted. This new approach was a first for Canada and, I believe, for North America. Several other provinces have now accepted it across Canada.

There were many more modest changes in the labour-management environment. They dealt with the effects of technological change, assisting employees to recover wages improperly withheld by employers, and trying to increase the number of working people who were represented by unions and reduce the number of unorganized workers, who are usually at the bottom of the totem pole when it comes to wages and benefits. I look back on what was accomplished with some satisfaction. In this area of labour legislation, as in others, imitation is the sincerest form of flattery.

'Celebrate Saskatchewan'

A happy interlude from dealing with the never-ending stream of mini-crises, which is the political life in office, was the celebrations surrounding the 75th anniversary of Saskatchewan as a province in 1980. The festivities were called 'Celebrate Saskatchewan.' Times had been relatively good for a few years, the land was green, and people flooded back from across Canada and beyond. There were many heart-warming little stories.

I recall the community day at Plato, which then had about thirty-five residents, depending on who was home. But for the homecoming day, bleachers were built and seven hundred people were there. All were wearing name-tags giving their name, their father's or mother's name, and a grandparent's name if there was a community connection. Everyone in the crowd was wandering about – older people looking at the name-tags of younger people and commenting, 'Oh, so you're Sam Shultz's grandson. I knew him well,' or, 'So you're Bessie Miller's girl,' and the chatter went on.

There were pancake breakfasts everywhere. They are a great institution for politicians. People line up to be served, and it takes about forty-five seconds to get your pancakes. A greeter could stand in one place, exchange names and a pleasantry or two – ordinarily asking the diners where they had returned from and what were their holiday plans – and the line moved on. Many were from Regina and Saskatoon. But Calgary, Edmonton, Vancouver, and Toronto were well represented. The relentless mechanization and modernization of agriculture had 'taken the boy out of the country,' but clearly it had 'not taken the country out of the boy.' For many, the homecoming was a nostalgia bath.

When the farm economy is prospering, the cities and towns are enjoying good times and people are remembering fondly their youth. Saskatchewan is not only green and pleasant but also warm and welcoming.

In my homecoming speeches, and I gave dozens of them – low-key and short – I frequently quoted a then well-known journalist, Jeanine Locke. She had written, 'Nowhere on earth are the good things of life more evenly distributed than they are in Saskatchewan.' I knew that this was not true, but it was probably true of Canada and perhaps North America. I regarded this as a very desirable objective and was pleased that when the tide of good times had come in, almost everybody's boat had risen.

There were the more formal events with the prime minister and the governor general, but the events in the smaller communities were the most fun. The government took the occasion to restore Government House, the original residence of the lieutenant-governor, to its original splendour circa 1910. It now serves as offices for the lieutenant-governor and a venue for quite a bit of small-scale government entertaining.

Urban Parks

Creating several urban parks in Saskatchewan cities was another happy accomplishment. In March 1981, legislation was passed creating the Wakamow Valley Authority and setting up a major urban park in Moose

Jaw. This was the third of the new parks we hoped to create in the four major cities: Wascana Centre in Regina (1962), Meewasin Valley Authority in Saskatoon (1979), and the Wakamow Valley Park. We hoped that there would be interest in creating a riverside park in Prince Albert, but it did not develop. We were tentatively calling it the Three Prime Ministers Park, to note the fact that Prince Albert is the only federal constituency that has elected to Parliament three sitting prime ministers – Sir Wilfrid Laurier, William Lyon Mackenzie King, and John Diefenbaker. King and Laurier were 'elected' in an earlier era when they were able to run in more than one riding in the same election. Prince Albert, with its parkland setting, has so many attractive recreational sites close at hand that its residents do not seem to have the same desire for urban parks as do the citizens of the prairie cities.

The three parks were established by legislation that provided each with a stable funding base that could be changed only by changing the legislation. This meant that in the press of setting a provincial or a civic budget, the park funds could not be cut except in the very public way of changing the provincial law.

The model was set when the park in Regina was formally set up as the Wascana Centre Authority in 1962. In 1960, the University of Saskatchewan reached the conclusion that it needed a new campus in Regina. The federal government's experimental farm on the outskirts of the city was the preferred site. I was minister of education, and I recall bargaining with the federal minister of agriculture, Alvin Hamilton, to acquire the property. The site bordered on extensive parks of the city of Regina close to the grounds of the Legislative Building. A small group, including Al Johnson, who was deputy provincial treasurer and served on the university's board of governors, and Jim Langford, who was deputy minister of public works, conceived of the idea of combining the new campus with the nearby parks owned by the city and the legislative grounds into a new and unified park.

I can recall Al Johnson working up a proposal over a weekend, so that I could circulate it on Monday and take it to cabinet on Tuesday. I got an agreement in principle, and we went ahead to organize a policy committee (the A committee) and an officials committee (the B committee). I acted as chairman of the A committee, which included the president of the University of Saskatchewan and the mayor of Regina. We went ahead with getting the best advice we could. A distinguished U.S. architect, Minoru Yamasaki from Detroit, a well-known landscape architect, Thomas D. Church from San Francisco, and Dean John A. Russell of the

Faculty of Architecture at the University of Manitoba made up the architectural advisory team. Yamasaki, with whom we worked closely, went on to become famous as the lead architect for the World Trade Center buildings in New York City, which were the targets of the terrorist attacks of 11 September 2001.

A master plan was prepared, and after extensive discussion, it was adopted. Meanwhile I had secured the services of Alan Gillmore as a special assistant to move this project forward. Gillmore spoke to dozens of groups in Regina and elsewhere and got acceptance not only of the master plan but also of the idea of having the park set up as a statutory body with guaranteed funds to be provided as follows: 55 per cent by the provincial government, 30 per cent by the city of Regina, and 15 per cent by the university. There was a superb job done of getting people to accept the idea and embrace the vision. The legislation came into effect in 1962, and the project moved forward as an unqualified success.

This same approach – a preliminary planning committee, engaging an eminent professional to prepare a master plan, taking the concept to the public, and then proceeding with legislation – was followed in the case of the Meewasin Valley Authority in Saskatoon. In this case the master planner was Raymond Moriyama of Toronto. (It was pure coincidence that Yamasaki and Moriyama were both of Japanese origin.) There was substantial opposition in Saskatoon from real estate interests. They were unhappy with the prohibitions against erecting buildings on the riverbanks in Saskatoon. Deputy Premier Roy Romanow and I hoped to shield the new authority from attacks on grounds that this was some sort of a plot by the NDP aimed against business, a common canard used when objections were really on other grounds. We sought a chairperson who would be very difficult to attack. Peggy McKercher agreed to chair the authority. She was (and is) charming, dignified, very competent, and not a New Democrat. She did an outstanding job in launching the new project. She went on to become chancellor of the University of Saskatchewan. Once trails along the riverbank had been built for walking and cycling, the public caught the vision of what could be done. Widespread public support for the concept developed and has been sustained. The project has made Saskatoon an even more attractive city.

The Wakamow Valley Authority in Moose Jaw was developed with less fanfare but with equal public satisfaction.

For people who do not live on the prairie, it is hard to explain the affinity with the land felt by people who dwell on these plains. They have a great sense of the bare elements of a landscape – earth and sky. But in

the same way that they cherish the broad horizon and big sky, they put
great store on the little oases of green that surround the few bodies of
fresh water that dot or snake through the prairie. The parks at Regina,
Saskatoon, and Moose Jaw are an effort to see that the bodies of water
and the grass and trees that surround them are havens of contrast with
the seemingly endless brown, green, gold, or white of the sequentially
monochromatic prairie.

9

The Universities

Universities have a role to play in the day-to-day life of a province like Saskatchewan. As a premier in a province with only two universities, each heavily supported by the provincial government, I faced heightened concerns about the relationships between the government and universities. We certainly had these issues during the 1971–82 period.

During the 1960–4 period of the Douglas-Lloyd government, I was minister of education for a time and as such dealt with the University of Saskatchewan, then our only university. It was a warm relationship. Our deputy provincial treasurer, Albert W. (Al) Johnson, sat on the board. He worked closely with Colb McEown, the university's vice-president. Johnson was diligent in taking the university's concerns to the government, while McEown explained the government position in university circles. This mutual respect and trust between the two groups made the relationship pleasant and productive.

The university plays a special part in the history of Saskatchewan. The decision to locate the university in Saskatoon was made by the newly created board of governors of the university in 1909. Premier Scott is widely believed to have guided this decision as a trade-off for the selection of Regina as the provincial capital in 1905. Out of this history grew a feeling in the minds of some at the university that it alone was entitled to make key decisions on university education in Saskatchewan, and that any involvement of the government in the process would be government interference. Having regard to the interaction of the university and the community, and the changing role of the university in society, this was a remarkable conclusion. Fortunately, it surfaced on only a few occasions.

The appropriate roles and relationships between our government and the university became an issue in the early 1970s. In 1972 we became aware of a good deal of discontent at the Regina campus of the University of Saskatchewan. The problem seemed to stem from a strong feeling that the people on the Saskatoon campus were not giving the people at the Regina campus enough scope to develop their programs in an appropriate way. The Regina campus was growing and attracting a new crop of academics. It was perhaps not surprising that tensions and rivalries would develop. The atmosphere became poisonous. There were some advocates of splitting the two campuses and restructuring the Regina campus as a separate university. I opposed that idea. I favoured developing a single university with two (or more) campuses. I was a little fearful that a separate university at Regina would begin to depart from the liberal arts and social science college concept that we had for the Regina campus. I feared that a separate university would want to compete with the Saskatoon campus in the 'heavy' sciences and in professional schools. I felt that Saskatchewan in the 1970s could afford only one full-service university.

We decided upon a single university with a single board of regents responsible for the major business decisions of the university – property management, salaries, pensions, fees, and the like – and for allocating funds to the campuses received from government grants. Each campus would have a board of governors, a chancellor, a president, a senate, and a faculty council, dealing primarily with academic matters. There are many universities with somewhat similar models, the University of California being perhaps the most well known.

A bill incorporating these concepts was introduced into the legislature in the spring session of 1973. There had been previous discussions with the two campuses, but no agreement was reached – indeed, their inability to agree on many matters was part of the problem.

Reaction to the bill was hostile at the Saskatoon campus. The ostensible objection was based on the transition clauses of the bill, which provided that until the boards of governors at the two campuses had chosen the presidents, the president of the university should be the president of the Saskatoon campus (by far the larger one), and the principal of the Regina campus should be the president there. We were uncertain whether university president Spinks, a distinguished scholar, would prefer to be the president of the Saskatoon campus or would prefer to be with the board of regents – the powerful administrative body. The transition provisions were represented, disingenuously, I thought, as interfering with university independence by naming transition officers. Right Honourable John G. Diefenbaker, the chancellor of the university, was vocal in his opposition to the bill.

I believed then that the objections were to the substance of the bill. I have come to believe something more. Some in Saskatoon thought the bill not only unwise but also somehow illegitimate. To them, it was not the role of the government, but rather of the university, to determine the direction of university education in Saskatchewan. At any rate, there was considerable public controversy. We felt it advisable to withdraw the bill and appoint a royal commission to study the issue. We appointed retired Supreme Court of Canada justice Emmett Hall as a single commissioner. Hall was a graduate of the College of Law at Saskatoon, had practised law at Saskatoon, and was a former chairman of the board of governors of the university (he later became chancellor from 1979 to 1987). Nobody could contend that he was unsympathetic to the concerns of Saskatoon or of the university community at Saskatoon.

As was his style, Hall tackled the job expeditiously. His report was clear. In effect he said to the government, 'You have the right diagnosis but the wrong prescription.' He agreed that the arrangement, as it then existed, between the two campuses was not working, and could not be made to work. He recommended that the campuses be separated, but that the separation should be complete – Regina should be established as a completely separate university. Many at Regina were happy with the proposal; many at Saskatoon less so. I felt that our proposal, set out in the bill, was to be preferred. But after the controversy and the royal commission, we decided it was best to move as recommended. And we did so. Emmett Hall has a claim to be the father of national medicare. He certainly has a claim to be the father of the University of Regina.

This whole incident of the inter-campus rivalry has always puzzled me. I simply failed, and to this day still fail, to understand the issues. I am reminded of a comment by Henry Kissinger. While at a university after his years as President Nixon's secretary of state, Kissinger is reported to have made this approximate comment: 'The intricacies of university politics make me long for the simplicity and transparency of Middle East negotiations.'

I think I know how he felt.

Our government attempted after 1973 to get some of the benefits of unified long-range planning by appointing a University Grants Commission to allocate grants between the two universities, and in so doing harmonizing their long-term planning and avoiding needless duplication. This worked passably well. The government of Grant Devine, which was elected in 1982, disbanded the commission.

Our government's relations with the University of Saskatchewan were a little cool for a brief time following 1973, but we got along well with both institutions during the remaining years of our term in office. The two universities have had their ups and downs but generally have prospered, and in the early years of the new century each seems to have charted a course for itself and is forging ahead at a healthy pace.

The University of Regina has developed colleges of education, social work, administration, and systems engineering. At Saskatoon, one of the important developments has been Innovation Place. I remember watching its origin and playing a part in its official opening in 1981, when it was known as the SEDCO Centre. It was an attempt to use the knowledge developed at the university to create new and innovative products for the marketplace; to make profits from professors. By almost any measure it has been a clear success. In 2005 it housed over 130 firms, large and small, developing and manufacturing products for sale to national and international buyers.

I've often pondered on what governments and the voters who finance them should reasonably expect from universities (and other post-secondary education institutions). These represent huge public expenditures. I've been serving on the board of an organization set up by Parliament, the Canada Millennium Scholarship Foundation. It was set up to spend 2.5 billion dollars, along with the investment earnings over ten years, to provide scholarships and bursaries to Canadians to pursue post-secondary education, mostly at universities. This is but a tiny part of society's spending on universities. Certainly society expects to get a stream of people educated and trained to deal with the many issues that arise to be dealt with by governments and other public institutions in our changing world. In this regard I like the formulation of the aims of a university set out by Professor Douglas Knott for the University of Saskatchewan some years ago. The university should seek

> to provide its students with a liberal education, or at least with the elements of one, by fostering in them, along with competence in their discipline or profession, a broadly informed, reflective and literate mind capable of independent and critical thought. The university should ensure that its teaching (and, in general, also its research) has a basically humanistic and philosophic orientation: scholars and students should have a broad understand-

ing of the place of their discipline or profession in the history of human knowledge and experience, of its meaning for society, and of the major theoretical and philosophical questions which it raises.

That must be a primary objective of any university – to speak to society's needs through the students it educates. But I want to suggest a further step. I believe that university faculties, acting as communities of scholars, have an ongoing obligation to be in dialogue with the public. I speak not only of faculty members individually, because, of course, they are already in dialogue with the public. I speak not only of faculty members, in series, giving their individual views on topics with which society is wrestling. That happens at symposia, in the media, and elsewhere. I speak of scholars at the university talking, discussing, and debating with scholars in different disciplines and offering their distilled wisdom to the public on important matters of public concern. We can hardly expect a comprehensive world view. But we could perhaps expect informed comment on topics such as genetic engineering of crops, or stem cell research, which may have genetic, theological, ethical, legal, and social aspects. There is only one institution that has experts in all such fields, and it seems to me reasonable for the public to ask these people with special competence to put their heads together and tell us what they collectively think.

What are needed are combined conclusions and judgments. Our society already has too many advocates and too few judges. We have too many people who are prepared to take a stand and too few who are prepared to explore the common ground among differing insights, particularly if these insights are informed by different disciplines. University faculties should see their role as offering their conclusions as a group of people with a wide range of skills and backgrounds.

It may be said, 'That is not the job of the university.' Then let me ask, 'If it is not the job of a university faculty, whose job is it? What other group possess the combination of knowledge, insights, and relative detachment and independence to offer views based upon the integration of all the available and relevant knowledge?'

The decline of religious authority has hastened the fracturing of society. The increasing specialization of knowledge has done the same. So, too, has the general decline in respect for, and acceptance of, the views of the social and governmental elites.

The university can help to fill the void. While this may initially embroil the university in controversy, it will in the longer run earn for it public recognition and respect as the place where scholars, as a group, consider and comment on the state of the human condition.

I turn to a second point. It is in the university's self-interest to respond to the public's *cri de coeur* as they find themselves awash in a sea of knowledge and of issues raised by this new knowledge. In our political life we are seeing a steady movement from representative democracy toward popular democracy. At one time, voters were generally prepared to elect their representatives and let those representatives wrestle with questions of public policy, such as, for example, the role of the universities in provincial society. Now, increasingly, the voters have opinions on all issues, manifested by regular polling. And elected representatives are relying not only on their own study and judgment but also on the opinions of their voters. The universities' arguments, which supported their worth to society, and accordingly their entitlement to funds, were once directed at a relatively small core of opinion-makers. They must now be directed at the general public as well. While the extent of this change can be disputed, I believe the direction cannot.

At the same time as democracy is becoming more popular or plebiscitary, the pursuit of knowledge is becoming more specialized. As scholars become increasingly specialized there is a danger that their work will seem to have less and less relevance to the lives of the voters whose general support they must now sustain. That represents a danger to the continued public support for large-scale public spending on universities (or, at least, on their core functions as I have described them).

Some universities enlist public support through athletic programs with which the public can identify. Some seek academic excellence and widespread renown with which the public can identify, even if they do not fully understand the basis of the renown. Some have extension programs of many kinds so that they may touch the lives of a good number of the public. And some continue to rely on their influence with the small core of decision-makers.

Universities will need to continue to address the matter of the techniques they can use to sustain broad public support. Their regular activities do that. They may increasingly use professional public relations advisers. But I suggest that they would gain public support in the longer term by their faculties attempting to address the felt needs of the public in dealing with complex issues requiring the insights of a range of disciplines.

Recognizing all the difficulties, I believe universities should give emphasis to the study of moral reasoning and ethical responsibility in the education of all students. I believe this would follow if university faculties undertook the role of integrating some of the torrent of knowledge that is flowing from their work, and from other disseminators of information, and sharing their combined insights with the public. Once one undertakes the task of making sense of the knowledge that is being produced, then the search for a framework forces moral and ethical reasoning.

We are all familiar with the question of whether nuclear scientists have any moral or ethical responsibility for the products of their work. The question begs a further question. If they do not, who does? I am not being critical here. I am merely making the point that somebody must undertake the job of converting knowledge into wisdom. It ought to be done at the university (although not exclusively there), and this process will involve moral and ethical questions. And when the faculty of the university wrestles with these questions, they then will become a matter of concern in the education of students.

If the university is a place congenial to a lively discussion of ethical and moral issues, the discussion will find its way into the classroom, the committee room, and into the public domain. While few of us like to preach, all of us have an obligation to bring the content of ethical reflections to our teaching, our decision-making, and our dialogue with the public.

The university is an institution created by society, and by which society provides a livelihood for scholars. In exchange, scholars pass on accumulated knowledge, add to the body of knowledge, and, one would hope, wrestle with the intellectual, ethical, and moral issues of the age.

In the course of so doing, the universities will spawn some heretics and some heresies. That, too, is part of their function. Every good university needs a few of each.

10

Northern Saskatchewan

One of our major efforts during the 1970s was to improve life for people in northern Saskatchewan. In order to put the problems of the North into context, it is useful to set out a few of the basic facts about this special and different part of the province.

Following the Second World War, civilization, as we are pleased to call it, was taken to the North. People from the South moved in, taking schools and modern health services with them. It's not clear whether the consequences, good and bad, of modernization were fully considered. Once it was decided that modern health services were to be taken into the North, and these services were put into place, infant mortality began to drop very sharply, and as a consequence population growth was very rapid. Once these things happened, the die was cast. Alternatives to the traditional way of life had to be provided. The resource base was enough to support the population that was there, but not to support the population that would be there. Accordingly, broadened educational services would be necessary, and steps to enhance the resource base would also be needed.

Programs to take roads into the North, to enhance the fur population, particularly of beaver and muskrat, and to preserve the northern fishery for northern residents would be required. These things were done with quite marked success. During the 1950s incomes of northerners grew sharply, but by the mid or late 1960s, the population was again outrunning the enhanced resource base. Other ways for northerners to make a living were clearly required. I am not sure that anything fundamentally different could have been done after the Second World War. Provincial authorities were no longer willing to allow the iron laws of infant mortality to keep the population appropriate to the resource base, and they were, over any long period, unable to expand the resource base, so that it might support the greatly enlarged population. Efforts were made by successive governments to involve Aboriginal people in the forest-extraction industry, with limited results. The interaction of northern Aboriginal people and non-Aboriginals from the South has continued apace, with some success stories and some failures.

Recognizing the need for an expanded economic base has proved easier than providing such a base for people with a very different history and culture than that of the rest of the population.

When we came to office in 1971, the Northern Administration District covered half of the province geographically and was populated by fewer than thirty thousand of the one million Saskatchewan residents. Approximately two-thirds of the people were of either Indian or Métis ancestry. They lived in fewer than thirty-five communities scattered over a land mass of more than 150,000 square kilometres. Roughly one-third of the population were registered Indians, historically and constitutionally the responsibility of the federal government. Another third were white, clustered mainly in the more developed communities of La Ronge, Creighton, and Uranium City. The other third were Métis.

Many of the Métis felt keenly that they were not fully accepted by either registered Indians or whites. They were not part of white society, yet they did not have the land base and recognition by the federal government that registered Indians had.

Northerners suffered under circumstances akin to those of people of the Third World. In 1971, major diseases such as tuberculosis and typhoid plagued northern residents at rates from two to sometimes as high as thirty times provincial norms. More than 60 per cent of northern children who were not white dropped out of school before grade six. Of eleven thousand persons of labour-force age in the North, fewer than half were regularly employed, and less than one-quarter of those employed earned over $2,000 annually. These wage figures make clear that the region was dependent upon subsistence activities such as hunting, trapping, and fishing. Full-time wage employment was concentrated in the three centres of La Ronge, Creighton, and Uranium City, where government administration and mining activities provided a focal point for some rudimentary service industries.

In 1971 northern Saskatchewan represented a classic case of colonialism and underdevelopment. Organizations and people from outside controlled almost everything in the North – government, the education system, businesses, and the churches. Those operating these institutions were, for the most part, accountable to people outside the North rather than to the community or its residents.

We set out to see whether we could change this, or some of it. It was very clear that the conditions existing in the North were special. It seemed to us that the problems in education in the North were more like the problems of health in the North than they were like the problems of education in the South. Most of the problems were very clearly specific to the North. In these circumstances, it makes sense to organize the government services on the basis of geography rather than function. Ordinarily a government has a Department of Education to watch over schools and school boards throughout the province. This is because we believe that the problems of education on the east side of the province are more like the problems of education on the west side of the province than they are like the problems of, say, highways on the east side of the province. An organization based on function makes sense. But we felt that this was not true of northern Saskatchewan. It made sense to set up a single agency to deliver most government programs there. So we decided to do that.

Legislation to set up the new Department of Northern Saskatchewan (DNS) was passed in the first regular session of our new government in February 1972. Just how we were going to make the changes we had in mind was not clear. We proposed two very different kinds of changes. The first dealt with infrastructure. We wanted to build some better roads, some new schools, and get some new houses. All this is fairly straightforward. For these things, you need an agency that can organize and deliver bricks, mortar, and gravel.

But we wanted also to make changes of a different kind. We wanted to see whether we could get northern people to take charge of many more of the activities that affected their day-to-day living, and to make or at least influence the decisions which shaped their lives. The activity of animating and empowering people who have been depressed and dependent for many decades is not a simple task. You're not likely to find people skilled at this kind of community development among those who can do a good job of delivering bricks, mortar, and gravel.

So we set up a department with a deputy minister who was a highly competent traditional old-line public servant, who would see that the 'normal' functions of government were delivered and delivered well. With him we had an associate deputy minister, whom we saw as essentially a social animator, a person who could head a staff which would go among the Aboriginal communities in the North and seek to organize them, so that we could have an elected council for the entire North, elected councils in the larger centres of a hundred to two hundred people, elected advisory committees in the small communities, and elected school boards in the centres which had major schools, with an overall elected school board for the North.

This approach was not fully successful. Some people felt that we should hold off on our infrastructure projects until northern people had been consulted and had given us their thoughts and priorities. Others felt that the basic planning for the activities of DNS should be turned over to a Northern Development Authority made up of northerners. The people who urged this upon us were indeed northerners, but they tended to be white people who had lived in the North a good number of years. We simply did not know whether they spoke for the majority of Aboriginal people in the North.

Our animators, or community development people, did indeed go into northern communities and worked with people to get organized. We knew that northerners, when they started to get themselves organized, would first organize against the power structure as they saw it. This is what happens when disadvantaged people organize themselves to assert their identities and to demand better treatment. The power structure in the North was largely represented by merchants, particularly the Hudson's Bay Company, the churches, particularly the Roman Catholic Church, and the government of Saskatchewan, now represented by DNS. So we had one group of employees of DNS organizing to help ordinary people express their dissatisfaction with what DNS was doing or not doing and to demand change. We knew this situation would arise. We thought it could be managed. We were wrong. We simply could not get public servants to accept that some of their own fellow public servants, with offices just down the hall, should be going about the communities organizing people to express their unhappiness with the way public servants of the same department were performing their duties, and to highlight the many perceived shortcomings of the public servants and the programs they were delivering.

I was not surprised that the first efforts at organization would be directed against the visible wielders of power. I had read Saul Alinsky, and particularly his book *Rules for Radicals*. But even though we were effectively forewarned, we could not manage the internal strife within the department. We had hoped that as northern people got some sort of control over their own destiny, they would fix upon some limited short-term objectives that we might well be able to satisfy, so that the general attack on the power structures would be modified. As it turned out, we simply did not have the time to see whether this process could have worked. We had to form some 'non-governmental' organizations that would be the employers of our community development people. We supplied the cash to these new organizations. The work of community development continued but without the community developers being formally employed by DNS.

As new organizations were created such as an overall Northern Municipal Council and the other elected local and advisory councils, there were immediate objections that the councils did not have sufficient authority or sufficient money. We took the view that the councils and school boards should have authority over operations, including hiring of employees such as teachers, but that capital projects should remain with DNS. We were by no means sure that these newly organized councils and school boards had the experience and the staff to plan and construct, for example, a new school. This was to come later.

We had established a school board in Ile-à-la-Crosse. We wanted to give them the opportunity to raise pride and create a sense of ownership in the community. This was a good community, but it had been riven by sharp disputes between the Aboriginal leadership and the white leadership structure. We decided to build a new school that would be a source of pride, and that would be not only a school but also a community centre. We engaged Douglas Cardinal, an Alberta Aboriginal architect, who has since that time become well known as the architect for the Museum of Civilization in Gatineau, Quebec. The school he designed was a little gem. It was a bit expensive, probably the most elaborate school of its kind in the province. But it served its purpose. The people of Ile-à-la-Crosse took ownership in the school. The library became the community library – something we have had great difficulty achieving elsewhere in Saskatchewan – and the facilities at the school, right down to the electric kilns for making pottery, became things which the community used and were proud of.

The story of DNS for the next eight or ten years is the story of some resounding successes and some impressive failures; a story of well-nigh constant comments from those who felt we were moving too fast and from those who felt we were moving too slowly. Virtually nobody felt we were moving too slowly in terms of getting new schools, new roads, and the like, but there were constant streams of advice that we should be consulting northern people more or getting them to do more. Conversely, auditors, and in one case a judge, were saying that projects were moving forward without being properly accounted for; that housing projects operated by Aboriginal housing companies were providing jobs and houses, but that their bookkeeping and accounting left a great deal to be desired. There is no way that we could win, but, in fact, we did win.

Because of substantial money from the federal government under the Western Northlands Agreements, because of the substantial investment by the provincial government, and because of a hugely increased involvement by Aboriginal people in the North in making the decisions that affected their lives, we did bring about major and useful change.

By 1982, much remained to be done to bring conditions in the North up to a level even approaching those in the rest of the province, but real progress could be seen in new facilities, new programs, and new services. But even more importantly, progress could be seen in reversing the patterns of colonialism and in having northerners take charge of their own destiny in a much more forceful way.

Through individual, corporate, joint venture, and co-operative ownership, northern people were actively involved in providing commercial services. They were producing radio programs, operating day care centres, serving as health workers, supervising construction projects, working in uranium mines and mills, providing substance abuse treatment, and actively participating in all aspects of northern society and northern development. Significant change did occur in the North. For example, over ten years the northern average annual wage increased 154 per cent, well over 10 per cent a year. The welfare dependency rate dropped from 47 per cent of the population to 14 per cent.

The single agency was far more effective than previous administrations had been in funnelling resources toward ignored aspects of northern development.

I travelled often in northern Saskatchewan. I travelled there because it is a land of lakes and trees, a land of boreal beauty, in contrast to the stark spatial beauty of the open prairie in southern Saskatchewan in the area around Regina, where I lived. I travelled there because we were engaged there in a fast-moving social experiment that was producing its full quota of successes and failures. I and other ministers would visit government offices, hospitals, schools, and businesses. I mentally told myself that whenever I saw a person in the position of authority or influence and that person had a white face, this was a sign of failure. The Aboriginal people of the North were inherently capable of filling all of those jobs, but we had not yet provided them with the opportunities for education, training, and experience that would allow it to happen. That was the road we were on.

I have spoken of success stories. A gymnasium was built for the school at Beauval. To build the gymnasium, we had one non-Aboriginal foreman from outside the community and one non-Aboriginal plumber, because we could not find a qualified Aboriginal plumber to meet the legal requirements. All other work was done by Aboriginal people, the great bulk of whom were from the immediate community. This included work normally done by other tradespersons. We used to say that from such a project we wanted four things: we wanted a good gymnasium; we wanted our money's worth; we wanted jobs for the local people; and we wanted training for those same local people, so that they would be able to undertake other construction jobs across the North when this job was done.

But not all was smooth sailing. Far from it. People elsewhere in the province assured us that they wanted us to transform the North, but not at the expense of changing long-standing rules. Contractors complained because many public construction projects were not put up for tender. Trade unions complained that a good deal of construction work was not being done by union labour. To each of these groups, we explained our position, and, except for a few individuals, they did not remain adamantly opposed.

One of the techniques used was to encourage Aboriginal people to form corporations or partnerships to perform work in the North. This usually meant that they entered into some kind of arrangement with, say, a construction company in the South, which was a minority partner but which effectively directed the project, using employees provided by the Aboriginal majority partners. It was not fully accurate to call these entities Aboriginal companies, but this type of arrangement worked tolerably well and has continued to this day. Major services such as trucking and catering are provided to uranium mines in northern Saskatchewan by companies in which the majority ownership is held by Indian bands, and a minority partner brings expertise in operating trucking companies, or catering, or as the case may be. Overwhelmingly, the employees are Aboriginal, and more and more supervisory and managerial people are drawn from the pool of Aboriginal employees.

All of these changes were made easier by a policy we adopted with respect to uranium development in the North. New mines were developed at Cluff Lake, Rabbit Lake, and Key Lake. In each case, in the surface lease that governed the operations of the mine, the government required the mining company to maintain a workforce at the mine site that was one-half long-time residents of the North. These were overwhelmingly Aboriginal.

Another practice put into place by the mining companies in consultation with the government was to have a largely fly-in workforce. We had real doubts whether we could get Aboriginal residents of the North to leave their homes, families, and traditional way of life for long uninterrupted periods. Further, we had no wish to see settlements spring up around the mine sites, where families would live and which would accordingly require health, educational, and some local government and security services. The solution arrived at was to have airstrips at the mine sites (required in any case) and to fly employees from their home settlements to the mine site and return. A typical pattern would be for an aircraft to pick up employees at their home community on Sunday afternoon and fly them to the mine site. The employee would work twelve hours a day for six days (or a little less on the Saturday) and then on Saturday be flown home, where he would stay until the Sunday eight days hence. Good accommodation was provided at the mine sites, but with such a work schedule, minimal recreation facilities were required. The employees worked, ate, and slept. The week at home allowed family connections to be maintained and some hunting, fishing, and other traditional pursuits to be pursued. It has worked remarkably well, largely because the mining companies have done their best to make it work.

The mines have provided a steady flow of income for northern communities and an opportunity for a growing number of Aboriginal people to pursue a career in the high-tech employment of modern mining.

Whenever there is a clash of cultures there is a potential problem. The fly-in method of staffing mines in northern Saskatchewan has been a successful way of bridging cultures – of allowing the benefits of a new technology to be enjoyed without destroying an older existing way of life.

Contractors and unions were not the only people who seemed to expect that social experiments in northern Saskatchewan could proceed without departing from the norms of southern commercial and business operations. When we first set up the head offices of DNS in La Ronge, the emphasis was to get on with the programs that we hoped to launch. Stories trickled down to Regina to the effect that the accounting systems left something to be desired. The Treasury Department set up SWAT teams, who found that, indeed, the accounting was not up to snuff. They sent back an internal memo, complete with a report that they had found money in shoeboxes and records in a rudimentary state. They remedied the problems before any damage was done. The provincial auditor, who had not uncovered any of the shortcomings, proceeded to publish in his report to the legislature the text of the internal memo from the treasury SWAT team to the central office of the Treasury Department in Regina. At the time I thought that action by the provincial auditor was unhelpful, unprofessional, and insensitive. I still do.

Another project involved the construction of houses by some of the Aboriginal-owned companies. We thought we got decent houses and decent value for our money. But once again the accounting was woefully weak. There was a minor judicial inquiry. The judge was sharply critical of the administration of this project.

The judge was a competent and decent man. His report was no doubt justified. But I remember thinking to myself that it would have been helpful if the judge had told me how we could organize projects in the North that would provide houses for the people, jobs for Aboriginal construction workers, and training in construction methods – and have done all this in accordance with generally accepted accounting principles. Perhaps it could have been done. But it was beyond our capabilities, at least in the early stages, and I suspect beyond the capabilities of the judiciary as well.

I contrast this with proceeding with public works projects by the book. Some years later, I was on the Indian reserve at Patunak in northern Saskatchewan and saw the installation of a sewer and water system there. At the time the unemployment rate on the Patunak reserve would have been well over 50 per cent. I saw a sewer and water system being installed by a contractor, who doubtless had been the lowest bidder, using all non-Aboriginal labour from outside the community, but who doubtless was keeping his books and accounts in a proper manner.

I had really no doubts that, with all its warts, the DNS experiment has had a positive and lasting influence on northern Saskatchewan.

After the election in 1982 of the Progressive Conservative government, DNS was disbanded. The end of the department meant, sadly, the end of virtually all further community development work and a decrease in the infrastructure construction that were features of the life and times of DNS.

A closely connected issue was the relationship generally between white society and people of Indian and Métis origin – Aboriginal peoples, to use today's language.

Mr Thatcher's government had taken some steps to help Aboriginal people. The government did what it thought best. It did little to find out what Aboriginal people thought was best for them. I, along with several ministers, tried to build a relationship with Aboriginal leaders. When one is trying to improve the lot of disadvantaged people, particularly when there are cultural differences between these people and mainstream government, it is important to get the perspective of the people you are trying to help. You may feel you know what the next step should be. And you may be right. But if they don't think that this would be the best next step, you are probably doomed to failure.

I had a standard line when I spoke to groups of Aboriginal people. In brief form it went: You have problems, some of them big problems. We (the provincial government) can't solve your problems. We don't know what the real problems are. You do. Only you can solve your problems or take the first steps to solve them. But we can help. What we ask you to do is to figure out what your problems are and what steps to deal with them should be taken first. If you think we can help, please call on us. We can work with you in sorting through the problems, but we can't decide what you should do.

The leaders came to accept this line of approach. I remember having a talk with Chief David Ahenakew, a wise and able leader, despite abhorrent views he later expressed about Hitler and the Holocaust. I was arguing that Aboriginal people had no alternative but to equip themselves to be part of the economic mainstream. (We were not talking about their retaining Aboriginal culture.) He said that he understood this, but that Aboriginal people could not integrate economically, one by one – not at this stage. They had to have a strengthened sense of their own identity, a stronger sense of their Aboriginal roots and a pride in those roots. Then we could talk about more integration. Meanwhile education should be pursued which would do both – raise pride in Aboriginal heritage and equip Aboriginal people to compete in the economic mainstream.

There gradually developed the idea of a separate Aboriginal post-secondary college associated with a university. President Lloyd Barber of the University of Regina was very supportive. Gordon McMurchy, the minister of education, who gained the respect of Aboriginal people, worked with Dr Barber and Aboriginal leaders to create the Saskatchewan Indian Federated College (SIFC), now the First Nations University of Canada. As I heard it put by an Aboriginal leader, 'Once we depended on the buffalo. The buffalo are gone. Education is the new buffalo.'

The SIFC was not the only new buffalo. In 1972, Dean Roger Carter of the University of Saskatchewan's College of Law established a Native Law

Centre. A major thrust was to set up a program whereby Aboriginal people of good intelligence, but little formal education, could be fast-
tracked to equip them to enter the college. Later, other law schools
sought the graduates of this crash course. By the late 1990s well over half
the lawyers of Aboriginal origin in Canada were graduates of the Native
Law Centre. It was a great tribute to Roger Carter. For his work Queen's
University in Kingston awarded him an honorary doctorate degree.

Aboriginal community colleges were set up, including the Gabriel
Dumont Institute, run largely by Métis organizations. I had a heart-warming experience when I attended a graduation ceremony at the Dumont
Institute and saw the pride exuded by the graduates, and especially their
parents, who clearly saw this as a milestone of hope in the lives of their
children. This is a common observation at post-secondary graduations,
but it was particularly powerful at the Dumont ceremony.

There has been a transformation in the state and status of Aboriginal
people in the last twenty-five years. Then, post-secondary attendance was
counted in dozens; now it's in the thousands. There is real hope, especially for the tens of thousands of Aboriginal people who are living successfully in the economic mainstream while retaining the core of their
Aboriginal identity.

Much needs to change, but great strides have been made.

11

Agriculture and Rural Life

In the 1970s, the major industry in Saskatchewan was farming. The chief products of the farms – wheat, barley, oil seeds, beef, and pork – were sold largely outside the province and often outside Canada. Most of these products were sold under international market conditions over which neither the people of Saskatchewan nor their government had any control, and at prices that were notoriously volatile. Economic stability for farmers was always sought after and rarely achieved. The uncertainty was added to by the unreliability of moisture and other weather conditions. Understandably, this made life in the smaller communities that depended upon agriculture uncertain and stressful.

A number of possible approaches to these issues were open to the government. We tried most of them. They included steps to deal with commodity price fluctuations; steps to deal with adverse weather conditions for field crops; steps to make farms and small towns more satisfying places to live and bring up children; steps to help retiring farmers sell their farms for cash so that they would have a secure retirement, and to allow people to enter farming who did not have the cash to buy a farm. We have here the interweaving of the broad objectives of improving economic security and of strengthening the sense of community.

With respect to achieving price stability, we worked with the federal government to get price support and supply management programs in place for dairy, poultry, and egg producers. We provided assistance for farmers to get into these areas of agricultural production so that Saskatchewan's quotas under national programs would be fully used and these relatively stable areas of agriculture would provide secure incomes for an increased number of farmers.

We encouraged farmers to broaden their production base from field crops to include livestock production. Livestock products are sold primarily in North America, where price fluctuations are not as dramatic as they are with grains that are sold on worldwide markets. We took steps to help farmers wishing to expand production of dairy, poultry, beef, and pork products by setting up programs of loans and grants operated under the name Farm Start. We provided a measure of price support for producers of beef and hogs through stabilization programs. The price supports sheltered farmers from the worst drops in prices, at the sacrifice of not being able to take advantage of some of the peaks, and provided a significant level of stability for both farmers and their bankers. One of the many adverse consequences of the boom and bust cycles in agriculture is that it can sometimes be very difficult for farmers to obtain credit from ordinary financial institutions. Credit is a necessity in highly capitalized industries like modern agriculture, especially for younger farmers, and price support programs greatly improve access to credit. The bankers liked more stability, particularly the reduction of the downside risks.

Turning to field crops, strenuous efforts were made to create new markets for crops other than wheat, barley, and oats. Rapeseed, and a particular variety of rapeseed called canola, became a major oilseed crop. Production of a wide range of other crops was pursued, with modest success.

Major steps to improve economic security for farmers included the reshaping of a federal-provincial-farmer-financed crop insurance program to guarantee against loss of yields because of weather conditions. The greatly improved crop insurance plan proved to be an absolute godsend to farmers in the 1980s. The other major effort was a federal program to provide broad general support for the western grain economy in times of depressed prices through the Western Grain Stabilization Program. With these programs, one year of drought or even two was not a financial catastrophe for most farmers; nor was a year or two of depressed prices a disaster.

There was a further ground for unease among rural people. Since the Second World War, they watched and conditionally welcomed the technological changes that transformed the way they lived and worked. Farming was no longer an activity carried on by a nearly self-sufficient family supplying many of its own necessities and using for their farm operations locally bred horses fed by crops they grew. It was now an activity carried out with massive and expensive machines produced outside the Prairies, and often outside Canada, fuelled by expensive petroleum products, and using methods requiring costly chemical fertilizers, insecticides, and herbicides. Technology allowed a farmer to cultivate huge areas of land, and economics forced the farmer to do so.

There were further grounds for unease in the farming community. The prices that farmers received for grain were effectively beyond their control. The cost of inputs used to produce the grain edged upward, and sometimes shot upward, as was the case when the price of petroleum and natural gas, and consequently the price of nitrogen fertilizer, rose sharply during the 1970s. One of the input costs – the rates charged by the railway companies to transport grains – was fixed by federal statute. These statutory rates, known as the Crow's Nest Pass freight rates, or the Crow rate, had been in effect for many years and were under constant pressure from the railway companies. Our government attempted to mount all the pressure it could to retain the benefits of the Crow rate for Saskatchewan farmers. We attempted, largely unsuccessfully, to make this a key issue in the provincial election of 1982. Eventually the federal government dismantled the Crow rate in the 1990s, to the great cost of Saskatchewan farmers who marketed grain outside the Prairies.

Another threat was the proposal by the railway companies to abandon a large number of the railway branch lines, which run like veins across the Prairie landscape. Their removal would see farmers transporting their grain by truck over much larger distances and over roads that were not designed for persistent heavy traffic. Again our government attempted to mount all of the pressure it could muster to prevent or delay rail-line abandonment. Abandonment required the consent of the federal government's transportation agencies. In order to grapple with this issue, the federal government appointed a Royal Commission on Grain Handling and Transportation in 1977. They appointed as the commissioner that redoubtable judicial jack-of-all-trades Emmett Hall, a judge retired from the Supreme Court of Canada.

Hall was a quite remarkable judicial statesman. He had been a successful practising lawyer in Saskatoon. His friend John Diefenbaker appointed him as chief justice of the Court of Queen's Bench of Saskatchewan in 1957. He moved on to become chief justice of Saskatchewan in 1961 and was appointed to the Supreme Court of Canada in 1962. While in this position, he chaired the federal Royal Commission on Health Services, and later the Provincial Committee on Aims and Objectives of Education in Ontario, which produced the Hall-Dennis Report in 1968. Judge Hall left the Supreme Court of Canada in 1973, having reached the compulsory retirement age of seventy-five. He was still very vigorous in mind and body. I recall our attorney general, Roy Romanow, approaching Hall to see whether he would chair an examination of the Saskatchewan court system to determine whether improvements might be made. Hall said that he would need a few weeks to move from Ottawa to Saskatoon and set up his new household, but then would be happy to undertake a study of the court system. He returned to Saskatoon in the spring of 1973 and commenced his court system study.

Shortly thereafter, our government found ourselves in difficulty concerning legislation that we had introduced to provide the Regina campus of the University of Saskatchewan with more independence. I referred to this in chapter 9. We felt that we needed a report by someone who was fully acceptable to the university community in Saskatchewan. Accordingly, we asked Hall to defer his court study and to undertake a study of the organization of the university system. He readily agreed and was just getting his new royal commission organized when there was a national railway strike that tied up the movement of all manner of goods by rail all across Canada, particularly the movement of Saskatchewan grain. The federal minister of labour asked Emmett Hall whether he would agree to be an arbitrator. Hall advised the federal minister that he would have to seek the approval of the government of Saskatchewan.

I remember Judge Hall coming in to see me and nominally asking permission. I laughed and I think he had the good grace to laugh. There was no possibility of any premier of Saskatchewan impeding the solution of a rail strike unless he was proposing to retire from politics within the week. So Hall deferred his work on the university royal commission. I asked him whether this would mean that he could not go forward with either the university study or the court study. He said no, he would dispose of the rail strike arbitration and then go on to the university study, and then complete the court study. So proceeded Judge Hall's retirement.

Some time after these jobs were out of the way, Hall undertook his Royal Commission on Grain and Rail. I remember this well. When we came to office in 1971, we wished to make some changes in the public service. The serving deputy minister of agriculture was Harold Horner, a very able person who was in the twilight of his civil service career. I asked him whether he would be prepared to step aside as deputy minister of agriculture, and head a small agency to study rail lines, particularly railway branch lines, the availability of railway cars, and other issues in grain transportation. I could see them as looming issues before many years had passed. Horner agreed to do this, and he made himself as well informed as anybody in Canada on these issues. I remember that when Judge Hall was appointed to chair the federal royal commission in 1977, he asked me whether he could have Harold Horner as the key person in his commission. I had to demur. The government of Saskatchewan had a vital interest in the outcome of Judge Hall's commission, and we needed to have all the expertise we could muster. Judge Hall was not upset. I think he simply wanted to get the best person he could get.

I recall an anecdote about Judge Hall and his wife, Isabel. They were off to Hawaii to the island of Maui for a January break. My wife, Anne, and I were on the same plane. It was a Canadian Pacific Airlines plane from Vancouver to Honolulu. We were delayed many hours, with the usual excuses mounted for the delay. We finally arrived in Honolulu late at night, dead tired. I happened to be behind Judge Hall in the line-up to get our assigned hotels. We would reach those hotels well after midnight. Judge Hall asked about his connecting flight to Maui in the morning. He was informed that he had to take the next available flight at 6:30 a.m. or else pay extra. He pointed out that this was grossly unreasonable, that the delays were not his doing and that he ought to be able to take, say, a 10:00 a.m. flight without extra charge. This proposal was peremptorily dismissed. I don't remember what argument was made, but I recall Judge Hall muttering to himself – I suspect only half in jest – 'The CPR will pay for this.' I'm sure the CPR continued to be treated fairly, but it showed that Hall was, as well as very bright, very human.

Judge Hall produced a report that was very helpful in restraining the railway companies from wholesale railway-line abandonment.

As the number of Saskatchewan farm families declined there was a gnawing and well-founded fear that the small towns that served them would also disappear, and with them the opportunities close at hand for education, health, recreation, and cultural services for farmers and their children. Farmers had been forced to expand to survive, and their life savings were invested in land and machinery. When retirement time came, they had no ready cash, and their children could not afford to buy the now valuable farm operation. This was the situation in rural Saskatchewan as it appeared in the 1970s.

Our government considered what it could do to preserve a good number of the towns that were the service centres for farm people. If some of their business functions were declining, perhaps we could preserve and add to their educational, health, social, and recreational functions, and thereby make life in smaller towns and the farms that they served a little more satisfying than it otherwise might have been.

We did our best to retain schools. We instituted province-wide collective bargaining for teachers' salaries, so that the salaries in the small towns were the same as they were in Regina and Saskatoon, making them very attractive salaries in the smaller centres. We improved the system of provincial grants to school boards, so that, up to a defined provincial standard, every school had approximately the same amount per student to spend on its schools. We also paid for the cost of bussing children to school.

We retained some small hospitals in rural areas when strict medical cost control criteria may have dictated otherwise. These hospitals helped to keep doctors in smaller centres and to provide some sense of security to families living on the isolated farms and in the villages of Saskatchewan. Changing medical and surgical standards forced a change in role, so that the smallest hospitals came to do most of their work in the areas of long-term and convalescent care and some emergency care, providing a sense of security. The road ambulance service was vastly improved, to add to the existing air ambulance service, and highways were improved, particularly those serving small-town Saskatchewan.

Nursing homes were constructed with a population base far below what federal authorities regarded as minimum. In the case of both small hospitals and small nursing homes, unionization of staff was encouraged and province-wide bargaining for wages and general working conditions was instituted so that, in general terms, working conditions were similar throughout the entire province. This made employment in hospitals and nursing homes in smaller centres financially attractive, with the result that competent staff was recruited and, for the most part, retained.

Grant programs were mounted. One that lasted five years, the Community Capital Fund, was directed to improving the social infrastructure of cities, towns, and villages. This was followed by another five-year program directed specifically to cultural and recreational facilities in these centres. The two programs produced a flowering of new hockey rinks, curling rinks, swimming pools, community halls, and smaller parks.

One could not help but be impressed by what some small communities could do with grant money. One community in southern Saskatchewan had constructed a rather fine outdoor swimming pool. I questioned the mayor as to where they got the money for that pool. He quoted me a figure for its cost. I scoffed at him and said that the bare cost of the materials would be quite a bit more than the figure he quoted, assuming that all labour was free. He advised me that all labour was indeed free, including that provided by the skilled tradesmen, and that while the community had paid for the pumps and filters associated with the pool, cement and some other components had been donated. It appeared that the town hardware and cement merchant also kept cattle. Surrounding farmers delivered feed grain to his cattle operation at no cost, in exchange for which the hardware merchant donated cement to the project, which, along with gravel produced from a municipal gravel pit and hauled by farmers in farm trucks, provided the concrete from which the pool was constructed by volunteer labour.

In another community, farmers and townspeople acquired some cutting rights over Crown land, went into the forest in the winter, cut the trees, pulled them out of the bush with their farm tractors, found a local person to saw the wood, and in due course used the wood to construct the huge rafters that were key components of their new skating rink. A skating rink organization was formed that hired people, many of them farmers who were 'temporarily unemployed' and who (perhaps) qualified to earn grants under federal and provincial winter works programs. Money earned and grants received were given back to the rink association, and so a first-class skating rink resulted.

Many, many communities found ingenious ways to turn the rules of provincial and federal grants into fine recreational facilities. Some of these projects seemed to be latter-day examples of the five loaves and two fishes biblical story. In the course of projects such as these, the sense of common purpose of the communities was further strengthened. In these towns, there was no grumbling to the effect that the town had to provide facilities for farm families who lived outside the community and did not pay town taxes. The facilities were community facilities in the full sense of the word.

Another initiative related to community colleges. When the government assumed office in 1971 there was no community college system of any kind. We did not feel that we could afford a conventional community college system with buildings at different locations throughout the province and faculties teaching at those locations. We devised a college system that had virtually no buildings and virtually no permanent academic staff. The province was divided into regions, and colleges were organized for each. The college consisted of an organization with an office and a handful of administrative staff to organize the program. Classes were offered in churches, schools, halls, and other public buildings. Instructors were obtained on a contract basis from the university centres of Regina and Saskatoon, and from technical institutes at Moose Jaw and Saskatoon.

As well, high-school teachers and other people with particular skills were contracted to give courses. In many areas the public response was overwhelming, with well over 10 per cent of the adult population enrolled for one or more courses. In this way, post-secondary and continuing education courses were offered in many hundreds of communities across Saskatchewan. The community college program achieved a great deal with limited resources and was a clear success.

To deal with the problem of assisting older farmers to retire with dignity and young people to get into farming without a massive amount of capital, we introduced the Land Bank plan. This was a scheme by which the government's Land Bank Commission would buy land from retiring farmers at market value and rent it to young people entering farming. Preference was given to members of the family from which the land was purchased. In these cases, the Land Bank was a way to finance a rollover of land from one generation to the next within the family. In other cases young people not connected to the farmer selling the land would rent it. We had an elaborate and, we felt, fair way to decide who could lease the land. Decisions were made by a board made up of local people according to a published point system. The person leasing the land for five years as a renter had an option to buy the land or continue to lease it. My thought was that as young farmers got established, they would buy their land from the Land Bank. This, in turn, would provide money for new purchases and leases to new young farmers. We failed to consider the strength of the forces of farm consolidation. Young farmers did get started. They did prosper and buy land. Unfortunately for the program, they bought land from private owners and retained their Land Bank leases, because they too felt the need for a larger and larger land base. As the Land Bank Commission bought more land and sold little, unease about government ownership of farmland grew. And, as farmers prospered, there were more and more applicants for each parcel of land that the Land Bank had available. It proved impossible to convince the disappointed applicants that the selection process was completely fair, although we felt it was.

The Land Bank was, therefore, only a partial success. It achieved some of its purposes, but many people were not convinced that it was the best approach to the acknowledged problem. It is not that the idea was superseded by a better one. Rather, it was that no approach to the intractable problem of getting farmland into the hands of the next generation was both effective and generally acceptable to the public.

I look back ruefully on all our efforts to try to stabilize farming and rural life. We were, it seems, King Canute trying to hold back the tide.

The economic forces at work leading to more highly mechanized and larger farms were too strong to be turned back by a provincial government and perhaps by any federal government. Preserving relatively smaller farms as a way of life and in order to preserve a particular visage of the countryside has been successfully done in Europe, but at very high cost. At times in the 1970s and thereafter, the cost of the Common Agricultural Policy carried on by the European Union represented half of its budget. I recall being in Germany and inquiring why they did not purchase more Canadian high protein wheat. The answer was that the import tariff together with shipping costs increased the costs to the German miller to about three times what the Canadian farmer received. Plenty room was left for European farmers to market their crop at a handsome price. Using different tools, a similar result was achieved for American farmers by providing them with billions of dollars from the U.S. Federal Treasury. The Canadian government has achieved some of the same results for egg and poultry producers by orderly marketing schemes that protect Canadian farmers from imports and require consumers to pay a price that yields a fair return to the farmer. But unless the Canadian government was willing to subsidize Canadian farmers to something like the level enjoyed by European and U.S. farmers, nothing could stop the iron laws of economics from forcing producers to seek the lowest possible costs, regardless of the effect on family farming and rural life.

Our government tried to take some of the risks out of adverse weather and sharp price fluctuations in grains, beef, and pork. We tried to retain the subsidy inherent in the Crow's Nest Pass freight rates. But the federal government was unwilling to continue the Crow rate subsidy. One can understand their point of view. With eggs and poultry, Canadian consumers pay the subsidy to Canadian producers. With the Crow rate, the subsidy was paid by Canadian railroads for the benefit, so it was said, largely of non-Canadian consumers. This is not a fair characterization of the effect of the Crow rate. The international grain prices were only moderately affected by Canadian production. Accordingly, the export price would not be significantly affected by freight rates paid in Canada. The Crow rate, therefore, was more accurately a subsidy by Canadian railroads to Canadian farmers. Nonetheless, the federal government took the view that Canada's international trade commitments made it difficult to maintain the Crow rate. This strikes Saskatchewan people as a poor argument. The same arguments would prevent both the United States and Europe from subsidizing products that enter international trade. But very clearly these countries subsidize their farmers, who produce a substantial volume of commodities that enter the international market.

In the absence of a national policy to support farmers whose products flow into international trade, their numbers will be dictated by the economics of production. The number of farmers will continue to decline, although the volume of production may not.

It may well be that the move to larger and larger farms could be slowed down if farmers as a group had a clear vision of what they preferred as a future for the producers of field crops. But consensus is lacking, and unless there is a change of heart on the part of governments and farmers, consolidation is likely to continue. Farm employment may not decline as much as the number of farm units. But it seems clear that farms will continue to get larger and more highly capitalized. The family farmer can be put on the list of endangered species.

12

Oil

Our election program in 1971 spoke of resources and our need to get benefits from them in the form of royalties, employment, and local control. But in our early years in office, resources did not occupy the central role in government decision-making that they did later in the decade.

In 1971 and earlier years, the value of mineral resources – oil, natural gas, potash, and uranium – on world markets was modest. Their market value over and above the costs of producing them provided only a small margin to be divided among the mineral owner, the producers, and governments. All this began to change in 1973. In preceding years, the demand for oil rose sharply – partly because of the war in Vietnam. Supplies became tight. Then many of the major oil-producing and oil-exporting countries combined in a cartel of Oil Producing and Exporting Countries (OPEC) to regulate production and, by doing so, to raise prices. And so we had the oil 'crisis' of 1973. Early in that year, the price of a barrel of oil was $2.00 (U.S. funds). By October it had risen to $3.00. This created a huge windfall of profits for oil companies, which owned billions of barrels of oil reserves. A 50 per cent increase in the sales price meant a doubling, tripling, or more of oil company profits.

These events were fast-moving. I wondered what Saskatchewan should be doing. I recall attending an NDP provincial convention in Saskatoon early in November of 1973. Returning home on the Sunday evening, I was tired and climbed into the back seat of the car, so that I could doze and think. What I arrived at was that we should study a royalty regime that left the oil companies with the benefits of the 1973 increases in oil prices, but that out of further increases, they should get only the increased costs of production and probably some allowances for exploration. The rest of the increase – what I thought of as windfall profits –

would come to the provincial government as added royalties (from Crown lands) or added taxes (from large blocks of freehold land).

The next morning I met with lawyers from the Attorney General's Department and asked them to come up with a rough draft of legislation that would take this approach. Out of this came a draft of The Oil and Gas Conservation, Stabilization, and Development Act (1973), which became known as Bill 42. The bill was introduced into the legislature on November 29th, and after a lengthy debate over fifteen days, third reading and royal assent was given on 19 December 1973.

In today's climate this bill seems draconian. And it was. But so were laws passed elsewhere. Alberta passed legislation abrogating existing leases and setting much higher royalties. We believed our leases permitted us to vary the royalty rates without abrogating the leases. And anything that Alberta or Saskatchewan did or might have done paled beside the actions of other governments in Venezuela, Libya, and elsewhere in expropriating the assets of oil companies.

There was vigorous opposition from the companies. But since world oil prices were rising, and sharply, we would have had no difficulty in arriving at a *modus vivendi* with the oil companies on a split of the 'windfall profits.' Some problems arose because we were adopting a new royalty plan. The chief difference in our approach was our reliance on graduated royalties. For decades, oil had been developed in North America on the basis of the oil company getting 87½ per cent of the value of the oil produced and the mineral rights owner getting 12½ per cent. The oil company paid all costs; the mineral rights owner had a 'carried' interest. If some oil properties were more valuable than would be fairly compensated by a 12½ per cent carried interest, then this was covered by a bonus payment to the mineral owner at the time the agreement was made between the oil company and the mineral owner. In the years when T.C. Douglas was premier there had been other approaches to royalties. Rather than the oil company bidding on a parcel of mineral rights owned by the Crown and naming a bonus payment along with a standard lease giving the Crown a 12½ per cent royalty, the oil company could bid by proposing a higher royalty than the stated 12½ per cent and a lower bonus payment. This served to encourage smaller oil companies with less cash on hand to bid for drilling rights.

In the 1970s we moved in the same direction. We felt that when the value of minerals was uncertain and rising, it was unwise to set a final price at the time when the initial contract was made. We favoured a relatively low base royalty combined with a graduated royalty that increased or decreased with the rise or fall of the price of the mineral as it was produced and with an adjustment for increases in costs of production. It seemed to us that a 12½ per cent royalty might make sense if the price of oil was $3.00 a barrel, but was too low if the price of oil increased to $6.00 a barrel and when there had been only a modest increase in production costs. We negotiated elaborate formulas for graduated royalties for oil, potash, and uranium. As prices increased, they yielded much more than fixed royalties plus bonus payments would have done.

Graduated royalty schemes are now fairly common. They represent, I believe, the fairest way to divide the return from mineral production among the producing company, the mineral owner, and the government. In many cases the issue is made simpler by the owner and the government being the same.

I said that we would have been able to get a working relationship with the industry even in a time of unstable and rising prices. But the federal government decided that the windfall profits should be shared by Ottawa and by all Canadians as consumers. There was a very sharp negative reaction in Alberta and Saskatchewan. People with long memories reacted with hostility: 'Here we go again. The feds think that Prairie resources still belong to them.'

It is difficult to appreciate the depth of this reaction without a consideration of the history of the Prairie provinces within Confederation. Seven of Canada's provinces, all but the three in the Prairies, were colonies (or, in the case of Ontario and Quebec, were created from one colony) at the time that they became part of the Canadian federation. They thus enjoyed independent colonial status when they became part of Canada. The Constitution Act, 1867 (British North America Act, 1867, or BNA Act, 1867) gave these new provinces the power to continue to manage their public lands and resources. But when the Prairie provinces were created from lands of the Hudson's Bay Company that had been previously acquired by the federal government, Ottawa did not give to them ownership and management of public lands and resources. All title to lands and all rights to mines and minerals and royalties were kept by the federal government.

A small annual *per capita* payment was paid to the three provinces instead of giving them management of the lands and resources. As you might expect there was strong opposition in the three provinces. Ottawa adopted this approach because it wanted to control the steps being taken to entice new immigrants to settle the 'empty' lands (empty, at least, of non-Aboriginal people). There was steady pressure by the three provinces to remedy the perceived injustices of federal control. When the settlement phase of the Prairies was largely completed, the federal government had less interest in controlling the public lands and resources. Finally, in 1930, by the Natural Resources Transfer Agreement and accompanying changes to the Constitution Act, 1867, the provinces gained the same control over their lands and resources that all other provinces had enjoyed since their entry into Confederation. That was the situation in 1930.

I am not aware of any incident in any non-Prairie province since 1867, or in any Prairie province since 1930, in which Ottawa sought to take to itself the economic rent due the owner of the resource, except through normal corporate taxes. Nor am I aware of instances in which the federal government sought to take to itself any of the economic rent when there were no corporate taxes because a provincial Crown corporation developed the resource.

Until the 1970s this was the situation. This was true whether the resource was developed for service to the people of the developing province by a Crown corporation, or whether it was developed for sale to another province or another country.

Ontario developed the electric power potential of the Niagara River (an international river) around 1900 and kept all the benefits for Ontario, even when on occasion power was sold to the United States. Ontario developed petroleum and natural gas resources in and around Sarnia and Petrolia and in Lake Erie (an international lake) without any claim by the federal government to any of the economic rent. Quebec developed massive hydroelectric resources and exported substantial amounts of electric power to the United States. British Columbia developed massive electric power resources for sale to the United States pursuant to the Columbia River Treaty (to which Ottawa was a signatory) without any attempt by the federal government to share in the economic rent.

Indeed, Saskatchewan developed coal resources near Estevan and on occasion sold the coal to other provinces, and also sold the electric power generated from this coal to the United States, without any claim by the federal government to any of the economic rent. The same is true for petroleum and natural gas development in Alberta prior to 1973.

The letter and spirit of section 109 of the Constitution Act of 1867 and of the Natural Resources Transfer Agreement of 1930 were fully respected – until the 1970s. This is the background to moves by the federal government to gain a share of the windfall profits.

The oil companies, of course, opposed Bill 42. They pursued remedies through the courts. The defining case was *Canadian Industrial Gas & Oil (CIGOL) v. Government of Saskatchewan*. The province was successful in the Court of Queen's Bench. Then Saskatchewan was successful in the Saskatchewan Court of Appeal by a five to zero margin. Chief Justice Culliton wrote the judgment. But Saskatchewan lost in the Supreme Court of Canada. A full panel of nine judges heard the case, and we lost seven to two. Throughout the court proceedings, we had eight judges on our side and CIGOL had seven, but theirs were in the better place.

Judge Martland wrote the majority judgment in the Supreme Court, and Judge Dickson, later Chief Justice Dickson, wrote the minority judgment. I won't try to outline the legal arguments. The case turned on the legislation, in which a provision calculated royalty on the difference between a base price and fair market price of oil, and gave the minister certain powers in setting the fair price. We set it up in this way to deal with the transfer-pricing problem – the possibility of an oil company in Saskatchewan selling oil to an associated company in the United States at an artificially low price, so that the purchaser rather than the seller would make the profit. This provision, it was said, interfered with international trade and commerce, a federal jurisdiction. I felt that on this key point the judgment of Judge Dickson was the better law.

Whatever the legal arguments, we had the Supreme Court upholding a very broad interpretation of federal power to regulate international trade. We felt that this was at variance with their holding in a Quebec case (*Carnation Milk*), where it was held that the province had a right to set a minimum price for milk going to a processing company and thereafter largely exported outside of Quebec.

The federal government took far more aggressive action to capture a large share of the increasing economic rent from rising oil prices. They imposed a ceiling price on all oil entering inter-provincial trade and an oil export tax on all oil being exported to the United States. This export tax was the difference between the world price of oil and the much lower ceiling price set for Canadian domestic consumption.

This amounted to a massive transfer of wealth from the producing provinces to the consuming provinces. I used to say it was a transfer of wealth from the good and prosperous burghers of Moose Jaw to the lumpen proletariat of Westmount in Montreal and Rosedale in Toronto. And a large transfer it was. In some years the export tax on Saskatchewan oil shipped to the United States was larger than the total take of the Saskatchewan government from that oil in regular royalties, royalty surcharges, corporation taxes, and all other sources of revenue from the oil.

It should not be supposed that oil was the only energy product that was increasing in value. As you might expect, other energy sources were increasing in value in an almost equivalent way.

Electricity producers were enjoying increases in revenues. British Columbia, Manitoba, Ontario, and Quebec were enjoying sharp increases in prices and profits on the electricity they exported to the United States without the federal government seeking to capture any part of these increases. So Ontario was enjoying oil and gas prices that were half the world price, electricity from their own public utility at low prices, and substantial profits from the export of electricity to the United States at increased full market prices. The level of federal-provincial controversy was intense. Saskatchewan issued pamphlets with titles such as 'Why just oil?' Our argument was that if the federal government believed that they had some right to share in the windfall profits from rising energy prices, why did they confine their grab to oil and gas? Why not electricity?

Commodities other than energy products were also increasing sharply in value. I remember arguing in a speech in Toronto in the late 1970s that Saskatchewan would be pleased to provide Ontario with oil at 1973 prices on one condition – that we were paid for the oil in gold mined in Ontario at 1973 prices. The price of gold had gone up by a much greater percentage than the price of oil. But the federal government claimed no share of this increase in price. Once again we asked, 'Why just oil?'

It was argued that if Alberta got its full increase in the value of oil, it would become so wealthy that it would unbalance the federation. We were sensitive to the argument. We knew all about trying to provide services somewhat equivalent to those provided in the neighbouring province of Alberta when Saskatchewan had to tax its citizens for most of the money spent by its government, whereas Alberta collected in oil royalties 60 cents of every dollar it spent and needed to tax much less. Again our argument was, 'If one province has too much wealth, find a way to tax the wealth – do not tax oil and gas in the hands of a relatively small, relatively poor province such as Saskatchewan.'

So the disputes surrounding oil and gas were intense.

The federal government dealt with the provinces of Alberta and Saskatchewan in bad faith, or so we thought – more on this later.

The combined effect of our loss in the Supreme Court and the relentless cash grab (as we viewed it) of the federal government caused us to seek other solutions. It seemed clear to us that if the resource was owned outright by the provincial Crown and developed by the provincial Crown, it would be more difficult for the federal government to claim the increase in the value of the resource. This is because the Constitution Act, 1867 provided in section 125 that no lands or property belonging to Canada or any province shall be liable to taxation. In 1974, we formed the Saskatchewan Oil and Gas Corporation (SASKOIL), a Crown corporation to acquire oil and gas prospects. This served two purposes. It immediately put some assets out of the grasp of the federal government, and it served notice on both Ottawa and the industry that significant public ownership was an option if we could not reach agreements in sharing the economic rents from oil and gas.

After the CIGOL case defeat in the Supreme Court, we were under obligation to return a massive sum 'wrongly' collected. With respect to this obligation, we recovered (in fact, retained) well over 90 per cent of the money by imposing, retroactively, an Oil Well Income Tax. This was admittedly playing hardball. But then those were hardball times, and we worked out some modest mitigation of royalties for the oil industry.

The situation was that we regarded the royalty paid as a fair price for oil extracted by the industry. We said we would be happy to return the royalty money if they would return the oil. This was clearly a rhetorical position. But the government and, more importantly, the public would not agree that companies extracting the oil should not pay a fair price for it. As prices rose, the royalties paid seemed a low price. The oil companies are hugely practical souls accustomed to dealing with governments of all stripes around the world. They accepted the Oil Well Income Tax and the modest adjustments we had made. This made sense to them because prices were rising, the federal government had made major changes to reduce the impact of the rule regarding the non-deductibility of provincial royalties (on this I will say more later), and they were making good profits. As a result, we lived more or less happily with the industry for the balance of the 1970s.

Our anger with the federal government was shared in equal or greater measure by the government of Alberta. Premier Peter Lougheed and I made common cause, grew to respect each other, and were able to resolve a number of issues, energy and otherwise, between our two provinces by sensible compromise.

A sidebar to this period of controversy was that as Alberta called for the world price for their oil rather than a 'Canadian' price set by the federal government, Ontario used its influence in Ottawa to keep the Canadian price for oil well below world prices. The oil export tax skimmed off for Ottawa the difference between the Canadian price and the world price of oil, all at massive cost to Alberta. Not surprisingly, relations between Alberta and Ontario became strained, to understate the situation.

Premier Lougheed and Premier Davis of Ontario were both gentlemen, and able gentlemen. In my view, neither province has seen their equal to this date. But while they continued to be respectful and polite, they were not able to muster the continuing confidence in dealing with each other that difficult negotiations sometimes require. As a result, during the constitutional negotiations of 1979–82, it became more difficult to bridge the gap between Ontario's position as the leading province in support of the federal constitutional reform proposal, and Alberta's position as a leading province of the four 'hard-line' opponents. It seemed to me that the bridging function fell, to a considerable extent, to me since I had been at pains to keep good relations with both Davis and Lougheed, both of whom I admire and like.

Just how much of a gentleman Premier Davis was (and is) is illustrated by what is for me a sad tale.

It was 1976 and the event was the Grey Cup game being played in Toronto at, as I recall it, Exhibition Stadium. Bill Davis, then Ontario premier, and I, then Saskatchewan premier, were with Prime Minister Pierre Trudeau watching the game. Bill Davis and I had a friendly wager. The three of us were up in the stands. The game was drawing to a close, and the Saskatchewan Roughriders were comfortably ahead of the Ottawa Rough Riders. The routine was that the prime minister and the premier of the winning province would be on hand when the cup was presented at the end of the game. With something less than a minute to play, Pierre and I started on our way down the aisle to get to the field level, where the presentation would be made.

We had just reached ground level when there was a great roar. Every older fan in Saskatchewan still remembers what happened. With twenty seconds left in the game, Tony Gabriel of the Ottawa Rough Riders pulled in a pass from Tom Clements and scored a touchdown that defeated the good guys 23 to 20. The pass may be legendary in Ottawa and referred to even today as 'the catch,' but in the Blakeney household, it is not the catch but the pits. Bill Davis had to hurry down to become part of the presentation ceremony, and I had to my make my way, head down and eyes averted, back to my seat in the stands to watch the Grey Cup being presented to Ottawa.

Think what had happened. I had lost my bet with Bill Davis. We had discussed the game. I had been humble, as befits any Roughrider fan. But as the game progressed, I may have allowed a note of triumph to

Allan Blakeney with Tommy Douglas ca. 1972.

Allan Blakeney and Queen Elizabeth II greet citizens of Saskatchewan during the royal visit of 1973.

Allan Blakeney, Queen Elizabeth II, and Prince Philip (standing behind the Queen) attend a formal banquet during the royal visit of 1973.

Premiers' conference in St John's, Newfoundland, August 1975. Allan Blakeney is in the foreground at right in conversation with Peter Lougheed, former premier of Alberta.

Ten Canadian premiers in front of the lieutenant-governor's residence in Winnipeg, Manitoba, 1981. From left to right: Brian Peckford (Newfoundland), Allan Blakeney (Saskatchewan), William Bennett (British Columbia), John Buchanan (Nova Scotia), Bill Davis (Ontario), Sterling Lyon (Manitoba), René Lévesque (Quebec), Richard Hatfield (New Brunswick), Angus MacLean (Prince Edward Island), Peter Lougheed (Alberta).

Ed Broadbent and Allan Blakeney at the opening of Tommy Douglas House, Regina, Saskatchewan, 1981.

On the campaign trail, Moosomin, Saskatchewan, 1986.
(Photo by Darlene and Fred Harrison)

Allan Blakeney.

creep into my voice. I had wagered a meal, but I had not intended the menu to be crow.

On the larger scene, if the Roughriders had won, back in Saskatchewan there would have been jubilation in the land. Confidence and contentment would have stalked the highways and byways. Any government in office likes this. But it was not to be. This state of grace was denied us – by twenty seconds and Tony Gabriel.

It is not my fondest football memory.

I return to the resource wars.

The federal government opened a new assault in 1980 with the introduction of the National Energy Program. It put in place new and fresh legislation that imposed a Gas and Gas Liquids Tax and a Petroleum and Gas Revenue Tax (PGRT). The latter was, in effect, a federal tax on each barrel of oil and each unit of production of natural gas. That tax added another swear word to vocabularies in the West – PGRT.

There was no way that there could be an agreement at this point.

For one thing, Mr Lougheed and I had lost our belief in the good faith of the federal government's negotiating tactics.

In early 1974 we had made clear that we were seeking for our province a large part of the increased value of oil and gas – the windfall profit, as I have called it. One tactic that we had heard might be used by Ottawa was to disallow as a taxable expense for an oil company the royalties they paid to a provincial government. This would be unprecedented and aggressive. Consider this: there are two parcels of land, one with mineral rights owned by the Canadian Pacific Railway (CPR), and one with mineral rights owned by the province of Saskatchewan. Oil Company 'X' produced oil from both. The royalties paid to the CPR are an expense for federal corporate tax purposes, as they should be. The royalties paid to the government of Saskatchewan are not an allowable expense. There could not be any reason in accounting, taxation, or government principle for this. I wrote to Mr Trudeau in March 1974 asking whether this was their intention. A few days later Mr Lougheed and I met with Mr Trudeau, and we believed we had his assurance that this was not so. Yet, in Mr Turner's budget a few weeks later, there it was. Mr Lougheed and I felt betrayed. So, future negotiations were in the mode of: 'Fool me once – shame on you. Fool me twice – shame on me.'

The governments of major resource-producing provinces – Saskatchewan, Alberta, British Columbia, and, to a lesser extent, Manitoba – were at daggers drawn with the federal government. We told our story over and over again to our voters. We spoke in other parts of Canada. There was a precipitous loss of faith in the government in Ottawa on the part of a large block of people in western Canada, defined here to include Manitoba, Saskatchewan, Alberta, British Columbia, Yukon, and the Northwest Territories (there was no Nunavut then). The public vented their wrath on the Liberal Party.

In the West, so defined, the Liberals won the following number of seats in elections prior to their defeat in 1984: 26 out of a national total of 264 in 1968; 7 of 264 in 1972; 13 of 264 in 1974; 3 of 282 in 1979; 2 of 282 in 1980; and 2 of 282 in 1984.

The Liberal Party was eliminated as a political force in the West. I do not believe that the caucus which launched the National Energy Policy in 1980 had a member who had a single barrel of oil produced in his or her constituency. Canadian politics has not recovered from this regional fracturing that the resource battles produced.

I turn to section 92A of the Constitution Act, 1867 (the BNA Act). This Act, along with its amendments in 1930, gave control of resources to the provincial governments. But the scope of this control came under fire in the 1970s because of Ottawa's policies with respect to resources, and because of decisions of the Supreme Court of Canada in the CIGOL and Central Canada Potash cases. I'll say more on the Central Canada Potash case in chapter 13. In the constitutional negotiations leading up to the patriation of the Constitution in 1982, our government tried to recoup some of the ground we felt we had lost by these federal policies and Supreme Court decisions. The best we could do was to get a new section in the Constitution, section 92A, which relieved some, but not all, of the sting of the CIGOL and Central Canada Potash cases.

The courts had suggested that some of the charges on resource companies by provincial governments were not direct, but rather indirect, taxes and therefore beyond the authority of a provincial government. This is a distinction that only a philosopher or a well-paid lawyer would appreciate. At any rate, the new section 92A fixed the problem. It allows provinces to levy direct and indirect taxes on resources so long as the tax does not mean that a province charges one tax for its citizens and another rate of tax for other Canadians. That was fair enough and acceptable to us.

The courts had also suggested that some of our charges to resource companies interfered with inter-provincial and international trade. Section 92A does not solve that problem. We did not believe that provinces should, in any real sense, interfere with inter-provincial and international trade. We just did not think that what we were doing did this. To us the Supreme Court arguments were not convincing. And they still aren't.

Despite its shortcomings, section 92A was a good step forward, both symbolically and legally. It was achieved partly by Ed Broadbent, the federal NDP leader acting as an advocate for the Saskatchewan government in this regard.

It is said that there are two things which you should never see made – sausages and laws – or so said Otto von Bismarck. This certainly holds for constitutions. Section 92A, referred to above, and section 35 of the Constitution Act, 1982, the latter dealing with treaty and Aboriginal rights, were among sections of the constitutional package that were subject to some raw wheeling and dealing.

The election of the Mulroney government in 1984 led to the repeal of the National Energy Program. Since that time we have not seen an overt move by the federal government to gain a major share of oil royalties.

But the scars still remain.

The resource battle represented a failure of our political system.

Time is healing the wounds. But we still don't have a party caucus that can perform the brokerage function so necessary in a disparate federation such as ours. The party in power in Ottawa should have a reasonable number of seats in all regions of the country for it to be able to take decisive action when required and still retain credibility throughout the country. It may be that proportional representation is the only way this can be achieved on any ongoing basis.

13

Potash

Prior to 1971

The potash story is one of the more interesting issues that our government was called upon to deal with during its eleven-year tenure. It is part of the struggle over resources and who would get the benefit from them that convulsed Canada during the 1970s, and which has influenced the political map to this day. An attempt to defend the Trudeau National Energy Program would earn a black eye in most Alberta bars today. Saskatchewan people are, for the most part, more peaceful. They would simply throw the offender out, if the publican, mindful of his premises, did not beat the patrons to the punch.

The potash story starts in the 1940s and 1950s. Largely as a result of oil and gas exploration, huge beds of potash were discovered over a large area of Saskatchewan. The government of Tommy Douglas gave fleeting consideration to developing them as a Crown enterprise but had decided by 1950 that the exploration of the resources should be left to the private sector. The government might have been willing to participate in a joint venture with a private sector company, but no offer was forthcoming.

The first exploration permit was issued in 1952. One company made sporadic attempts to sink a shaft near Unity, Saskatchewan. Two other companies pioneered the sinking of shafts to mine potash in the conventional way – Potash Corporation of America (PCA) and International Minerals and Chemical Corporation (IMC). They experienced huge technical problems in driving their shafts through a geological formation about 1,800 feet below ground – the Blairmore formation – which held saline water under high pressure. The water eroded cement-lined shafts. IMC brought a technology from Germany, which involved sinking a series of holes around the shaft and freezing the ground and water, then sinking the shaft through the frozen soil and lining it with a heavy steel liner, a process called tubbing. The German owners of the technology incorporated a company in Canada to deal with their interests – Associated Mining Consultants. It was represented here by Davidson, Davidson & Blakeney, the law firm with which I was associated from 1958 to 1960.

Eventually PCA and all other companies that sunk shafts in later years employed tubbing. One company, Kalium Chemicals Limited (KCL), used a very different mining technique. They drilled holes into the potash bed, pumped hot water down into those holes to dissolve the potash, pumped up the potash-impregnated water, and boiled it to get rid of the water. Using the knowledge that salts have different temperatures at which they precipitate out, KCL was able to produce potassium chloride of a good level of purity. Moreover, by using this method, KCL could tap potash deposits as deep as 6,000 feet, whereas the shaft mines average perhaps 3,300 feet in depth, and would have substantial difficulties going more than a few hundred feet below that level.

Favourable royalty rates were negotiated with those three pioneers, PCA, IMC, and KCL, and were guaranteed until 1981.

During the period between 1960 and 1964, when I served in the Douglas-Lloyd cabinets, the mine at Lanigan was approved. This was a French-German consortium that used the name Alwinsal. They pressed for the same royalty arrangement as the pioneers. The cabinet decided that Alwinsal should not get the preferential rate and that the regular royalties would apply. The pioneers had, unfortunately, incurred a great deal of extra expense solving the mining problems by methods that were now available to newer entrants like Alwinsal. The company accepted the decision and went ahead.

When the Thatcher government took office in 1964, they pursued policies designed to fuel economic development. One of their targets for expansion was potash mining. They gave the preferential royalty rate and guarantee to all new entrants but announced that it would be available only to companies that committed to new mines by 1 December 1967. The result was that ten mines were in operation by late 1970. Well before that date, capacity had outstripped market demand, and mines were in serious financial trouble. With capacity being at least twice that of effective demand, prices tumbled. In four years potash prices (I refer to muriate, the commercial product) dropped from $21 a ton to $12 a ton. With mines operating at less than 50 per cent capacity and with prices dropping by 40 per cent, the companies were facing extremely tough times. But there was a further problem. The low prices were devastating the U.S. potash industry based in New Mexico. Premier Thatcher, who was a major author of the debacle, was somewhat disingenuous when he stated: 'Seldom in the economic annals of Canada have we seen such responsible corporations get into such an economic mess. Lack of co-operation and lack of planning have brought major corporations to the brink of disaster.'

These developments in the late 1960s caused bills to be introduced in the U.S. Congress to impose potash tariffs and to restrict the quantities of potash that could be imported into the United States. Anti-dumping proceedings were instituted.

The potash companies, mainly U.S.-based, were unwilling to come together to restrict production and maintain a realistic price. They believed, probably correctly, that potash consumer groups would generate anti-trust proceedings.

Premier Thatcher moved to do what he felt was necessary to save the industry. He was clearly frustrated by receiving encouraging signals from the companies, only to receive formal letters and telegrams, clearly drafted by anti-trust lawyers, refusing to participate in framing any joint plan dealing with the production, export, and pricing of potash. The premier's frustration was understandable. In his mind he was dealing with Canadian companies, albeit subsidiaries of U.S. companies, producing a Canadian resource for sale both within and outside of Canada. Yet it was clear that U.S. lawmakers were asserting jurisdiction in a manner that caused the companies to decline to discuss such issues as levels of production and price in a meaningful way with the government of Saskatchewan.

Mr Thatcher introduced a plan based upon the productive capacity of each mine and the assured markets that each operator had captured. There was to be a quota for production from each mine and a floor price at which the potash could be sold. Effective 1 January 1970, each mine was given a production allowance that tended to be about 40 per cent of capacity. The minimum price was to be $18.75 per ton. The plan was referred to as the pro-rationing plan.

The plan went into operation and worked reasonably well.

There were questions about whether or not a provincial government could establish such a marketing scheme. Since virtually all potash produced in Saskatchewan is sent outside the province to the United States, to other countries, and other parts of Canada, and since constitutional jurisdiction to regulate international and inter-provincial trade rests with the federal government, there were real doubts about a province's ability to set up a legally valid regulatory scheme of this nature. The minimum-price provision was clearly open to attack. There is general agreement that a province can regulate the production of a resource for conservation purposes. This has been recognized with respect to oil and gas. But with respect to potash, for which resources are estimated in terms of hundreds of years of production, it is harder to make a conservation argument.

The federal government showed a lively interest in the issue, probably because it was likely to arise in relations with the U.S. government. Both Jean-Luc Pepin, the minister of industry, trade and commerce, and later John Turner, when he was federal minister of justice, came to Regina to discuss the issue with provincial politicians. Notwithstanding the interest, and the issues arising in the House of Commons on more than one occasion, I know of no instance prior to the election in June 1971 when Ottawa took a public position stating that what the government of Saskatchewan was doing was beyond its constitutional jurisdiction.

1971–1982

Such was the situation when we came to office on 30 June 1971.

While in opposition, the NDP had been strongly critical of the potash pro-rationing plan. In our election program, 'New Deal for People,' we had made clear references to potash. 'Regina Liberals,' our platform said, 'make deals with U.S. potash interests whereby American mines run at full capacity while Saskatchewan's American-owned mines lay off one-third of their workers.'

We promised to restore employment in the industry by '[ending] the present government collaboration in a potash cartel that restricts Saskatchewan output and jobs.'

We accused the mine owners of showing their 'unconcern' about jobs for Saskatchewan miners, and of using 'their power to force farmers to pay exorbitant fertilizer prices.'

We promised that 'an NDP government would consider the feasibility of bringing the potash industry under public ownership.'

We ended by saying that an NDP government would 'review existing royalty and other arrangements with a view to renegotiating, where necessary, those not in the interests of Saskatchewan people. Where feasible, we will reclaim ownership and control of foreign-owned resources.'

Even making some allowance for the forthright language common to election manifestos, these phrases were likely to cause unease in potash industry circles, and they did. Almost immediately after we assumed office, I had a stream of senior officers of the potash industry coming to see me. I was able to reassure them that we had no immediate plans to acquire ownership positions in the industry – and I did not detect real concern on their part with respect to the ownership issue. They were concerned about whether we would retain the pro-rationing plan. They, uniformly, urged us to do so, with the possible exception of one company, Central Canada Potash.

In opposition we had not fully considered all the issues at play. We were clearly unhappy with a deal which saw Canadian mines operating at about 40 per cent capacity, with a consequent loss of employment, while U.S. mines in New Mexico operated at virtually full capacity. In retrospect, I suspect that some of our views, including my own, were affected by a bit of a pro-Canadian, anti-U.S. attitude that was, and is, part of the thinking of many people in the NDP. I recall that when Premier Thatcher was negotiating the potash arrangement, he had dealings with Governor Cargo of New Mexico. Doubtless as a gesture of goodwill, Governor Cargo had made Mr Thatcher an honorary colonel in the New Mexico National Guard and gave the premier a plaque to mark the appointment. Mr Thatcher had it displayed in his office. I felt that the display of the plaque was vaguely demeaning to the office of premier. I'm sure others would simply regard it as an indication of goodwill. I was conscious that we all have different built-in reactions to events, major and minor, and that it is useful to keep that in mind.

We saw the options as increasing production in Saskatchewan, thereby increasing jobs, economic activity, and, perhaps, royalties, at the expense of price and at the expense of U.S. producers in New Mexico. Alternatively, we could reduce production in Saskatchewan with a consequent loss of jobs and economic activity, but with increased company profits, more jobs in New Mexico, and higher prices for potash for both U.S. and Canadian farmers.

Perhaps this statement of the issue did not fully capture the matters in play. Perhaps the U.S. producers, over the objection of U.S. farmers, would have been able to curtail the import to the United States of Canadian potash at low prices.

We knew when we came to office that we wanted to unwind the pro-rationing plan as soon as feasible, but this was not an urgent priority. Our strong advice from our officials, the same officials who had advised Premier Thatcher, was to retain the pro-rationing plan, but to alter it to give less weight to markets which the companies said they had secured and more weight to plant capacity – so-called flat pro-rationing. All of the companies but one, Central Canada Potash, urged the same change.

We adopted this advice from the industry and from our officials. In retrospect, I think this was a mistake. The advice in favour of the change was based on the fact that companies were being less than frank in estimating their markets and were thereby increasing their quotas at the expense of other producers. Plant capacity could not be so easily fudged.

But Central Canada Potash contended that it was in a position different from other companies. Central Canada was 51 per cent owned by Noranda, a long-established Canadian mining company, and 49 per cent owned by C.F. Industries. C.F. was the industrial arm of Central Farmers Co-op, a large farmers' co-operative based in the corn belt of the United States and possessing an extensive potash-distribution system. When C.F. Industries said it had a market, it probably did. Central Canada Potash contended that it had built its mine on the basis that it had secured its market by joint ownership, and should not be required to share that market to support companies that had expanded without taking the precaution of securing their market. Other companies said that they, too, had made market connections and that since the issue was industry over-supply, all companies should share in the industry stabilization effort.

At the outset, I tended to treat the industry as one entity. This was unwise. There were more cross-currents than I had believed there to be. I have often thought that the potash story in Saskatchewan is one in which, at various stages, all the players made decisions as if they were seeing the future through a glass darkly. Not even the hindsight was 20/ 20.

During our first few months in office there were many pressing issues to be handled. My purpose in the short run was to find a way to stabilize the industry and, at the same time, extract more revenue for the province. We were to launch an ambitious set of new social programs, and in the next several years costs would be rising.

Our cabinet started as a small group of ten. I added two ministers in January 1972, including Kim Thorson as minister of mineral resources. In June, Mr Thorson announced that we would continue pro-rationing, but based on plant capacity only. He also announced a pro-rationing fee of 60 cents per ton of muriate. Central Canada Potash made very clear that it opposed our plant-capacity-only, 'flat' pro-rationing, and it applied to the Court of Queen's Bench for a *writ of mandamus* requiring the government to permit it to produce all the potash it required to fill its orders. This application was eventually denied.

In December 1972, Central Canada Potash launched an action to have the pro-rationing regulations declared *ultra vires* – that is, beyond the legal powers of the province to enact.

Meanwhile our government was having some difficulty getting from the Department of Mineral Resources any well-developed policy options other than the policy we were pursuing. We moved to add to our corps of advisers in late 1972 by engaging John Burton, an economist with some specialized knowledge of potash. He had been a Member of Parliament from 1968 to 1972 and had been defeated in the election of that year.

I felt that we needed some new insights on potash. I was anxious to get rid of our regulations setting a minimum price. I felt that they were open to legal attack. Respecting pro-rationing generally, I hoped to be able to drop these regulations in due course, but in the meantime to use them as a method of raising revenue.

My goal was to arrive at a longer-term strategy whereby the industry would provide Saskatchewan with both a stable economic base and a source of dependable revenue to finance social programs. This strategy might involve a marketing agency, public ownership of the potash resource and private development pursuant to contracts, public production and sale of potash, or any combination of these and other options. Over the next two or three years, relations with the industry, and particularly relations with the federal government and interventions by the courts, came to dictate our choices among the options. We did support what amounted to a common selling agency called Canpotex for all Saskatchewan potash sold outside North America.

We took steps to get a rational tax and royalty regime in place. To date, we had had only a royalty based upon tonnage mined and a pro-rationing fee based upon tonnage sold. In October 1973, we announced a requirement that financial statements for each mine be filed with the government.

Our staff and some of the consultants we engaged were considering a wide range of options. Professor Arne Paus-Jenssen of the University of Saskatchewan did important work that was the basis of a tax on potash reserves introduced in 1974.

In the eyes of the government, potash assumed a role of lesser prominence after the emergence of the oil crisis of late 1973. There are only so many battles that can be fought at one time. We turned our attention to the sharply rising value of oil. We introduced legislation called An Act Respecting the Conservation, Stabilization, and Development of Oil and Gas in Saskatchewan, commonly known as Bill 42, in November 1973. It was designed to capture for the people of the province a large part of the windfall profit that was flowing from the sharp increase in the international price of oil precipitated by the formation of the OPEC cartel. The controversy surrounding oil was to spill over into the world of potash.

With potash we confined ourselves to continuing the pro-rationing plan but made modest changes to allow more production than we thought would be sold. We believed that this would modestly relieve the problems of Central Canada Potash and that it would put pressure on prices so that we could increase Canada's share of the world market. We moved to get modestly more revenue with an increased pro-rationing fee and sought to learn more about the industry by gathering financial and other information, so that we could devise a rational tax regime based upon the industry's ability to pay. We also hoped to reach a joint venture arrangement with one or more producers. When sales exceeded productive capacity in the future, we hoped to be a part owner of the new capacity.

The next issues arose largely as a result of actions by the federal government and, later, the courts.

I mentioned earlier that the federal budget delivered by finance minister John Turner in May 1974 provided that royalties and like provincial taxes paid by taxable Canadian corporations to provincial governments were no longer deductible as expenses for the purpose of calculating corporate taxes payable to the federal government. This created a huge problem in dealing with the potash companies. They took the position – a reasonable one – that the combined federal-provincial tax load on their company should be even-handed and bear an appropriate relationship to their ability to pay. The province took the position that provincial royalties and like taxes were payment for a resource being sold by the government, as agent for the people, to the resource company, and that clearly the resource was valuable as evidenced by rising resource prices on world markets. The province was perfectly willing to concede that the federal government should tax profits of corporations. We were not prepared to concede as appropriate the federal government's practice of calculating profits for taxation purposes on a basis wholly inconsistent with any business or financial method of determining profits. We would not accept a practice designed to capture for the federal government a part of the increased value of the resource being sold by the province to the resource companies. We determined to carry on in what we felt was a totally appropriate way, based upon our well-understood constitutional position and on past practices since 1930, when, by constitutional amendment, the province gained control of its resources. We felt that we could not be responsible for the clearly unfair taxes being levied by the federal government on a basis which bore no relation to generally accepted accounting principles.

During this period some of our planning people were doing work on methods of moving toward public ownership and control of a portion of the industry. At that time we were not discussing taking over existing mines. We were to be partners in plant expansions, and we gave some thought to a new government-owned mine. We had made a change of minister in the Department of Mineral Resources, from Kim Thorson to a new young MLA, Elwood Cowley. Our oil policies were not well received by the oil industry. Accordingly, it was not wise to have Mr Thorson, who represented the oil city of Estevan, identified with these policies. Mr Cowley represented Biggar, which was not an oil-producing constituency.

Meanwhile there was a development on the legal front. I have mentioned that Central Canada Potash had launched a legal action to attack the potash pro-rationing as *ultra vires*, or beyond the legal jurisdiction of the government of Saskatchewan. In November 1973, the federal government, acting through the office of Otto Lang, attorney general of Canada, moved to be added as a co-plaintiff along with Central Canada Potash. So far as I am aware, this was, and is, wholly unprecedented. It is not uncommon for the federal government or provincial governments to ask to be added as an intervener in cases that involve constitutional questions. This is a status that, in effect, says, 'We do not wish to become involved in the issues between parties. We do, however, wish to advance legal arguments dealing with the constitutional issues raised by the case.' This is a well-understood procedure used by all governments on occasion. This role does not permit the intervening governments to bring forth their own evidence dealing with the questions at issue between the parties, nor does it allow the interveners to collect costs from the parties to the action.

Asking to be added as a co-plaintiff was a startlingly aggressive act. When Premier Duplessis promulgated the Padlock Law in Quebec, giving the government power to shut down premises where communist ideas – so-called – were discussed, and when this was attacked in the courts, I recall no action by the federal government to be added as a co-plaintiff to oppose the Duplessis bill on constitutional, human rights, or any other grounds.

It was particularly galling that Ottawa was taking this stance with respect to regulations that were introduced by the Liberal government of Premier Ross Thatcher with the full knowledge of the federal government and, in particular, Ministers Pepin and Turner, and with the tacit consent of that government. The new NDP government that came to office in 1971 had done absolutely nothing to change the regulations to make them less constitutional. Indeed, the changes we made were designed to make the regulations more directed to resource conservation and less directed to market considerations, and accordingly to the regulation of inter-provincial and international trade – areas of federal jurisdiction.

The conclusion to be drawn seemed to be that what was constitutional if done by a Liberal provincial government became unconstitutional when done by a NDP provincial government. In our view, it was clearly inappropriate for the office of the attorney general of Canada to be used in this way. It was not a case in which a plaintiff of limited means might need help in marshalling evidence for a constitutional challenge. Central Canada Potash represented the combined resources of Noranda Mines Ltd, one of Canada's largest mining companies, and the Central Farmers Co-op, one of the largest farm supply co-operatives in the United States.

Ottawa's action seemed to us a declaration of war that clearly signalled, when combined with the Turner budget of May 1974, how the federal government proposed to move to appropriate for itself a major part of the increasing value of resources in western Canada. Ottawa seemed to be willing to use constitutional law and far-reaching tax law changes in the battle.

People in western Canada could not fail to notice that it was only some resources that were being targeted by the federal government. If a date is to be set for the rise of western alienation, it would be November 1973 and May 1974 in Saskatchewan and, I suspect, May 1974 in Alberta. The rise was fuelled by the federally maintained low domestic price of oil, the export tax on oil, the formal National Energy Program in 1980, and other strategies in the federal Liberal government's war on the West.

Meanwhile our government was pursuing ways to raise more revenue from potash. We hoped to disband the pro-rationing plan in short order and with it the pro-rationing fees. We did not wish to raise royalties because of the royalty guarantees given to the companies by the previous

Thatcher government. We had been considering other tax vehicles, and in April 1974 we announced a new tax to the industry – the potash reserve tax. The government continued to press for a role as a joint venture partner with companies in the industry. We indicated that we proposed to set up a corporation to market potash and that the potash could be obtained by receiving royalties in kind rather than in cash.

The potash reserve tax was to be a tax on individual potash deposits. We were attempting to get money and participation in new ventures. The industry was pushing back. We were using our tax proposals, and our proposals for a new corporation to enter potash marketing, as bargaining chips. We had taken a bargaining position and were prepared to move from it. But the expected bargaining failed to take place. There were a couple of reasons. John Turner's 1974 federal budget caught the companies in a squeeze not of their own making. Ottawa was taking a new and unprecedented position, and we were unwilling to concede that much of the value of the resource belonged to the federal government. I'm not sure that Ottawa was targeting potash in its budget; rather, it was targeting oil and gas, and potash was simply caught in the crossfire. 'Collateral damage' is the term sometimes used in other wars; but certainly not 'friendly fire.' There was nothing friendly about the federal attack.

The industry suggested that taxes like the potash reserve tax be replaced by taxes on net income, a tax to be divided between the federal and provincial governments. This approach, while reasonable from their point of view, left completely unanswered the question of how net income was to be calculated. Was it to be calculated according to normal accounting rules, or according to new, and in our view, outlandish rules set by the federal government?

These dealings were taking place in a climate of sharply rising potash prices. Mr Thatcher had to contend with ruinously low prices of $12.00 a ton. The support price under the pro-rationing regulation was $18.75 a ton. By April 1974 prices were in the range of $40.00 a ton, and by late 1974 the figure was $60.00 a ton. It was this massive increase in the value of potash that added the sizzle to the three-way debate among the provincial government, the federal government, and the potash companies.

Our initial proposal for the reserve tax, before the Turner budget, would have left the potash companies with a return on investment in the 17 per cent range, based on information then available. We anticipated that there would be representations by the industry, and further bargaining, and that we would arrive at a tax level with which the industry could live. It became clear after the Turner budget that our new tax, combined with the new federal rules (that provincial royalties and taxes would not be deductible as business expenses), would impose a hardship on the companies. We were convinced that, in principle, provincial royalties and taxes on natural resources extracted by resource companies were entirely proper, that the royalties and taxes paid were clearly business expenses for the purposes of calculating corporate income, and that taxes should be paid on that corporate income to federal and provincial governments. Our view was that the problems of the potash companies were wholly due to inappropriate actions by the federal government. The companies appeared to take the view that it was up to the provincial government to compensate for the federal action. We did not share that view.

The companies asserted, undoubtedly correctly, that they were being badly treated by both governments, taken together. They declined to show us any meaningful financial material. And things began to get difficult.

In October 1974 we announced publicly a new potash policy, including the reserve tax that had been disclosed to the industry in April. All minimum price provisions in the pro-rationing regulations were removed, and all mines were authorized to produce at full capacity. There was a restatement of the need to expand capacity and the desire of the government to participate in the expansion.

We continued to await some response from the industry to the October 1974 announcements. We waited in vain. The companies did not put forward any counter-proposals for a tax regime. They did not provide us with any financial statements. And they went one step further; they began to withhold information on how much potash they were in fact mining, so that we had no way to calculate royalties on the old basis. This was wholly unacceptable. No company can remove a public resource and decline to pay for it where they do not deny their obligation to pay, on the grounds that they have a quarrel with the government on another issue. Every citizen, individual or corporate, must be prepared to pay taxes that are acknowledged to be owed. This situation continued for a short period.

In February 1975 some ministers and I had a formal meeting with the industry in the cabinet chamber in Regina to hear their grievances and to state again the position of the government. They continued to be adamant and continued their position of non-payment of any taxes.

We were commencing a legislative session.

It was an open secret that there would be a provincial election in June, and I assumed that the industry was taking a hard-line position in hopes of our electoral defeat and, from their point of view, having a new, more reasonable government with which to deal. We decided that we would not precipitate a confrontation until after the election. I fully expected that immediately after that election, the industry would indicate it was time that our differences were resolved. And so the situation continued in a stand-off mode until the election of 11 June 1975.

I was very surprised when following our re-election there was not a contact from the industry indicating a desire to bargain. Instead, nine days after the election, the companies launched a legal action to attack the potash reserve tax regulations. Shortly thereafter they launched a legal attack on the constitutional basis for the pro-rationing regulations as well. I regarded this as a very low blow. These were the same companies that in 1971 had come to the government and to me personally asking that the pro-rationing regulations be continued. I had come to office with the intention of considering dismantling the regulations, and this had been made clear in our election manifesto. The companies persuaded me that such a move would not be in the best interest of the industry, and we continued the regulations and made the changes that the large majority of companies requested. This had caused one company, Central Canada Potash, to launch legal proceedings to attack the legal validity of the regulations. The companies had urged us to hang in with the regulations, and we had done so. Admittedly there had been other intervening events, but none of them could possibly affect the legal right of the province to pass the pro-rationing regulations. I regarded it as bad faith in the extreme for companies to attack the legal basis for regulations that they had urged us on so many occasions to retain.

What we were seeing was an industry lashing out against a government that they felt was abusing them. We felt that the industry was laying at our door the sins of the federal government and were declining even to enter into negotiations with us. In addition, they were withholding taxes that they fully acknowledged were due and payable. All of these events were the background for a decision that we made in August 1975 to acquire, if we could, a significant part of the potash industry of Saskatchewan. Such a move would accomplish a number of important objectives. The first would be to place beyond the reach of the federal government the returns from that part of the potash industry that was owned by the Crown. Secondly, it would signal to Ottawa that the vehicle of public ownership was available for other industries, namely oil and uranium, if they persisted in their policy of attempting to get for themselves a substantial part of the increased value of these resources. Thirdly, it would signal to the potash industry that it was wholly unacceptable for the industry to withhold taxes that were acknowledged to be due and owing, and would signal to them also that there were other options for developing the potash industry in Saskatchewan, and accordingly that they could not name their own terms. Negotiations were required. Fourthly, it would signal to other resource industries that our government considered public ownership of some of the resources as an option, and we believed that this would be part of their thinking when negotiating with the government.

Finally, some of us felt that the public ownership of some resource industries would cause some in our party and other groups in the community, particularly the academic community, to consider the economic future of Saskatchewan in a different light. We hoped that we could encourage people to regard the future as not wholly determined by decisions made by foreign resource companies but to be partly determined by Saskatchewan people themselves. This is the germ of the idea that later became the 1978 election slogan, 'We Can Do It Ourselves.' It was, in an inchoate way, a declaration of independence from the federal government and of more independence from the international resource companies.

We began to plan in earnest for the public ownership of some of the potash industry. There had been plans developed for a government-owned mine at Bredenbury in eastern Saskatchewan, and these were dusted off. We had consultations with people throughout the world, including Maurice Strong, George Cadbury, and officials of the Manley government in Jamaica, about problems that might arise should it be necessary to expropriate any properties, particularly those owned by U.S. companies. There were extensive legal consultations.

We did our preparation in private so that the issue would not be bandied about in the media before we had assembled the relevant information and before the final decision was made.

Finally, we were in a position to announce our new policy in the Speech from the Throne delivered on 12 November 1975. Almost immediately we introduced legislation to provide a stronger statutory basis for the Potash Corporation of Saskatchewan and to provide for the development of potash resources in the province.

I was aware that the reference in the speech to possible expropriation of the Saskatchewan assets of companies with headquarters in the United States might raise some concerns in Washington and elsewhere that could lead to questions being directed at the Canadian government. Accordingly, I had one of our people go to Ottawa. I called Prime Minister Trudeau the day before the speech, read him the portions that might provoke enquiries, and suggested that our person in Ottawa might brief officials at External Affairs (as it then was) on the issue as we saw it. We had a cordial chat. The prime minister expressed no views on the policy question and thought consulting with the department was a useful idea. The consultation proceeded, and I think External Affairs appreciated the opportunity to avoid being blindsided.

Throughout our term in office, I was meticulously careful to respect the role of the federal government in dealing with foreign countries. Before I went to China and Japan in 1976, I had External Affairs send me briefing material. I read it and spent a full day with an official from Ottawa going over all the points of sensitivity. When in Japan, I had close contact with our embassy, and the ambassador accompanied me when I spoke with groups who would question me about uranium policy. The ambassador was Bruce Rankin, a man from Saskatoon, and we spent a convivial evening, along with the late Bud Estey, also from Saskatoon. Estey served as a justice of the Supreme Court of Canada. That evening the prospects of the Toronto Blue Jays loomed larger than matters of potash or uranium.

In the same vein, I recall a period when the government of France was refusing to sign the Nuclear Non-Proliferation Treaty dealing with uranium. I recall speaking with the then undersecretary of external affairs, H. Basil Robinson. He was a friend – we having played together on the Oxford University ice hockey team. I recall telling Basil that while we hoped to sell uranium from Saskatchewan to France, if the federal government decided to ban sales of Canadian uranium to the French, Saskatchewan would make no public objection.

I simply did not approve of provincial governments sending representatives abroad who acted to undercut the role of the federal government in managing our external relations. Beyond our borders we are one country. We should keep our fights at home.

The debates on the Speech from the Throne and the two potash bills were protracted and acrimonious. But the bills were passed and became law in January of 1976.

We set out to put some flesh on the idea of the corporation. To understate the matter, the companies were upset with our move. They reacted in quite different ways. The European partnership – Alwinsal – simply decided to adjust. International Minerals and Chemicals was the single biggest player, and potash was their major product. They, too, decided to adjust, as did the companies with Canadian roots – Central Canada Potash and Cominco. The others appeared to decide that if the price were right, they would sell to the new provincial Crown corporation. Alwinsal made the same decision on financial grounds. In the ensuing two years, the Potash Corporation of Saskatchewan (PCS) purchased the mines usually described as Rocanville, Allan, Cory, and Lanigan, and acquired about 40 per cent of the producing capacity of the industry. It was our hope that as mines expanded, we would get something approaching 50 per cent of capacity.

I had no wish to have all or almost all of the capacity in PCS. Many problems come with being the clearly dominant operator and marketer. We expected that some customers in the United States would not wish to buy from us on ideological grounds. Conversely, the Chinese government preferred to buy from a state-owned trading corporation. They operated their own state-owned corporations and understood that world. We felt that there was real merit in having private operators, against whose performance we could measure the performance of PCS. And we felt that we did not need to own all or most of the industry to send a clear signal to the resource companies and the federal government that public ownership was an option in pursuing our policy to get for Saskatchewan people the largest possible return from the resources being exploited.

In the following few years, we saw the fruits of our potash policy.

On the one hand, the bruising battle with the industry had possibly harmed the reputation of Saskatchewan as a place for investment by foreign capital. This is hard to measure. Certainly the potash companies continued to invest, as did the oil and gas and, particularly, the uranium companies. But it is quite possible that some others did not.

In commercial terms, the Potash Corporation prospered. It became an influential player on the world potash scene. And it was profitable. On an equity investment of about $420 million, it made profits of $78 million in 1979 and $167 million in 1980.

The U.S. government took an interest in any possible expropriation of assets of U.S.-based companies. The ambassador to Canada, Tom Enders, visited me in Regina. He was a tall man with a commanding presence. He was cordial but insistent that any acquisitions be at fair prices. We never intended to do anything less. We were aware that our primary potash markets were in the United States. So we had no difficulty agreeing in principle. He acknowledged our right to acquire the assets; we acknowledged the obligation to pay fair prices. In any event, all assets were acquired by bargaining, and prices fair to seller and buyer were paid. No assets were expropriated.

More broadly, a new bargaining climate had been created for dealing with both the resource companies and the federal government. Ottawa continued to insist that payments of provincial royalties and like taxes by resource companies were not deductible for federal income tax purposes. (Soon after the Turner budget of 1974, we moved to make such royalties and taxes deductible for the purposes of provincial income tax.) The federal government introduced a series of other deductions that relieved much of the pressure on the resource companies, and left room for our potash reserve tax.

Once negotiations were established, we were prepared to make adjustments to the potash reserve tax. Financial statements were provided, taxes were paid, and a *modus vivendi* was established. I do not suggest that the potash companies were happy. But they remained and they prospered. And so did the treasury of the government of Saskatchewan, and therefore the people of Saskatchewan.

Since the capital cost paid by PCS for its mines per unit of productive capacity was much higher than for companies who had constructed their mines many years previously, and since PCS enjoyed good profit margins, it can be safely concluded that the potash companies made very satisfactory profits, while still paying the potash reserve tax.

Drawing Conclusions

Looking back on the potash dispute, one is forced to conclude that all of the players acted less than adroitly. This stemmed partly from a lack of a full understanding of the objectives of the other parties and the pressures under which they were operating. It stemmed also from the fact that the potash dispute occurred at the same time as that surrounding oil revenues, in which the stakes were much higher.

The overwhelming event leading to the disputes was the sharp rise in the value of resources that saw the price of a barrel of oil rise from $2.50 to $10.00. The value of a ton of potash rose from $15.00 to $60.00, and, a short time later, the value of a pound of yellowcake (the uranium product sold by Saskatchewan mines) rose accordingly.

The amounts involved, particularly in the case of Alberta oil, were staggering. Under those circumstances, governments in Canada are under great pressure. The Alberta government, by legislation, abrogated thousands of oil leases that provided for a fixed royalty of 12.5 per cent. Saskatchewan leases allowed the government to adjust the royalty figure, but the court held that the parties did not contemplate changes of the kind that we made. The federal government felt that it should require Alberta and Saskatchewan oil to be sold in Ontario and elsewhere at well below the prices it could have been sold for in the United States. Everybody used arguments based on equity, fairness, historic precedent, or whatever argument came to hand.

In Saskatchewan we believed we had solid arguments. Referring to potash only, we believed that the government had assisted the industry for years when it was in trouble, and that the industry should not have resented sharing some of the newfound wealth. The industry no doubt felt that the government in the 1960s had given them royalty holidays and were now trying to destroy the benefit of low royalty guarantees by imposing other taxes. Each was convinced that the other was acting in bad faith.

I believe the government was resentful of the unwillingness of the industry to present a coherent industry wide-position but, as we would say, was offering instead conflicting positions put forward by different companies in, so far as we were aware, the same circumstances. I think our government did not fully appreciate the pressure that the U.S. companies felt due to ongoing antitrust actions by agencies of the U.S. government. It is not easy for Canadians to appreciate fully that, in many respects in trade matters, there is not one U.S. government, but several. At one point, an agency of the U.S. government was taking proceedings alleging that Saskatchewan potash was being dumped in the United States at prices below the costs of production and below the prices at which it was being sold in Canada. At the same time, another agency of the U.S. government was alleging that officials of the Saskatchewan government were conspiring to operate a cartel to maintain the price of potash at an artificially high price. U.S. potash companies have to navigate that morass of trade law, and I don't think we were fully appreciative of all the difficulties that this created for them.

Conversely, I felt that the companies failed to appreciate the complexities of federal-provincial dealings in Canada. They may perhaps be forgiven for that. But it was in the highest degree unrealistic for them to expect the government of Saskatchewan to produce a royalty and tax regime that incorporated both federal and provincial taxes when the federal government was asserting a right to get a share of the increase in the value of resources in a totally unprecedented way. They should have known that this assertion was being resisted, particularly by the governments of Alberta and Saskatchewan, and that potash revenues were only a small part of the total stakes in dispute.

Elsewhere I have referred to the lack of sophistication of the potash industry in dealing with governments, compared to the oil and gas and uranium industries. This undoubtedly played a part.

And there may have been unacknowledged and largely unappreciated factors at work. Up to the beginning of the 1970s, Saskatchewan people who long had shared some quiet pride in their accomplishments in curling and social policy had reluctantly accepted the fact that in economic terms our star was not rising. Our fortunes were tied to agriculture, and we seemed doomed to suffer the swings of world grain markets and the results of increased mechanization and the steadily falling rural population that followed it.

And then came the 1970s. We had some oil and gas. And that was good. It provided money and with it hope. And there was potash and later uranium. In potash, perhaps, we could be a major player on the world stage. Perhaps even with uranium. And in some way, perhaps, this sense of growing pride and self-confidence found its way into our dealings with the resource companies. When matters of provincial government participation arose, the oil industry exhibited little concern. On a project basis, they have a bewildering array of farm-ins and farm-outs that allow what might be thought of as floating partnerships. At a corporate level, they have dealt with and partnered with many state-owned enterprises. The uranium industry had no concerns with provincial government participation. In the world of potash, the Europeans had no problem with government participation. Indeed, a person I dealt with in the state-owned French potash company, which was a partner in Alwinsal, and someone with whom I had dinner at his downtown Paris residence, went on to be the foreign minister of France. But the U.S. companies did not seem able to consider the idea of a partnership with a provincial government. This rejection may have had a greater effect on our approach than we acknowledged.

For whatever collection of reasons, an effort that on our part started with a desire to dismantle the pro-rationing plan as soon as practicable and to get substantially more revenue from potash ended with these objectives being achieved, along with the establishment of a Crown enterprise, which during our term in office was a solid success.

14

Uranium

In Saskatchewan the story of uranium is a sharp contrast to the story of either oil or potash. While our government in the 1970s had robust disputes with the petroleum and potash companies about royalty levels, I often thought that I could not have had a real dispute with the uranium companies even if I tried. They were so sensitive to the political aspects of uranium development, and accordingly so willing to have government partners, that dealing with them was a serene and simple activity.

I recall some of the negotiations of a new royalty schedule. We put out a proposal to them that provided for a sliding scale of royalties depending upon uranium prices, but with a minimum royalty of 5 per cent. They protested that the minimum of 5 per cent was too high. We felt that any mining operation should be able to provide 5 per cent of the sale price of the product to pay for the mineral in the ground. They offered to show us where we were wrong. At the next meeting, they appeared with computer printouts of all the financial statements of the uranium companies and the impact of our proposed royalty schedule on each. They were able to show that for the Eldorado mine at Uranium City, in times of low prices, a 5 per cent minimum was very high. We were talking about one mine that had been in operation for twenty-five years, so not a lot was at stake. It was the complete openness of the companies about their financial position that contrasted so sharply with other resource companies, particularly the potash companies, which at one point refused to disclose to us how many tons of potash they were mining, so that we had no way of knowing how much royalty they should pay.

Our issues with uranium mining were very different from those of potash or oil. We wished to see that uranium development provided the greatest possible benefit for the people of the North, and we wished to deal effectively with the sensitive environmental issues that are associated with mining uranium, refining it into yellowcake, and shipping it outside the province.

There was a lively dispute within the NDP as to whether Saskatchewan should mine uranium at all. The opponents had a range of objections. I felt that at their root the objections came from a feeling that mining uranium contributed to the nuclear arms race, and that the possibility of nuclear Armageddon was the greatest threat faced by the world. I am not sure that the opponents would have advanced this position as a logical argument; nonetheless, I felt that it provided the underlying basis for their formal arguments under the broad headings of nuclear non-proliferation, nuclear reactor safety, and the disposal of nuclear waste.

I tried to deal with these arguments, and others, head on, and to explain what the government was doing and why. I think I can best put the position that we took at that time by quoting at some length from my report to the provincial NDP convention in November of 1979. In a section on uranium and a section on the environment, I reported as follows:

'I want to talk about uranium – first by reporting on developments, and then by discussing with you some of the larger issues involved.

As you know, uranium has been mined in Saskatchewan since 1953. We now (1979) have mines in operation in the Uranium City area and at Rabbit Lake near Wollaston. Amok's mine-mill complex at Cluff Lake will be in operation by 1981.

We know that the mines currently operating, and those which might be developed, will contribute greatly to the Saskatchewan economy. Just how great is not certain because uranium prices and demand are bound to vary. But, conservatively, we are looking at a half-billion-dollar industry by the middle of the 1980s.

This industry will create jobs for Saskatchewan people, particularly Northerners, and, we believe, without greatly disrupting the Northerner's way of life. It will lead to other jobs in the construction and service sectors and this industry will help build, through royalties and taxes, our Heritage Fund, which will be used to find alternative energy sources for future generations.

The development of uranium is taking place with three objectives in mind, the same objectives which apply to all resource development.

The first objective is that the people of this province receive the maximum benefit, not only from revenues, but also in opportunities to participate in all phases of particular projects – as employees, as contractors, and as suppliers of support services.

The second and equally important objective is the protection of the physical environment in which the development occurs.

Third, we insist that the occupational health and safety of workers be protected during both construction and operation.

Through the Saskatchewan Mining Development Corporation, which we set up 5 years ago, we have the option of public participation in every post-1975 project in Northern Saskatchewan. SMDC has the option of taking up to 50 per cent of any project. As of July 1, 1979, it is involved in a total of 245 exploration and development projects. We are assured a public presence to monitor and control events at each stage of development; from exploration right through to actual mining should a project reach that final stage.

There are broader economic problems for Saskatchewan. They relate in part to uranium – but also to other resource development: heavy oil and potash in particular. I tried to address those problems when I spoke to the Resources Conference in Saskatoon in late August (1979).

Simply put, I said Saskatchewan – with its boom and bust history – was looking to resource development opportunities to provide greater stability and balance in its economy. I argued that this could not happen if development proceeded without planning. I called for a staged development – to avoid overheating our relatively small economy for a period, followed by an economic 'bust.' Staged development also gives us the opportunity to train Northern people and to proceed with the greatest possible margin of safety.

Stability and balance. These are our prime economic objectives.

I submit those are also appropriate measures to apply – stability and balance – when considering the moral questions related to Saskat-chewan as a source of world supply of uranium for nuclear power generation.

It is not with any regret that I acknowledge that objections to uranium development on moral grounds are more prevalent among democratic socialists than among people of other political convictions. Indeed, I would be disappointed were it otherwise. It is true in Canada. I believe it is also true in the United Kingdom, in the Federal Republic of Germany and in Sweden, countries which I recently visited.

But social democrats, like other mortals, are not blessed with moral certainty. Nor are we likely to attain such certainty in this life. The problem for each of us is to make the best informed judgment we can, considering not just one side of the question, but all sides.

Balance.

There are risks associated with nuclear power generation and the nuclear cycle. Undeniably.

There are risks associated with all human activity. And with the failure to act.

The appropriate question for the government and people of Saskatchewan to consider and keep considering, I believe, is this: How will all the risks be affected by the mining and export of our uranium under achievable safeguards, and, conversely, how will they be affected by our failure to mine and export?

We moved to address these questions with the Bayda Commission.[1] *To some it was not persuasive. I can tell you, however, that it is a highly regarded assessment, both as to method and scope, in both Europe and Australia.*

We have followed Bayda with the progressive implementation of the Commission's environmental and safety recommendations.

That is not persuasive to some because it does not answer all the questions about: non-proliferation; reactor safety; the disposal of nuclear waste; and other very important concerns.

I do not intend this morning to attempt to deal with this range of issues. Many will undoubtedly arise later in this convention. What I do propose to do is put before you another set of issues which are part of the whole.

These issues have to do with the risks of not proceeding with uranium development in Saskatchewan – the risks of withholding our uranium from the world pool of energy reserves.

These issues have to do with the global problems of an expanding population, with the vast disparity between the industrialized and the developing nations, the selfishness or at least self-centredness of the wealthy minority of mankind, and with the hopes and aspirations of the vast majority of the world's people. And they have to do with a very real and growing world shortage of conventional energy supplies – particularly petroleum. And whether a particular shortage is real or contrived, it is clear beyond question that there is a looming world shortage of oil.

It is not terribly difficult to sit here in affluent Saskatchewan, in the heart of a continent which has the highest per capita energy consumption in the world – in affluent Saskatchewan, which has more energy resources than we could consume in the next hundreds of years – and to say we will not share our energy surplus in the form of uranium. Because it's too risky.

Some anti-nuclear protagonists will say there is no real energy shortage – that renewable alternatives can fill the gap.

---

1 I was referring to a Royal Commission appointed by the government of Saskatchewan to examine into all aspects of uranium development in Saskatchewan, with particular reference to the proposed mine at Cluff Lake. The Commission was headed by Mr Justice Ed Bayda of the Saskatchewan Court of Appeal. It was probably the most detailed study done in uranium development in the world up to that time.

I say that the preponderance of evidence is that in the medium term – over the next 50 years – there are insoluble problems in bridging the gap without nuclear fuel. Even with serious application of conservation measures, more serious than are likely to be accepted or imposed in democratic countries, even with the substitution of coal for our diminishing stocks of oil – the gap cannot be filled – without nuclear fuel.

The anti-nuclear proponents' answer to that is to offer the no-growth option. Stop consuming energy to promote economic growth.

That might be an answer to us in affluent Saskatchewan – in affluent North America. But are they also saying 'no-growth' to the people of Sri Lanka? Are they saying 'no-growth' to the people of India?

I think that's unacceptable to those people and morally unacceptable for us to impose upon them.

If we were talking about supplying a hungry world with food, I think there would be near unanimous agreement in this room that we were morally obliged to export as much as we could.

What we are talking about is whether or not we have the moral right – however highly motivated – to withhold our uranium from the energy pool of an energy-short world.

I think on balance – balancing all the knowable risks – that we have not.

Caucus members will be familiar with my argument on this issue.

Let me put this argument in other terms:

What happens if Saskatchewan uranium is withheld from world markets?

The most likely result is that the uranium will simply come from other sources. There is after all no scarcity of uranium in the world. Some uranium – like Saskatchewan's – is just cheaper to mine than others.

But let us leave that argument completely aside. Let us assume that if Saskatchewan's uranium is withheld there will be less uranium used for power production.

What then?

There will be less energy in the world. Some will go short. Who will go short? Will it be the Canadians? No way. Will it be the Swedes, or the Germans, the Russians, or the Japanese? No way.

It will be the people of South East Asia, of Africa – the people of Bangladesh and Mozambique. You will answer: Nobody need go short. If we all share there will be enough for all. That may be.

But I say to you: can you make Canadians or Americans or Japanese share? And if you can why aren't you doing it in the oil crisis which is even now wreaking havoc on the economies of the third world?

It is entirely responsible and moral for a citizen or any group to urge wealthy nations to share their wealth with the poor of this world.

But it is entirely irresponsible and immoral for any government to act as if that sharing would certainly take place.

Make no mistake about it. To reduce the energy available to the world is to consign the poorest nations to untold misery and privation. It is more than significant that the opposition to nuclear power for the world is strongest in the most affluent countries with the most alternative fuel supplies.

Don't misunderstand me. I am not saying that poor countries should use nuclear power. That may or may not be appropriate. What I am saying is that if a country like Japan does not use nuclear power it will use coal and oil that would otherwise be available to poorer countries.

Even greater shortages will appear. Prices will rise still further. And the poor will be crushed still further. Not to recognize this is folly and folly which will have disastrous results for the poorest on this planet.

Certainly there are risks to using uranium. But in the absence of other assured energy sources there are grave risks to not using uranium.

In the absence of any risk-free activity, the government has to make a decision on uranium development. We indicated our position and our proposed involvement clearly. For example we introduced at the 1976–77 session of the Legislature, and debated a bill to set up the Saskatchewan Mining Development Corporation and announced clearly that it would participate in uranium mining. We consulted the people of Saskatchewan through the Bayda Commission. We consulted the members of this party at annual conventions. I believe that the policy decision of the 1978 NDP convention was the correct decision – both technically and morally.[2]

I believe this party and your government has grappled with this difficult issue and has arrived at the right decision.

The Environment

These decisions present challenge.

We meet parts of the challenge by putting stiff environmental safeguards in place, and then enforcing them, not perfectly, but well.

We have Canada's most comprehensive and most open environmental assess-

---

2 The decision was that uranium should be mined and exported, subject to appropriate safeguards.

ment process. It covers all significant resource projects, not only in the North, not only with uranium.

This process attempts to make sure that the public is aware of each project proposal and that the environmental studies are made available for public review and comment.

It provides that the economic, social, and environmental implications of each project be subject to rigorous technical review. Major projects, such as Cluff Lake – a uranium mining project in north-west Saskatchewan, are given a third review by an independent board of inquiry that holds public hearings. All of these are done before any final decision is made.

This is not the case across Canada. One comparison may serve to illustrate the difference. Recently, we appointed a board of inquiry to review Saskatchewan Power's proposals for a power transmission line from Squaw Rapids (Saskatchewan) to The Pas (Manitoba). On the basis of that review, and of public opinion, we decided to route the line around the environmentally sensitive Cumberland Delta.

By comparison, in Tory Ontario, the Darlington nuclear power plant was cleared for development without public hearings.

For uranium development in Northern Saskatchewan, we have placed on developers the most stringent conditions in the world. These protective measures demand minimum impact on the surrounding environment and restoration of the disturbed area when mining is completed.

The safety of workers is protected by the toughest rules in Canada, if not the world.

We have an energy and resource development strategy, and the most open and comprehensive project assessment process in Canada. We recognize the need for vigilance. We do not intend to relax that vigilance. We believe that, with care, we can have balanced development and environmental protection, and we intend to pursue both those goals with dedication and persistence.'

That was what we were saying in 1979. Looking back, the emphasis was on energy shortages. We now know that there was not a shortage of petroleum. There was a shortage of inexpensive petroleum. Our term in office had seen oil prices rise from just over $2.00 a barrel to a price several times higher. There were wild suggestions of oil reaching $50.00 a barrel or even $100.00. In the climate of 2007, they do not seem so wild. A thirty-fold increase in the price of oil has wreaked havoc on the economies of many developing countries.

The concerns of global warming had not yet fully emerged. If I were

giving that report today, this would have featured largely when considering the wisdom or otherwise of uranium development.

In the 1970s and until we left office in 1982, we were sensitive to the
nuclear non-proliferation arguments – the concern that Canada was
somehow contributing to the possibility of the spread of nuclear weapons by producing uranium and exporting it to countries that were using
uranium for producing electricity. The world was attempting to deal with
this threat by means of a nuclear non-proliferation treaty regarding
weapons, which all countries pursuing nuclear plans were asked to sign.

I did not believe then, and don't believe now, that nuclear technology
can be somehow restricted to a few nations, but its spread for use in
nuclear weapons can be inhibited. However, it is not easy to contain
nuclear growth while the United States is increasing its nuclear arsenal
and while it continues to be aggressive in its foreign policy. A policy
whereby existing nuclear powers would agree to reduce their arsenals,
and non-nuclear powers would agree not to acquire weapons, might be
made to work. It is clearly harder to bring this about when existing
nuclear powers are increasing these arsenals of warheads and improving
their delivery systems.

In the 1970s, when these issues were at the forefront, the proliferation
of nuclear weapons was constrained by the two great powers, the USA
and the USSR. Each was trying its best to see that the balance of terror
would not be destabilized by the entry of new nuclear powers.

Today's threats come more from non-state groups who may acquire
relatively unsophisticated weapons and use them for the purposes of terror, and from the possible overreaction by states that are the victims of
terror.

There is little connection between developing nuclear weapons and
generating power by using nuclear fuel. If one wanted to produce plutonium for weapons, a small reactor could be constructed at one-tenth
of the cost of a CANDU electric power reactor (the kind of reactor
developed in Canada) and be a more efficient producer of plutonium.

I now turn to the matter of electric power reactor safety. Here in Canada and in the Western world, the production of electricity by using
nuclear fuel has proved remarkably safe. Mine accidents have been minimal, as have accidents during refining activities. Nuclear reactors in all
Western countries have proved exceptionally safe. I see no likelihood of
these activities becoming unsafe.

Certainly the loss of life by producing electricity by using uranium –

from mine to reactor – is far less than the loss of life by producing electricity through using coal.

In Wales, where my mother was born, there are cemeteries full of people who have died in coal mining accidents. The same is true in Nova Scotia, where I was born. And almost weekly the news of coal mining disasters in China and Russia, but also in Western countries, reminds us that 'the price of coal is blood.' So, in terms of producing the fuel, there is no dispute that electricity produced using nuclear energy is far safer than electricity produced by coal. This is true in total, or as measured per million kilowatt-hours or per million mega-joules of electricity produced.

It might be argued that I do not mention the nuclear reactor disaster at Chernobyl on 26 April 1986. I believe that safety systems in Soviet nuclear reactors have very little relevance in considering the safety of modern nuclear reactors. Soviet safety standards have been notoriously low, and not only in nuclear fields. At a time in the 1980s when Soviet men in other occupations had a life expectancy of 64 years, the average Soviet coal miner had a life expectancy of 48. Only 5 per cent of miners lived to age 55.

It may be argued that the real hazards of nuclear power are not in mining or in reactor operations but rather in disposal of the spent fuel bundles from nuclear reactors – the reactor waste. Here it is harder to be definite. Reactor waste has been stored for half a century successfully in water containers – 'swimming pools' – usually on the reactor site. It is well accepted that radioactivity declines very rapidly in the water storage.

While the radioactivity of fuel bundles declines rapidly once they are removed from the reactors and placed in water, some radioactivity, constituting a safety hazard for humans, continues for thousands of years. So there is a long-term threat to people and the environment that must be managed.

Several methods are available. If we agree that we do not wish to reprocess the spent fuel bundles, then the most promising method for Canadians to manage the spent fuel bundles is to bury them in Precambrian rock that has been stable for millions of years. But I readily concede that nuclear reactor waste in the form of spent fuel bundles is a hazard.

Other methods of generating electricity create other hazards. Aside from hazards associated with producing and transporting fuels such as coal and natural gas referred to above, giant hydro dams present risks. They can rupture. They rarely do, but when they do, they can cause massive damage in the often heavily populated river valley below. And we are coming to accept that there are other major hazards that may be part of generating electricity from burning fossil fuels. For many years we have been aware of the dangers to forests and lakes from emissions of sulfur compounds from fossil-fuel power plants that cause 'acid rain.' Now we are becoming increasingly aware of carbon dioxide emissions and their contribution to trapping heat in the earth's atmosphere and accordingly their contribution to global warming. We are unsure whether the effects will be short-lived or whether they could last for hundreds or thousands of years. But the evidence is mounting that global warming will be a major long-term hazard. Since the potential effects could be very dangerous for the planet, there is justifiable concern about power plants fuelled by coal, oil, or natural gas.

There is no question that electricity can be produced by wind, solar, and geothermal means, but in relatively small and sometimes uncertain amounts. I've often thought that the next major breakthrough in electricity technology should be a way to store electricity more effectively – better storage batteries or some other technology. Wind is intermittent. The sun shines only sometimes. And river flows are variable. We've solved some of these problems, but by no means all. When we do, the electricity produced by these means might make more of a contribution to our seemingly insatiable demand for electricity.

All of these issues need to be dealt with in the context of the democratic institutions that govern us. I've heard people express the opinion that if leaders showed 'political will,' they could enforce conservation measures to reduce the consumption of electricity substantially. Certainly some marginal but useful reductions could be achieved. But I am very far from convinced that the voting public will accept sharp reductions in electricity consumption in some 'war' on global warming. And if they do not, then any 'political will' will have only a short-term effect, if any.

The clear conclusion to be drawn is that there is no effective method of reducing in a major way the consumption of electricity in Canada in the short or even medium run; nor is there any way of producing large volumes of electricity that is risk free. We are left with choosing from among the risks – which risks are greatest, which are most manageable.

As a world, we have dealt with spent fuel rods from nuclear reactors without incident for fifty years when stored at reactor sites. The proposals for burying them in stable geological formations seem to offer a high degree of safety.

While we do not know with any certainty how much our carbon dioxide emissions are adding to global warming, the scientific community is reaching the opinion that it is substantial. Once it happens, climate change seems to be completely beyond our control. Accordingly, I regard global warming as a major hazard. And the evidence seems to be getting clearer that we humans should be putting less carbon dioxide into the atmosphere. The most obvious way to reduce the escape of carbon dioxide to the atmosphere is to burn less coal for the production of electricity. And this can happen easiest if we substitute nuclear power. If countries such as the United States and China produced electricity by substituting uranium for coal to the same extent that France does, the drop in carbon dioxide emissions would be enormous.

I have noted that an increasing number of environmental groups are embracing nuclear power as a better option for producing electricity than coal-burning plants. The question is not whether we in Canada or throughout the world should develop solar, wind, geothermal, and other alternative power sources. Of course, we should. The question is whether we should substitute uranium for coal in thermal plants. I believe the answer is equally clear – of course, we should, at least until we know a great deal more about global warming than we now do.

This seems to me to be the course of prudence in protecting the environment of our planet.

15

Some Thoughts on Resource Policies

As I reflect on the resource controversies of the 1970s and early 1980s, I am struck by the differences in approach used by the different resource industries, oil, potash, and uranium, in their dealings with the government of Saskatchewan.

The oil industry spokesmen were hardened veterans in dealing with governments. When the Saskatchewan government increased royalties sharply by Bill 42 in late 1973, and when the federal government, in the spring of 1974, introduced a rule about the non-deductibility of provincial royalties, the oil companies, in effect, said that they would continue to produce from existing wells, but they would sharply curtail their exploration activities until these matters were 'straightened out.' And they did just that. The number of wells drilled dropped from 770 wells drilled in 1971 to 290 wells drilled in 1976. We expected that oil prices would rise, and, as we said, 'The oil will not rot.' Oil prices did rise. After some bargaining, matters were 'straightened out,' and they came back.

With the oil companies, you might not like where you were, but you usually knew where you stood.

The uranium companies were acutely conscious of the fact that, at least in the 1970s, they did not want to fight with any government. They were perfectly prepared to disclose their financial information to governments and were not concerned about a Crown corporation being involved in uranium mining. Eldorado Nuclear, a federal Crown corporation, was a pioneer in uranium mining. Negotiations with the industry were sometimes sharp but never laced with latent distrust.

The potash industry was in sharp contrast to the other two. Much of the industry was not experienced in dealing with governments and seemed to exude the view that government ought not to be involved with the industry except to offer support when required and to collect modest royalties. The potash company based in Europe took quite a different approach. Indeed, it was half owned by the French government. But the U.S.-based potash companies were remarkably unsophisticated compared with U.S.-based oil companies. Perhaps we as a government expected resource companies to fit into a common mould. If we did, we were wrong. They were markedly different. And that accounted for some of our challenges in dealing with them. I attribute the differences largely to the amount of worldwide exposure each industry had had to governments of many stripes.

The U.S. potash companies did not appear to have dealt with politicians who had some experience with private sector, co-operative, and public sector business corporations. I had a discussion with the president of one company who had been a governor of Colorado. It was polite and civil. He emphasized the role of government in encouraging initiative and development. While conceding this, I put more emphasis on the role of government in dealing with the inevitable casualties produced by a highly competitive economy. It was a difference in emphasis only, but perhaps an important one.

To a lesser extent, the differences between the approach of potash companies and oil and uranium companies may have related to their confidence and perhaps their clout in dealing with U.S. authorities. The potash people were clearly concerned about falling afoul of U.S. antitrust laws and perhaps the U.S. farm lobby. The oil companies showed no concern about U.S. antitrust laws. Perhaps their activities did not attract antitrust concerns. Perhaps they were more confident in treading the paths of power in Washington.

Our experiences were a classic case of the complexities of a small Prairie government dealing with transnational corporations with sharply different approaches to relations between business and government.

One of the issues that must be dealt with by governments in resource-rich provinces is setting royalty rates. At first sight, this seems a simple question. To keep the discussion simple, I will speak only of mineral resources. The resource, be it oil, potash, uranium, or some other mineral, is (usually) owned by the Crown (the government of the province on behalf of its people). It would seem to be straightforward. If a government is selling a resource – and that is what is being done when a resource company produces a mineral and pays a royalty – it should sell it at the highest price possible. It is not easy to see why the people should sell their resources at a price lower than what could be obtained. If I was managing somebody's business and I sold assets at less than what could be had, I don't think I would be doing my job as manager.

There are always counter-arguments. It is said that our royalty rates should be competitive. I would ask why? If another province is willing, for whatever reason, to sell (say) its oil in the ground at less than its value, that is hardly a reason for Saskatchewan to do so. The rejoinder is that development in our province may be lost. I have rarely found that argument persuasive. I agree that development might be delayed, but only at certain times. In the 1970s, Saskatchewan royalties were always higher than those of other provinces. But oil was produced and, but for brief periods, produced steadily. Saskatchewan royalties were such that, again but for brief periods, resource companies could make profits producing oil in Saskatchewan. The fact that they could make more money producing in another province did not stop them from producing and exploring in Saskatchewan. The argument that our royalties must be competitive is based on an either/or argument. Either the resource companies will produce in province A or in province B. This is rarely true.

Resource companies, particularly oil companies, produce oil in many provinces, states, and countries around the world at the same time and at widely different profit margins. As I see it, a province should not try to set its royalties at a 'competitive' level but, rather, at the highest level that will attract production, if that is the desired goal. As I said more than once in the 1970s, 'The oil won't rot.' If production is interrupted, it is doubtful that the people of the province – the owners of the resource – will lose much. With hindsight, I sometimes wish that we had produced less oil in the 1970s and 1980s, and had it now to produce and sell in this era of $100+ per barrel oil. Foresight is not given to us to enjoy. Otherwise we would all be wealthy, or so it is said. But as a general proposition, the value of mineral resources increases over time. The U.S. humorist Will Rogers used to advise, 'Buy land – they ain't making any more of it.' In the same way, it might be argued that we should be reluctant to part with our mineral resources – they ain't making any more of them either.

This is an argument for close and careful husbanding of our mineral resources and getting the highest royalties possible. The counter-argument is that resources and their development can be a springboard for economic development that our province and its people need. And certainly there is some merit to this argument. If lower royalties generate more development than higher royalties do, and not just more profitable development for the resource companies, then this is an argument for lower royalties. But this does not end that calculation. This additional development must be balanced against the other development that would come from higher royalties and the use of the additional royalty money to generate that development. If the money is spent as additional money for, say, highway construction, university expansion, tax cuts, or a dozen other uses, those can all be expected to stimulate economic development. Which approach produces the most development? The calculation is not always easy to make, but a few general principles can be identified.

If the province has a virtual monopoly on the resource, then development is likely to take place in any case and royalties should be higher rather than lower. This allows the province to have the benefit of both the development activity and the extra activity that can be generated by spending the additional royalty money either as extra services (say, highways) or on lower taxes. Similarly, if the development of the resource is done in such a way that many economic spin-offs occur outside the province, then royalties should be higher rather than lower, since the extra royalty money will very likely yield more development than any lost development in Saskatchewan because of higher royalties.

As an example, if oil companies centre their operations in Calgary and when drilling around let's say Kindersley, Saskatchewan, they use drilling companies centred in Alberta and employing Alberta-based workers, then the lasting development for Saskatchewan can be quite limited. In cases like these, maximum royalties would seem the best approach.

The setting of royalties requires consideration of a number of factors, including the sale price of the resource produced, the cost of production, and the costs of exploring for new fields or deposits. It is the margin between sale price and costs or, in the economists' terms, the economic rent, that is to be split between the owner (the public) and the producing resource company. I make this point because whether royalties are higher or lower needs to be determined by the relationship of the royalty to the margin and not to the sale price.

In the 1970s I thought it was a good idea for the provincial government to own some producing oil wells and potash and uranium mines. This gave us a very good idea of what the costs of production were and, as we participated in exploration consortia, what the costs were of finding new fields and deposits. Then we did not need to be dependent on figures supplied by the resource companies. Understandably some of the companies shaped their figures to produce the result they wanted. I would add that there is nothing inherently wrong about this. Accounting is not an exact science. There are huge areas for judgment. If an international resource company makes a profit, it is often a pure matter of judgment to determine where or when the profit was made. Was it made when the resource was produced, or was it made when it was transported to, say, the United States, or when it was sold, or when the buyer paid the seller? Arguments can be made many ways. Indeed, it is the normal thing to do for resource companies to keep one set of books showing one level of profit for presentation to their shareholders and another set for presentation to tax authorities for the calculation of taxes. This does not suggest any wrongdoing. It just makes the point that financial statements are prepared for different purposes, and different purposes will produce different financial statements, using the same facts. So, as long as we don't fool ourselves into believing the financial statements are 'accurate' in some scientific or precise sense, then we are in less danger of misunderstanding what we are being told.

There is merit in trying to structure royalties so that resource companies maintain head offices in Saskatchewan. It is a good idea, too, to see that reductions in royalties are in the form of development incentives. If royalty reductions can be earned by resource companies that drill oil wells in new fields or develop a new potash or uranium mine or pursue a new mineral opportunity, there is a good chance that foregoing current royalties will produce economic development over a longer term.

Every province must make its own calculations, and these will change over time. In the 1970s I felt that the numbers favoured a plan of higher royalties and using the money for projects that would stimulate economic development and add to the quality of life in the province. There was no doubt that spending money on a new swimming pool in, say, the town of Lafleche provided not only jobs but also enjoyment to the people of the town.

There may well be sound reasons for lowering royalties and thus lowering provincial revenues. Arguments based on higher cost of production are often valid. It is a matter of the extent of the higher costs. Arguments based on competitiveness are true only to a minor extent. I think it is unlikely that higher royalties would have a major effect on levels of production. This issue cannot be properly dealt with by slogans about 'thousands of new jobs,' on the one side, or 'subsidizing foreign multinationals,' on the other. Hard-headed analysis by the government and forthright debate in the legislature and by the political parties seem to me to be what should happen if the interests of the Saskatchewan public are to be protected.

16

Constitution: Introduction

One of the great events of my time in public life in Canada was the patriation of the Canadian Constitution in 1982, complete with a Charter of Rights and Freedoms, a new amending formula, and other important changes. Two major changes dealt with the control of natural resources and with the legal rights of aboriginal peoples of Canada.

On a rainy morning in April 1982 on a platform erected in front of the Parliament Buildings in Ottawa, the Queen signed a proclamation bringing into force the Constitution Act, and so cutting the legal cord that bound Canada's Constitution to the Parliament of the United Kingdom. The events over many months leading up to the ceremony have been written about extensively. A good account is found in *Canada ... Notwithstanding*, written by Roy Romanow, Howard Leeson, and John Whyte, members of the Saskatchewan negotiating team. I propose only to add some comments on three areas: Saskatchewan's dealings with Mr Trudeau, and what I came to believe were Mr Trudeau's minimum objectives; some reflections on the week in November 1981 which led to the agreement among the federal government and nine provincial governments; and the events later in November 1981 as they relate to the section dealing with equality of men and women, and the section dealing with the Aboriginal and treaty rights of Aboriginal peoples, introduced into the Constitution at that time.

In September 1980 there was a federal-provincial conference on the Constitution. Mr Trudeau hoped to achieve some agreement among the federal and provincial governments that could be the basis for a resolution of our federal Parliament calling upon the Parliament of the United Kingdom of Great Britain and Northern Ireland (the U.K.) to pass an act providing that no further laws of that Parliament would have effect in Canada.

In 1980 the only laws of the U.K. Parliament that had any effect in Canada were ones changing our Constitution – the British North America Act (BNA Act) of 1867 and later BNA acts. Any possible application of British laws to Canada had been formally done away with in 1931, with the exception of the BNA Act. Everybody, especially the U.K. Parliament, agreed that the Constitution should be 'patriated' – that is, that all matters respecting the Constitution should be decided in Canada. But for patriation to happen, it would have to be accompanied by provisions to allow the BNA Act to be changed in Canada. We Canadians would be forced to come to an agreement on how changes were to be made in the future. These provisions for constitutional change have come to be called amending formulas (I'll refrain from using the Latin plural, formulae), or, more simply, an amending formula. Since 1931 Canadian governments had talked about an amending formula on dozens of occasions but had never agreed. Mr Trudeau also sought to add to the Constitution a statement of rights and freedoms (usually called the Charter).

Mr Trudeau called a conference of first ministers for September 1980. The opening dinner was held in the (then) External Affairs building in Ottawa and chaired by the governor general, the Right Honourable Ed Schreyer. I remember it well. It was on September 7th, my fifty-fifth birthday, and somebody provided a cake. It was about the only festive note of the evening.

Premier Lyon of Manitoba, chairman of the premiers' group, put forward a proposal that he and Mr Trudeau should jointly chair the conference sessions. Mr Trudeau reacted angrily at this display of *lèse majesté*, and as the discussion proceeded and tempers flared, Mr Trudeau rose and left before the dessert and before the governor general had taken his leave. The niceties of protocol were taking a beating, and the prospects for a useful conference were receding by the minute.

The conference was not a success. Agreements were not reached either on an amending formula or a Charter, the basic matters at issue. At the close of the conference, I had an opportunity to put forward my position that any general amending formula that called for the unanimous consent of the provinces was a bad idea. The formula should provide for a majority in Parliament and a consensus of provinces, and we should seek such a formula. At this point, this was not a popular idea.

Following the conference, Mr Trudeau decided to go it alone. He introduced into the House of Commons a resolution which, if enacted into law by the U.K. Parliament, would patriate the Constitution with an amending formula and a Charter. Up to this time Canadian governments had operated on the understanding that major changes in the Constitution affecting the position and powers of the provinces required the consent, or perhaps the acquiescence, of the governments (the cabinets, not the legislatures) of all of the provinces.

Mr Trudeau decided to test this understanding and to have the Canadian Parliament send a resolution to the U.K. Parliament in London without unanimous provincial agreement or a consensus among provinces. This unilateral approach was opposed by the Progressive Conservative Official Opposition in Parliament and ultimately by the governments of eight of the provinces. Two of the provinces, Ontario and New Brunswick, had reservations about the process but were prepared to support the Trudeau initiative.

Six of the provinces – Newfoundland, Prince Edward Island, Quebec, Manitoba, Alberta, and British Columbia – firmly opposed the initiative at the outset, and took the position that the rule of unanimous provincial consent should apply to any constitutional changes as comprehensive as those proposed. Two provinces, Nova Scotia and Saskatchewan, opposed the initiative but sought to see whether some compromise position was possible. This resulted, after efforts to build a compromise consensus failed, in the two provinces joining the other six to, as we termed it, 'stop the Trudeau train.' The eight provinces, dubbed the 'Gang of Eight' by the Ottawa media (perhaps at the suggestion of the federal government), formed an alliance to put forward their joint proposals and to oppose the federal initiative. The label 'Gang of Eight' always amused me. It was clearly copied from the label 'Gang of Four' given to four left-wing communists in China involving the wife of leader Mao Tse-tung. To associate Premier Sterling Lyon of Manitoba with left-wing communism, even by inference, had its hilarious aspect.

During the period from October 1980 until the Gang of Eight came together in the spring of 1981, Saskatchewan had a number of dealings with the federal government to see if there was any common ground between the federal position and that of the dissenting six provinces. It was not an easy position to take and was one that attracted some criticism. Anyone who tries to build a bridge between two warring camps is likely to be shot at from both sides.

One of the challenges was to discern just what the federal government was aiming at. Clearly they wanted, as did we all, patriation. This required an amending formula. But which formula? Ottawa favoured a Victoria

Charter–type formula. That was the name given to a formula contained in a charter put forward at a federal-provincial conference in Victoria, BC, in June 1971. It was based upon four regions of Canada: Ontario, Quebec, the four western provinces, and the four Atlantic provinces. In general terms, any constitutional amendment would require the approval of Parliament, the legislatures of Ontario and Quebec, and the legislatures of at least two of the four Atlantic provinces and two of the four western provinces that have 50 per cent of the population. It was unclear how strongly the federal government felt about this type of formula, which served to give each of Ontario and Quebec a veto.

The federal government favoured a charter of rights and freedoms. The October 1980 resolution contained a charter patterned off the Canadian Bill of Rights adopted in 1960, to which had been added a codification of democratic rights and new parts dealing with equality rights, with the use of the French and English languages in Canada, and some mobility rights, so called. There was no override or notwithstanding clause equivalent to section 33, as finally enacted.

It was not a comprehensive charter. It was enough to be respectable and to provide a place where language rights could be embedded. Early on in the lengthy negotiations, Mr Trudeau visited me in Regina. I asked him why the language rights provisions were in the Charter, because language rights are not human rights. It is no more a human right to speak English than, say, Spanish. I said that I was not aware of language rights being in bills of rights of other countries. I made clear that I thought language rights should be in the Constitution, as part of the Confederation bargain. I suggested that he was embedding them in the Charter because it was easier to argue for a charter than it was to argue for free-standing language rights. He readily agreed. Since he clearly wanted the language rights provisions, he had decided to wrap them in a charter. From that, I concluded that the language rights provisions were part of Mr Trudeau's bottom line. He therefore would hold out firmly for a charter, but he might be open to changes in its content, and to a notwithstanding clause, as long as it did not apply to language rights. We were learning more about the bottom-line position of the federal government.

Looking back on the constitutional negotiations, I think I was deluding myself for two or three months from November 1980 to February of 1981. I agreed with much of what Mr Trudeau was trying to do. I thought it was high time that our Constitution was patriated. I had no strong objections to an amending formula that required all amendments to be adopted by Ontario, Quebec, two Atlantic provinces, and two western provinces (with half of the population of the region, in each case) – a four-region concept. I would have preferred other formulas giving more recognition to the idea of the equality of provinces, but I could have accepted a four-region model basic amending formula. I had no great affection for a charter of rights. But I did favour putting into the Constitution English and French language rights. This might help to prevent Canada from descending into two very distinct language solitudes and so making the country even more difficult to govern. I did not like the idea of embedding the language rights in a charter of rights and freedoms, but I understood the pure political argument for doing so. So perhaps we could live with a minimal charter with an effective notwithstanding clause. And after decades of debate and a year or two of bargaining, I felt the first ministers owed it to the Canadian people to arrive at an agreement of which they could be proud.

The unilateral process was clearly unacceptable, but I did not accept the idea that all provinces had to agree to all changes. I felt that a rule that all provinces must agree to every constitutional change was far too rigid. A reasonable majority of provinces should be enough. My position is stated with clarity in the documents that Saskatchewan put before the Supreme Court of Canada when the court dealt with the issue of patriation in 1981. As noted, I had stated that position earlier at the conference in September 1980. So I felt that it might be possible to put together a package to which the federal government and perhaps six or seven provinces could agree. Accordingly, during the months after October 1980, some of the Saskatchewan team made contact with officials from Ontario, British Columbia, and Nova Scotia, with some tentative contacts elsewhere.

My reading of the situation was this: I feared that Quebec would never agree to anything. I did not think it was politically possible for René Lévesque to agree to any proposal that Pierre Trudeau put forward.

I feared, too, that Sterling Lyon had such a hostile view of Mr Trudeau's concept of Canada that it would not be easy to get Manitoba support.

Alberta had a rational, well-articulated position but held a more confederal view of Canada that would make agreement difficult. Relations between Alberta and the federal government had been further soured by the announcement in October 1980 of the National Energy Program, which many felt, with good reason, was aimed directly at Alberta. Saskatchewan and British Columbia were caught in the crossfire. Any coalition that could be cobbled together should include British Colum-

bia, Saskatchewan, Ontario, Nova Scotia, New Brunswick, Prince Edward
Island, and possibly Newfoundland. But it was not to be.

At about the same time, the federal government seemed to change
their strategy. They were continuing to discuss issues with provincial governments, but they began to pursue a parallel strategy of marshalling
Canadian public opinion to support a resolution to be sent to the U.K.
Parliament without provincial government support. To this end they
arranged that a special joint committee of the House of Commons and
the Senate (the Parliamentary Committee) would hold public hearings
on the merit and the contents of a charter of rights and freedoms and
arranged that these hearings be televised. Submissions were solicited
from groups who saw the Charter as a means of having their particular
concerns as a disadvantaged group recognized and protected. Many
groups made submissions. There were some who had a vested interest in
an expanded charter – the so-called 'Charter Canadians.' To provinces
concerned that each addition to the Charter was a subtraction from their
legislative powers, this was an unwelcome development. It certainly was
not designed to get provinces to join the federal government's patriation
initiative.

As part of Saskatchewan's search for some middle ground, I presented
a detailed brief to the Parliamentary Committee in December 1980. I
made many familiar points. Canada needs a strong central government
to pursue national goals and strong provincial governments to respond
to distinctive needs across this vast land. A few quotes will give the flavour
of the brief:

> Canada can work neither as a centralized state nor as ten principalities: one
> defies our diversity, the other our common goals.

> If the contents of the resolution [the resolution tabled in the House of
> Commons in October 1980] are substantially improved, we will be in a posi-
> tion to consider acquiescing in the process in the interests of lessening the
> level of controversy. If the contents are not substantially improved, we will
> have no option but to oppose both the process and the contents.

We put forward an amending formula that required, for the general
formula, the approval of a majority of the provinces, including two from
Atlantic Canada and two from western Canada. Further, the approving
provinces had to contain 80 per cent of the population of Canada. This
preserved a *de facto* veto for each of Ontario and Quebec.

We opposed the constitutional entrenchment of a charter of rights, and favoured including in the Constitution English and French language rights, protection for the rights of Aboriginal peoples, and clarification of matters respecting resource taxation. We also favoured the inclusion of provisions respecting equalization – programs to have the federal government provide extra funds to poorer provinces to allow them to provide essential services of reasonable quality without an undue burden of provincial taxation.

I presented the brief at some length at the televised meetings of the joint committee. It was an attempt to set out our basis for negotiation with the federal government and (we hoped) some of the provinces.

I have often been asked why I objected to the introduction of a charter of rights and freedoms into the Constitution. I did not, of course, object to citizens being able to enjoy the rights and freedoms protected by the Charter. Indeed, many of these rights and freedoms were already protected by the Canadian Bill of Rights, introduced by Mr Diefenbaker, and by the Saskatchewan Human Rights Code, introduced during our period of office in the 1970s. But I had two broad concerns. One was that our system of government cannot work effectively unless citizens regard themselves as being responsible for how the system works and for what values are put forward and protected. If citizens are encouraged to believe that somehow a constitution protects them and they no longer need to be vigilant about how our political system works, either to protect personal rights and freedoms or otherwise, then we will all be the poorer. If voters depart from the idea that democracy is about free people governing themselves and that constant vigilance is the price of liberty, and rather come to believe that somehow their liberties have been (sometime in the past) protected by a constitution with a charter so that vigilance is no longer necessary, then liberties are endangered. I freely acknowledge that a charter can be something that unifies all citizens around values set out in a document phrased in inspirational language. And this is no small benefit. But it carries with it the belief that somehow a constitution or charter protects freedom. Only citizens and vigilant citizens protect freedoms. A charter may or may not assist them to do so.

I like to cite the example of how Canadian and American citizens of Japanese origin were treated during the Second World War. Each group of people had their property seized, and numbers of each group were removed to camps far from the Pacific Ocean, and on no grounds except racial profiling and fear. The United States had a constitutional bill of rights. Canada had no such constitutional protection. As has been widely recognized in both countries, the way Americans and Canadians of Japanese origin were treated was a gross violation of their rights and freedoms. But when fear gripped the public, rights were violated and constitutional provisions provided no protection. I believe that if Canada had had a charter of rights in the 1940s, the treatment of Japanese Canadians would not have been different. The way that Canadian authorities and courts have acted after the terrorist attack on the World Trade Center in New York in September 2001, when there was only a low level of public fear in Canada, tends to support this belief.

The other broad objection deals with the content of the Charter. It is a document that is in many ways based upon the Bill of Rights included in the Constitution of the new United States of America in 1789 (it came into effect in 1791). That was a document drawn up in the days when there were very few centres of private power. Power rested with governments, and it was the abuse of this power against which that document was aimed. Today it is a very different world, where national, provincial, and local governments are powerful, but so are giant corporations and international organizations. The original American Bill of Rights protected only against governments. For close to seventy-five years of its existence, it allowed the widespread ownership of slaves in the United States. Their most basic rights and freedoms were not protected from abusive private power.

In 1941, President Franklin D. Roosevelt gave a famous speech based upon the theme of four freedoms – freedom of speech, freedom of religion, freedom from fear, and freedom from want. This was an acknowledgment of changes that had come about in the preceding 150 years, and of the need to broaden our horizons about the meaning of freedom. I would have hoped that if Canadians proposed, in 1980, to set down their idea of rights and freedoms, they would have embraced the vision of President Roosevelt. But that was not to be. The Charter protects citizens only from abusive exercise of power by governments. If a great corporation such as Shell Oil or Wal-Mart should decide that none of its employees could vote in a national election in Canada, on pain of being dismissed, it might be an outrageous violation of the civil rights of the employees, but it would not be a violation of the Charter of Rights and Freedoms. If a government decides that people of Chinese origin cannot use a hospital in Toronto, this is a violation of the Charter. If governments provide no funds or facilities for any hospitals, then this is not a violation of the Charter, or so I believe. The Charter protects only negative freedoms, not positive freedoms, and only breaches by government, not breaches by others who have the power to interfere with rights and freedoms. It is because we need a broader understanding of freedom and a wider sense of our obligations to our fellow citizens that it is unwise to put into our Constitution for special protection a list of negative but not positive freedoms, and to protect freedoms only against governments, and not against other powerful groups who abuse freedoms.

In 1980, I felt that Canadians were not ready for a positive social charter. Progress was made in that direction during the negotiations for the Charlottetown constitutional agreement ten years later, but Canadians rejected that agreement largely on other grounds.

One can hope that Canadian society will come to accept the idea that laws should guarantee a minimum right to food, clothing, and shelter, as they guarantee the right to speak, to write, and to practise one's religion. That is a challenge for the future.

In January 1981 I had some discussions with Mr Trudeau and Mr Chrétien about what would make the Charter then under discussion in the House of Commons less objectionable. I suggested that the clause protecting property rights that had been recently inserted should be withdrawn. That was done. Discussion turned to the Senate. I was strongly opposed to the Senate, as then (and now) constituted, having a permanent veto on all future constitutional change. At about the same time, I learned that Mr Trudeau had given senators the assurance that they would retain their veto. I then realized that Mr Trudeau was negotiating on several fronts and that no deal could be made on a bilateral basis. One would be committed, at least in the public mind, to deals Mr Trudeau made with other groups. I reluctantly abandoned what was probably a faint hope at best of gathering a few provinces to accept the process if the substance was satisfactory. Saskatchewan then joined the 'Gang of Six,' soon to be joined by Nova Scotia to constitute the Gang of Eight. It was at all times understood to be a defensive alliance to derail the Trudeau initiative. The accounts of the references to the courts of appeal in Manitoba, Quebec, and Newfoundland and Labrador have been dealt with elsewhere, as has the accord reached by the Gang of Eight in April as a basis for resolving the constitutional confrontation.

The decision by the Court of Appeal of Newfoundland and Labrador, written by Chief Justice Mifflin (a classmate of mine at Dalhousie Law School), holding that the proposed federal patriation process was unconstitutional, meant that there would be real trouble getting the U.K. Parliament to act on the proposal without some substantial provincial support. In the result, the federal government referred the issues to the Supreme Court of Canada, whose decision was rendered in September 1981. Their Delphic decision, to the effect that what the federal government proposed to do was legal but unconstitutional, forced a resumption of negotiations under very different circumstances. No longer could the federal government assume that the U.K. Parliament would readily act on a resolution from our Parliament that did not enjoy substantial provincial support and which the Supreme Court had declared unconstitutional. Similarly, no longer could the provinces assume that substantial changes to the Constitution required unanimous provincial consent, since the Supreme Court had held that a consensus of provinces was sufficient. Neither group had as good a hole card as they had earlier thought. So it was back to the bargaining table. The conference was resumed on 2 November 1981.

I've often wondered what would have happened to Canada if the Supreme Court had confined itself to the pure legalities of the federal position. It is likely the federal government would have proceeded to the U.K. Parliament, who, I suspect, would have held their noses and approved the proposal.

I was strengthened in this belief by a conversation I had had with the Right Honourable James Callaghan. Jim Callaghan, when he was prime minister of the U.K., visited Canada and included a visit to Regina. My wife, Anne, and I had the opportunity to have Jim and Mrs Callaghan, along with Roy and Eleanore Romanow, to our house for dinner. We had a pleasant meal and talked about the success of his party, the Labour Party, in Britain. During the course of the evening, I asked what would be the reaction of the British Parliament to a request from the Canadian Parliament to repatriate the Constitution if the request was opposed by many of the provinces. He made clear that he felt that the British Parliament would simply go along with any resolution of the Parliament of Canada, regardless of the position of the provinces. I got the impression that he was expecting someone to ask such a question and had given a little thought to his answer. He was, of course, not giving any official response. Nonetheless, it was not a comforting reply.

If Mr Trudeau had proceeded unilaterally and if the Imperial Parliament had given their assent, the eight dissenting provinces would have been incensed. I know the Saskatchewan government would have been.

The government of Quebec would have been particularly angry. But they would not have been alone or isolated.

Would Canada have been better served by eight angry provinces or just one – an angry and isolated Quebec?

I'm sure many people have pondered that possibility. But to no point. Nothing is as remote as the what might have been.

17

Constitution: The Week That Was

The week of constitutional negotiations in November 1981 was as highly charged as any in which I have participated, except those leading to and then terminating the Saskatchewan doctors' strike of July 1962. We who were involved in the constitutional negotiations and had invested so much blood, sweat, and tears into them regarded them as very important indeed. But I suspect that the public were less involved. I remember a quip in the 1960s of Premier Ross Thatcher in Saskatchewan. He is quoted as saying that if he asked the public in Saskatchewan what their 100 most pressing problems were, the Canadian Constitution would rank 101. Nonetheless, the patriation of the Constitution, with an amending formula, substantive constitutional changes respecting control of resources and the rights of Aboriginal people, statements with respect to equalization of provincial revenues, and a Charter of Rights and Freedoms, was an important milestone in the political life of Canada. It has made a major difference in how Canadians see themselves.

The events of the week have been recorded elsewhere. There are several sources available for those wanting to pursue those events in more detail. They include: *Canada ... Notwithstanding*, by Romanow, Leeson, and Whyte (referred to in chapter 16); legal oral history materials gathered by Christine Kates and stored in Library and Archives Canada; 'Constitution-Making as Intergovernmental Relations: A Case Study of the 1980 Negotiations,' by A.D. McDonald; 'Canada and the Constitution 1979–1982: Patriation and the Charter of Rights,' by W.F. Dawson, available through JSTOR (Scholarly Journal Archive).

I want to touch on a few of the events as they transpired. The federal government very much wanted an agreement. Mr Trudeau was reaching the end of his term as prime minister and, I felt, wanted to achieve patriation (which involved adopting an amending formula or formulas) and a symbolic charter of rights which, at minimum, protected language rights across Canada and perhaps the right to seek and hold a job in any part of Canada. I believed that he felt that these were important both in symbolic and in practical terms. Perhaps, but perhaps not, Mr Trudeau wanted an amending formula which preserved a veto on constitutional change for Quebec.

The provinces, on the other hand, had a good deal less emotional and political capital tied up in any particular constitutional change. Mr Lévesque would, I suspect, have been happy if negotiations had broken down. I felt that Premier Lyon did not appreciate Mr Trudeau's style or his tactics and would have been happy enough for Manitoba to deal with his successor. Some of us felt that it was important for Canada to complete the patriation exercise to strengthen Canada and add to the sense of national confidence with which Canadians viewed themselves. Other premiers shared this view but felt that Canada had done quite well for over fifty years without this matter being resolved and that no great harm would be done if the matter were further delayed.

So the dynamics were tending, but not strongly, toward settlement. I feared that Mr Trudeau would proceed to the U.K. Parliament without support from a consensus of provinces. If he met with opposition and delay in the U.K. Parliament, as I suspected he would after the ruling of the Supreme Court of Canada in the Patriation Reference (referred to in chapter 16), he might be tempted to hold a national referendum on the patriation package. I felt that such a referendum would be hugely divisive. It had too much potential to become a pro-Trudeau/anti-Trudeau decision in the public mind. In parts of Quebec and in much of western Canada, the dislike of Mr Trudeau was deep and visceral. In the 1980 federal election, the Liberals had, in all of Saskatchewan, Alberta, British Columbia, Yukon, and the Northwest Territories, won no seats. In Manitoba they won two, both in greater Winnipeg.

Much of the anger arose out of the energy policies pursued by the federal government since 1974, culminating in the National Energy Program announced in 1980. I did not want a referendum, and I certainly did not want a referendum in 1982. On some issues it was (and is) not easy for a provincial politician to argue for a pan-Canadian view. I certainly did not want the patriation of the Constitution to become a partisan regional issue, as I felt (and still feel) it would have become.

With this background, we headed into negotiations on 2 November 1981. The week started with Ontario and New Brunswick making some conciliatory statements. We had no doubt that these were inspired by the federal government. But we couldn't quite read what they meant. In retrospect, perhaps we should have read a signal that the federal government was willing to consider an amending formula that was not regionally based, but based on a formula requiring changes to have the approval of a stated number of provinces representing a stated proportion of the Canadian population. This would have been a formula of the type advanced by the Gang of Eight provinces in April 1981. But any such formula meant that probably no one province would have a veto. The federal government, understandably, did not want to put forward the idea that Quebec would not have its historic veto. So the apparent plan was to float this idea, lightly, by having Ontario suggest that, in some circumstances, Ontario would be prepared to give up its historic veto. The signal seemed to be that the federal amending formula was not carved in stone.

New Brunswick talked about some parts of the proposed Charter being firm and some parts being subject to being set aside by Parliament or a provincial legislature by use of a *non obstante* clause (as the lawyers call it), which came to be referred to as a 'notwithstanding clause.' In these proposals was the germ of an agreement. But there was still lively controversy. Mr Lévesque and Mr Trudeau began to goad each other on the matter of who would win a referendum. Since some others and I wanted no part of a referendum, either for adoption of the changes or as part of a new amending formula, I found these dogfights unhelpful. I still did not understand the way politics in Quebec was conducted. I was reasonably sure that the protagonists did not mean what they said, but that gave me little help on what they did mean. By Tuesday evening the conference had reached an impasse. I advised my colleagues in the Gang of Eight that on Wednesday morning I was going to put a revised proposal on the table. Its contents hardly mattered: I had no expectation that it would be adopted. I did think it would keep the discussion going for a bit longer.

Some of my colleagues disagreed with the tactic. They felt that we should not depart from the position agreed upon by all eight of us in April. I don't think any of the eight premiers felt that my proposal represented the breaking of any understanding given. It was well understood that if our alliance of the eight premiers succeeded in getting Mr Trudeau back to the bargaining table, each of the eight was free to advance his own proposals for change. We had agreed at the beginning of the week that if anyone proposed to depart from the April agreement, he would give his colleagues advance notice. Mr Lévesque later stated that the agreement was otherwise. Some months later, Mr Lougheed had an exchange of letters with Mr Lévesque on this point, and Mr Lougheed published them in a small volume. I agreed with his view of the agreement reached on this matter. Mr Lévesque, in debate, agreed at one point to a federal proposal for a referendum, which was clearly not part of the April accord of the Gang of Eight. I did not regard this as a breach of the understanding among the eight, except to the extent that he gave no advance notice to his colleagues.

In the event, my proposals went nowhere. They were met with some odd reactions – comments starting with a welcome of the proposals and then rapidly moving to clear disagreement with the contents. They did seem to get some discussion going. The federal government was making informal overtures through Mr Chrétien speaking with Mr Romanow, through Mr Trudeau and Mr Davis speaking with me, and with Mr Chrétien, Mr Romanow, and Mr Roy McMurtry, the attorney general of Ontario, discussing several options. The discussions seemed to gel into a proposal for the federal government to accept an amending formula close to the April consensus of the Gang of Eight, with the provinces accepting a charter with Mr Trudeau's minimum of language rights and probably mobility and additional fundamental, democratic, legal, and equality rights, which might be subject to some opt-in or notwithstanding provision.

On Wednesday afternoon, Mr Chrétien put forward a proposal to Mr Romanow, who spoke with ministers from some other provinces and then spoke to me. I asked him to get Mr Chrétien to put the proposal in writing in brief form. Mr Romanow came back with a brief proposal. We discussed whether it was even worth talking about with the others. We concluded it was. Mr Romanow and I decided that it would go nowhere unless Mr Lougheed agreed to discuss it. In general, we felt that Mr Lyon, Mr Peckford of Newfoundland, and Mr MacLean of Prince Edward Island would probably follow Mr Lougheed's lead. This was not assured by any means. Each was his own man, but probably it would work that way.

I spoke with Mr Lougheed privately. We agreed that it was at least worth a look. By now it was around 5:00 p.m., and we were all dead tired. I suggested that we go our separate ways to have a meal, a shower, and probably a nap. I asked him to send someone to my suite at the Chateau Laurier Hotel at 9:00 p.m. to do some work on the proposal. We got word to some of the other delegations. I had no sense that we were going to flesh out a solid proposal. But as the evening wore on, the proposal looked more promising. I relayed proposals by telephone to Premier Davis, who was at the Skyline Hotel (as it was then called).

He kept indicating that some provision was, or was not, acceptable. I did not know, and to this day do not know, to what extent, if any, he was in touch with Mr Trudeau, Mr Chrétien, or Premier Hatfield. As drafting continued and some agreements seemed to be emerging, I began to speak to some premiers. Premier Peckford joined the group in my suite. He took the position that it was 'deal time.' If Premier Peckford could see a possible basis for a deal, I thought it should be pursued. At some point, I spoke with Premier Buchanan of Nova Scotia, who was about to leave Ottawa for perhaps a day because of a family bereavement. I convinced him to stay because we might well have a solid basis for negotiation by morning.

As an aside, I remember the response that Prince Edward Island attorney general, Horace Carver, had to my suggestion that Premier MacLean join the group. He demurred, saying that Premier MacLean was tired and that a stressful day such as we had had was difficult for him, considering his Second World War experiences. He recounted that Angus MacLean, then in the RCAF, had been shot down over Holland, had been hidden by the local residents, and had, in a harrowing journey lasting a year, been smuggled to Spain through Holland, Belgium, and France, all occupied by German forces. He had found his way back to the RCAF in Britain and resumed his duties. That is a story I had not known. As I recall it, Premier MacLean did join us at one point.

At no time during the evening and night did I see or speak with Prime Minister Trudeau, Premier Hatfield, Premier Lougheed, Premier Lyon (who was in Manitoba), or, I believe, Premier Bennett, although some of them were represented by officials. I did not see, but spoke several times with, Premier Bill Davis. I mention this because there have been stories circulated that the prime minister and most of the premiers met and ground out a deal without including Premier Lévesque in the discussions. This myth has acquired a colourful name – the 'Night of the Long Knives.' This is pure fantasy. Its grain of truth is that officials of most of the provinces did participate in the ongoing discussions in my suite at one time or another, but, as I recall it, these did not include Quebec. The officials were certainly not making commitments on behalf of their premiers. I did not for a minute believe that any official could commit, say, Premier Lougheed to a constitutional text without his having seen it. Our world did not work that way.

I certainly did not believe that the proposal we were hammering out was even close to its final form. I expected that what we were working on was a proposal to present to the Gang of Eight premiers at breakfast in the morning. (The Gang of Eight had a practice of meeting together for breakfast each morning to plan strategy.) At that time we hoped to reach a general consensus to bargain with the other side.

Breakfast was a bargaining session. Mr Lévesque was dismissive of the proposal and said Quebec would not agree. Mr Lougheed called for the reach of the notwithstanding clause to be widened somewhat. This was agreed. We agreed that Premier Peckford would introduce the proposal. I felt that this was sound strategy. It should come from one of the provinces – Quebec, Alberta, Manitoba, and Newfoundland – who had taken a fairly firm line throughout the negotiations, as opposed to the 'willing to compromise' provinces of British Columbia, Saskatchewan, and Nova Scotia. Prince Edward Island was less easy to categorize. These classification categories were only generally accurate. But it seemed prudent to suggest that this proposal had some backing. It would be up to Premier Davis to speak for himself and Mr Hatfield. Perhaps the proposal would be a basis for negotiating a settlement because many parts of it seemed to have been 'pre- cleared,' totally unofficially, with Mr Davis.

Mr Chrétien raised an objection or two, which were later abandoned. Saskatchewan and several other provinces were prepared to have the federal government, with as much agreement as they would get from Quebec, sort out the intricacies of minority language education rights. I remember having a private conversation with Premier Davis and Mr Trudeau on this point. My closing comment was, 'All right, but be it on your head.' Premier Davis's reply was to the effect, 'Yes, that's right. But, Allan, I wouldn't put it just that way to the public.'

After a morning's bargaining, we arrived at an agreement. We included the provisions in earlier drafts dealing with equalization payment and control over resources (which became section 92A of the Constitution Act, 1867), but much to my regret, I could not get agreement to include a provision on the rights of the Aboriginal people of Canada. We checked the draft to see whether we all agreed on which provisions would be subject to the notwithstanding clause and which would not. That was it. The deal was made. Nobody was happy with the contents. The agreement was somehow anti-climactic. We had done our best. We had a deal. The government of Quebec was not in. I was sorry but not surprised. Mr Trudeau assured us that almost all Quebec MPs would support it (73 out of 75 did).

It is easy now to suggest that 'Quebec' was left out. Certainly the gov-

ernment of Quebec was out. But it was far from clear whether Mr Trudeau or Mr Lévesque spoke for the people of Quebec. This was 1981. In
1980 there had been a federal election in which constitutional change
had been part of the election debate. For the ten previous years, Mr
Trudeau had been talking about constitutional reform, and his views
were widely known. In the election in Quebec, the Trudeau Liberals
received a massive 68 per cent of the votes. The next party was the Progressive Conservatives at 12.6 per cent, with the New Democrats polling
9 per cent. The Social Credit Party got 5.9 per cent, with the Rhinoceros
Party next at 3 per cent. In the light of these 1980 results, it was not hard
to accept Mr Trudeau's position that on constitutional matters he spoke
for the people of Quebec.

At any rate, a settlement was arrived at. Nobody got what he wanted. It
was far from perfect, but nobody could figure out how to get any agreement to make it better.

So a new constitution was born – and born, not out of the head of a
legal scholar crafting elegant and hortatory prose, but out of a toughly
bargained compromise that is so often the basis of democratic government. We then agreed that the agreement by the federal government
and nine provinces was a package deal. Drafting changes could be made,
minority language education rights could be clarified, but no one of us
would support any other changes to the agreement without other signa-
tories being free to suggest still further changes that might be made.
This decision that the deal was a package was to raise its head before
long. And so a week in the life of Canada was to reverberate through the
next decade as we debated proposed Meech Lake and Charlottetown
accords, and lived through a referendum in Quebec, the passage by the
federal Parliament of the Clarity Act, and other events that put strains on
the federation.

I attended the events when the Queen visited Canada in April 1982 to
preside over formal patriation ceremonies. After fifty years, Canadians
had decided on a way to make the Constitution our own. Like almost
every other important event in Canadian constitutional history, it was
met with a mixed response. Almost everywhere there was relief. Some
were close to jubilant. Some were incensed. Others felt it was an event
that called for clapping with one hand. But it was done.

18

Constitution: Aftermath

We returned to our homes after the marathon negotiations of November 2nd to 6th, pleased that an agreement had been reached but sorry about some clear failures. I was keenly disappointed, but not at all surprised, that we had not arrived at something that the government of Quebec could agree to. We understood that a very large majority of MPs from Quebec would accept the agreement, but that was not the same as having agreement of the Parti Québécois, which was the government of Quebec. I was sorry that I had not been able to persuade my colleagues to include the Aboriginal clause that had been discussed and that I had included in my proposal put forth to the conference on Wednesday, November 4th. But agreement required compromise, and I felt that it was important for Canada that an agreement be reached.

Soon after my return to Regina, I met with Aboriginal leaders and outlined to them why I had been unsuccessful. I was not clear on their position. From public announcements, it was by no means clear that they favoured the terms of the Aboriginal clause we were debating. I went on to say to them that if another opportunity came up for me to press for an Aboriginal clause, I would do so. I had the distinct understanding that they wanted me to do so. I didn't expect that such an opportunity would arise soon, but with constitutional matters, one never knew. And quite unexpectedly an opportunity did arise.

In the week of November 7th to 14th, some groups in Ontario, led by the National Action Committee on the Status of Women (NAC), began pressing for a change in the November 5th agreement to remove section 28 (providing for equality of men and women) from the ambit of section 33 (the notwithstanding clause). There was some contact between officials of the federal and provincial governments as to what wording might be necessary if this idea was to be followed up. On Monday, November 16th, Mr Chrétien, the minister of justice for Canada, spoke to me about what was called 'a free-standing section 28.' I expressed my reservations that if section 28 was 'free-standing,' the logical interpretation was that there could be no affirmative action programs to benefit women as provided for in section 15 of the Charter.

Section 15 set out a general rule that every individual was equal before the law and had the right to equal protection of the law without discrimination based upon several grounds, including sex. It went on to say that this non-discrimination rule did not preclude affirmative action programs for the benefit of individuals or groups who were at a disadvantage on several grounds, including sex. Thus it would allow for 'reverse' discrimination in favour of women who had been disadvantaged because of their sex. The proposal was for a free-standing section 28, which stated that notwithstanding anything said in section 15 or elsewhere, men and women were to be treated equally. That seemed to me to wipe out the possibility of affirmative action programs in favour of women.

Perhaps other interpretations were possible. I am sure that NAC took a different view, but I did not (and do not) understand what it was.

On November 17th the deputy minister of justice for Canada advised that all but three provinces had agreed to the proposed wording for the new 'free-standing section 28.' In a telephone conversation that I had with Mr Chrétien on either November 16th or 17th, I talked about the agreement all parties had made – that if the substance of the November 5th agreement was changed, all participants had the right to put forward other suggested changes. Mr Chrétien confirmed that this was his clear understanding. He then agreed that the change proposed for section 28 was a change in substance to the November 5th agreement.

Meanwhile, NAC and others were mounting pressure for a free-standing section 28. On Wednesday, November 18th, we made our decision, and at 3:30 p.m. we set out our position in a long telex from Mr Romanow to Mr Chrétien. I will quote the key parts:

> The accord of November 5, 1981, agreed that the charter of rights would remain intact, but that sections dealing with fundamental, legal, and equality rights later identified to be section 2 and section 7 to 15, and section 28 would be subject to a notwithstanding clause, this has been incorporated into the official working draft of November 5, 1981.
>
> On 17 November 1981, during a conference call, federal officials suggested a compromise wording which would more clearly delineate the respective applications of section 28 and section 33, the purpose being to

ensure that sexual equality was not brought under the ambit of section 33 in respect of sections other than section 15. Saskatchewan agreed to that compromise.

Since yesterday some now wish to eliminate the application of section 33 to section 28 entirely.

This is a change in substance, and therefore, a change to the agreement itself.

Premier Blakeney has stated that the Saskatchewan government is prepared to accept the accord of November 5, 1981, even though, as with any compromise, there were elements he would have otherwise preferred. If the accord of November 5, 1981 were to be changed in substance, then it is incumbent on us to consider another change of substance, too.

More specifically, if the agreement is now to be re-opened and if changes to section 28 are to be agreed to, it seems only fair to change the agreement to include section 34 (*now see section 35*) for the native peoples of Canada. To change the substance of the agreement in this way, without further considering a change to reinstate section 34 is not acceptable to us.

To summarize, we are quite willing to maintain the original agreement and to accept the compromise wording on section 33, worked out and agreed to by officials on November 17, and telecopied to us later that night, however, if you propose to change the substance of the agreement and amend section 28, we would agree to it only if another change in the substance of the agreement is accepted as well, namely the reinstatement of section 34 on native rights.

A copy of this telex was delivered not only to Mr Chrétien but also to the federal NDP caucus. On the evening of Wednesday, November 18th, the public campaign for a free-standing section 28 began in earnest. A federal cabinet minister proceeded to state the position of the government of Saskatchewan as being opposed to their initiative, but without contacting us or without, apparently, contacting her colleague Mr Chrétien. The CBC, in a news story replete with inaccuracies, again stated the Saskatchewan position, without contacting anyone in Saskatchewan. They included in their story a short clip of my voice recorded when I was giving a presentation to the Joint Parliamentary Committee in 1980 on another document and in totally different circumstances. It was done in a way that suggested to the listener that the comments were current. Stephen Lewis, a friend of long standing and then active in the Ontario NDP, called me and complained about the quote. I had difficulty convincing him that I had not given any television interview on the current section 28 issue. It was just another example of the CBC's all too often being 'his master's voice' in echoing the views of the federal government on constitutional issues, whatever these issues might be.

I noticed that same tendency later with respect to events that in no way concerned me personally. I can recall Mr Trudeau giving his views on the place of Quebec in Confederation and particularly his disdain for including in the Constitution any recognition of special status for Quebec. This was duly reported by the CBC with a slant that suggested that those calling for special status were wrong and bordering on being disloyal Canadians.

I recall later the discussions surrounding the Meech Lake Accord. Mr Trudeau was gone and Mr Mulroney was prime minister. A Trudeau adviser, Deborah Coyne, had gone to work for the Liberal premier of Newfoundland and Labrador, Clyde Wells. He opposed the Meech Lake Accord and began to express his opposition for including in the Constitution any recognition of special status for Quebec. He used words hauntingly similar to those previously used by Mr Trudeau. This was duly reported by the CBC with a slant that suggested that those opposing special status were wrong and bordering on being disloyal Canadians – a 180-degree turn.

I am a warm supporter of the CBC, but not of their constitutional reporting.

The pressure mounted in the media. In vain did I put out press releases stating our position and calling for recognition of Aboriginal (then referred to as Native) rights. Gradually opinion began to turn. The *Regina Leader Post* ran an editorial setting out our position with clarity.

By Friday the pressure was beginning to turn on other governments – why were they opposed to Native rights?

· On Saturday, NAC had scheduled a rally in Regina on the steps of the legislature. I asked to speak to the rally. I gave what I hoped was a clear day-by-day statement of our position. Apparently, this was news to many people who had taken their 'facts' from the Ottawa media. The chair of the meeting was Lucie Pépin, later Senator Pépin. She graciously noted that NAC was not in possession of the full facts. Some of the demonstrators chided me for 'trading rights.' I chided them for not using the very considerable lobbying talents of NAC (which I ruefully conceded) on behalf of Aboriginal people.

I received several hundred telegrams inspired by NAC. I prepared a form letter telling our story and sent it to everyone who sent a telegram and for whom we could find an address. I did not receive a single reply.

I came across a book setting out the accomplishment by NAC in securing a 'free-standing section 28.' The book suffered from tunnel vision, gracelessness, and, at its kindest, a restricted view of the facts.

By early the following week, all governments had agreed to the inclusion of both a free-standing section 28 and the Aboriginal clause, with a minor but important insertion of the word 'existing' (I believe at Mr Lougheed's suggestion) to make clear that the Aboriginal clause was meant to recognize existing treaty and Aboriginal rights and not to resurrect rights that may have existed in the past. I welcomed this clarification. The constitutional resolution was amended to include a free-standing section 28 and an Aboriginal rights clause.

By late November, I was able to report to Aboriginal leaders in Saskatchewan that the Aboriginal clause was in the constitution as section 35. It has been used many times before the courts to define and delineate Aboriginal rights.

I take some personal satisfaction in how events unfolded. I don't like clauses in a constitution as imprecise in its meaning as section 35. Yet I felt and still feel that it was important to give Aboriginal people some legal tools to improve their lot in Canadian society. As I've noted elsewhere, I believe that the best hope for Aboriginal people is for non-Aboriginal society to help those who wish to do so, to participate more fully in the mainstream Canadian economy. It is important that progress be made on all fronts, including the constitutional one.

19

Democracy after the Charter

One of the greatest accomplishments in the history of the Western world during the last two centuries has been the development of institutions by which free people can govern themselves in a democratic way. If by democracy we mean the participation by the great majority of adult citizens in their own government, then this is a comparatively recent development. The legitimacy of democracy as an idea owes its birth in recent centuries to the philosophers of the Renaissance and to the American and French Revolutions of the 1770s, '80s, and '90s. Prior to that time, many held the view that only a select group of people should direct and control government.

And even after the American and French Revolutions, the development of government based on a broad franchise took a very long time to come about. The right to vote was denied to large groups of people until well into the twentieth century. There have been many hurdles to overcome – hurdles that restricted the right to vote to people of wealth or property, of higher levels of education, or of freeman status rather than slaves; to men rather than women; or to those who were not registered Indians, and so on. Indeed, it was in 1982 in Canada that the legal right to vote was given to convicted felons, people suffering from mental illness, and superior court judges.

Why was it that what we might call universal franchise took so long to develop? At least two reasons can be identified. The first is simple. People who already exercise power rarely like to share power, and they can find many reasons to justify their exclusive exercise of that power. The second reason is a little more complex. It is counter-intuitive to believe that giving the right to vote to everybody is a good idea. Surely decisions should be made by people who have an interest in and knowledge of the issues, and not by the ignorant.

We started with the belief, once widely and honestly held, that the right to govern is given by the deity to only a select few. God had given to monarchs a divine right to rule. Later, landowners and men of substance in the feudal system insisted on a right to participate in government. There was no suggestion that this right be shared with vassals and serfs. Still later, when merchants became wealthy from trade and commerce, they insisted on a share of power. Once again there was no suggestion that their menial employees be included in the group exercising governmental authority. Gradually the group exercising power was enlarged. In the parliamentary tradition that we have inherited from Great Britain, substantial changes began in Britain with the Reform Act of 1832. But the progress was slow. In Canada women were not given the franchise until the First World War and then in a limited way. This right was gradually expanded. Women did not attain the right to vote in provincial elections in Quebec until 1940, and registered Indians could not vote in federal elections until 1960.

There have always been a great number of people who felt that ordinary individuals could not be trusted to make rational and prudent decisions on public affairs. And surely this is understandable. We must admit that many ordinary people of little education, little wealth, little time to pursue the issues, and little interest in them cannot always be relied upon to make prudent judgments. As the belief goes, we should leave these decisions to people who are interested and informed about them. But this is the siren call of those with little faith in democracy. In earlier times the belief was that decisions were best left to people of wealth and substance. Just a few decades ago, the belief was widely held that public matters were very complicated and that most decisions should be left to people with a technical knowledge of the facts. This view found its expression in the theories of technocracy, popular in the 1930s and 1940s, and to some extent in the theories of the Social Credit movement.

Admittedly it is an act of faith to believe that politicians chosen by voters exercising a very wide right to vote will, in the long run, make better decisions than those with more knowledge, be they monarchs exercising a perceived divine right of kings, or the landed aristocracy, or merchant princes, or technical experts. People who share this faith in democracy believe that it is almost inevitable that people exercising power for an extended period of time will exercise that power to benefit themselves or the groups or classes which they represent. In short, wisdom and impartiality are wasting assets, and society is wiser to rely upon the inherent good sense of the mass of the people, even though they are less well informed than the experts. I believe that this is one very valid interpretation of the Churchillian comment that democracy is the worst system of government except for all the others. But it is, at any particular time, a counter-intuitive idea that we should trust the broad electorate. It always seems that we would be more prudent to trust our fortunes to the wise and well-informed. Each generation or two seems to bring forth yet another siren call to give government over to the experts.

The history of attempts by governments to deal with human rights, and particularly the rights of minorities and the powerless, has produced our latest burgeoning of faith in the experts. Who can we now trust to protect human rights? Once again we express distrust for the wisdom of the ordinary voter, and we cast around for a wise expert. Judges are now being cast in this role.

In Canada, parliaments and legislatures, as they became the voice of the mass public, recognized that they were majoritarian in their approach to many issues. They, too, realized that they were governing for the benefit of the groups and classes that they represented. True, they represented the majority, but not necessarily all voters. And they realized that this process sometimes did not recognize the legitimate rights of minorities and the powerless. So parliaments and legislatures groped for ways to build special safeguards for minorities and the powerless into their majoritarian democratic system.

In 1947 the province of Saskatchewan adopted a Bill of Rights and, a little later, laws to improve equity in employment and public accommodation. The Parliament of Canada adopted a Bill of Rights in 1960, into which principles of rights for minorities and the powerless were incorporated. The law was stated to be paramount over any other law passed by the Parliament of Canada unless specifically stated to the contrary in a later act of Parliament. And the courts were given the obligation to implement this paramountcy. Provinces passed similar legislation in their areas of legislative jurisdiction. Saskatchewan enacted a human rights code in 1979 that was similarly made paramount over ordinary legislation.

Particularly in the case of the Canadian Bill of Rights, the courts did not give a robust and vigorous interpretation to the legislation. This led to a campaign for a similar bill of rights to be enshrined in the Constitution. Mr Trudeau became prime minister in 1968. He was a product of

the Quebec of Maurice Duplessis and the Union Nationale. That government was a strong argument for the need for a bill of rights enshrined in
the Constitution of Canada. Mr Trudeau also believed that in order for
Canada to survive as a united nation, it would be necessary to give additional protections to the French language, and that these protections
should be included in the Constitution. He did not feel that he could get
sufficient agreement to include the French language provisions in the
Constitution if they were introduced on their own. So, as I have outlined
in chapter 16, he contrived the plan to introduce a bill of rights, which
he called a Charter of Rights and Freedoms, and insert into the Charter
the language rights that he wished to see in the Constitution. From a logical perspective, these language rights are ill placed in the Charter. But,
as a practical matter, it made sense to regard language rights, which
should be a part of the Confederation bargain, as 'human' rights to be
enjoyed by all Canadians in a bilingual federation. So the Charter of
Rights and Freedoms was introduced into the Constitution.

The Charter, in broad terms, re-enacted the Canadian Bill of Rights. It
included as well: additional protection against discrimination for minorities and the powerless; certain democratic rights which political leaders
felt might not be fully protected by parliaments and legislatures; some
mobility rights; Mr Trudeau's language rights; and some provisions to
enforce the Charter. That is what the people who negotiated the Charter
believed they were doing, and that is what they explained to the Parliament, the legislatures, and the public.

Section 7 of the Charter is in substantially the same terms as section
1(a) of the Canadian Bill of Rights of 1960. It has been the law of Canada
since 1960. It was given some judicial interpretation. Since 1982, the
same words, included under the heading 'Legal Rights in the Charter,'
have been given a very substantially different interpretation by the courts
than was previously the case. I believe that the drafters of the Charter and
the parliaments and legislatures that adopted it had the right to assume
that the same words as used in 1960 would bear substantially the same
interpretation when used in the Charter. In particular, the draftspeople,
parliaments, and legislatures had the right to assume that the words of
section 7 of the Charter would be interpreted to protect what has been
called procedural due process. They had the further right to assume that
the words would not be interpreted to mean that the courts had a general
supervisory role over all acts of parliaments and legislatures.

Section 7 of the Charter provides that 'everyone has the right to life,
liberty, and security of the person and the right not to be deprived

thereof, except in accordance with the principles of fundamental justice.'

A great many laws passed by parliaments and legislatures affect the life, liberty, and security of the person. A great many activities of governments and their public servants and police similarly affect the life, liberty, and security of the person. Many of these are the normal activities of government that affect all or most of the public and that, almost by definition, cannot be executed without some hazard to the life, liberty, and security of the person. There are not enough resources to perform all activities of government in a way that does not affect personal security. Indeed, deciding the extent to which one objective can be pursued without unduly affecting other objectives is the very essence of government. Government is all about making choices. And rational choices cannot be made unless the persons making the decisions can weigh the strengths and weaknesses of competing claims. Thus, if a government provides for health care, there are never enough resources to avoid some threat to personal security. If a government builds and maintains highways and streets, there are never enough resources to avoid some such threat. Similar arguments arise when deciding how many police officers or child welfare workers should be employed. All of this is weighed against the level of taxation – the level of resources gathered from the citizens in order to provide for the citizens the communal services which they want and are prepared to pay for.

It is simply not rational to suggest that appropriate decisions on whether or not sufficient resources are being devoted to a particular objective of government can be made by resort to the judicial process. A recent case decided by the Supreme Court in 2005, *Chaoulli v. Quebec (A.G.)* [2005] SCC 35, illustrates the problem. The reasoning set forth by the court in the *Chaoulli* case clearly suggests that if any activity of government poses a threat to personal security, then 'Section 7 of the Charter is engaged,' and it is appropriate for the court to determine whether sufficient resources are being devoted to this activity of government. In the *Chaoulli* case, a decision was arrived at without any reference, so far as can be gleaned from the reasons for judgment, to other demands on the government of Quebec. For example, would providing additional resources to the medical care system have meant a reduction of spending on, say, highways in a manner so as to create even greater risks to personal security? Was the Quebec government spending too much on highways and too little on health, so that personal security is threatened? The recent collapse of a highway overpass in Laval suggests that this was not the case.

It might be argued that too little was being spent on highways. These are the issues of priorities which the government of Quebec is daily being called upon to deal with. I saw no evidence that the Supreme Court of Canada recognized this. Nor was there any reference to levels of taxation or other means of financing government activities. It may be argued that the *Chaoulli* case did not purport to require the government of Quebec to spend more money on medical care. Rather, it provided that if the government of Quebec did not spend more money on medical care, then private care supported by private medical insurance must be permitted. I did not read any clear analysis as to whether the promotion of private care financed by private insurers would or would not increase the pressure on the government of Quebec and thereby render it less able to provide for the personal security of its citizens.

Several provinces in Canada have reached the conclusion that the parallel private health care system would increase the difficulties in providing medical care for their citizens, accordingly threatening personal security, and as a consequence they have prohibited the sale of private medical care insurance.

This is precisely the kind of decision that can best be made by people who have all the facts at their command or who can secure them from people well versed in the field. It is the kind of decision that does not lend itself to being disposed of in a one- or two-day hearing before judges who are necessarily unaware of the many complex issues involved.

In particular, if it is conceded that private medical care insurance might improve the personal security of a particular citizen – be it a physician (Chaoulli) or a patient (Zeliotis) – surely another question immediately arises: does private medical care insurance increase or decrease the personal security of the great majority of Quebec residents? I read no analysis of this question.

I believe that the problem in cases like *Chaoulli* arises because of the perverse interpretation given to section 7. That section was included in the legal rights portion of the Charter because it was intended to ensure that legal proceedings were conducted in a way that respected high standards of due process. I believe this is the way that the provision was drafted, the way that it was understood in Parliament and in the legislatures, and the way that the public understood it. This is the way that substantially the same words in the Canadian Bill of Rights were interpreted by the courts for well over twenty years. I do not believe that Parliament or the legislatures or the public intended that the courts would use the words in section 7 to erect some general supervisory role over all governmental activities. This is the effect of the interpretation given by Chief Justice McLachlin in the *Chaoulli* case.

The chief justice bases her argument on whether any particular activity of government significantly affects the life and security of a particular citizen, and if such is the case, then the court is entitled to review the activity. Since a very substantial number of activities of government affect the life and security of its citizens, then it would appear that a very substantial range of government activities are subject to review by the courts to ascertain, not whether they are for the general benefit of the public, but rather whether they adversely affect the position of any individual citizen. Surely this is a startling proposition, and one, I submit, which does not reflect the intention of Parliament or the legislatures.

It may be argued that judges, when they interpret a constitution, should not be guided by the original intent of the document. I think this is a false argument. The proper argument, in my view, is that over time the courts should feel free to depart from the original intent. Because the language used is in a constitutional document and because it is therefore difficult to change and is often phrased in general, visionary, and hortatory terms, courts should feel free to change the meaning to make it accord with changing circumstances. This idea is often put in terms of the constitution being a living tree that has the capacity to change and mature over time. This does not mean that within a few months of Parliament and the legislatures adopting a constitution, the courts should give it a sharply different meaning. This is to change an acorn into a giant oak in an indecently short period of time.

Our system cannot work effectively if the courts believe that their role is to supervise all activities of government. To extend the court's argument in the *Chaoulli* case, are we to assume, if Parliament after informed and earnest debate decided that war should be declared against North Korea, that the Supreme Court should review this decision on the basis of it threatening the personal security of individual citizens, and that Parliament should outline to the court why this threat to security should be permitted in a free and democratic society?

The Charter, in my view, was intended to restate the provisions of the Canadian Bill of Rights, to add democratic rights which had largely been honoured but not codified, and, in particular, to add the equality rights of section 15 of the Charter. There were additional rights with respect to mobility and language rights that are not relevant to this argument. The Charter was intended to make sure that the laws passed by parliaments and legislatures and the activities carried out by employees of governments fully respected the rights of minorities and the less powerful, people who may well be treated unfairly or discriminated against in the majoritarian climate of government because of their minority or powerless status. These objectives are fully consistent with the Charter if section 7 is given the meaning intended by the draftspeople. The Charter was not intended to replace the preamble to the Constitution Act, 1867, which gave us a system of governance similar to that of the United Kingdom. It was not intended to provide for a general supervisory role to be exercised by the courts over the bulk of governmental activities, where such activities do not affect in any special way the rights of minorities or the powerless, but simply involve the general weighing of the competing claims of the general citizenry to have government resources expended in their particular area of interest. It should not be so interpreted.

20

Defeat

In the provincial election of April 1982, the NDP was soundly defeated. I did not see it coming until well on in the campaign. I was not aware of any widespread unhappiness with the government. Certainly there were danger signs. The support staff in the some seventy-one major hospitals called a strike that continued for over sixteen days in March of 1982. With so many hospitals not in full operation over such an extended period of time, we felt that we had to ask the legislature to pass back-to-work legislation and provide for binding arbitration if a negotiated settlement was not arrived at within eight days. The back-to-work legislation was passed on March 26.

The trade union movement was unhappy with the back-to-work legislation. I was always mildly aggrieved that the trade unions took this position on this and other occasions when back-to-work legislation was passed. In every other province of Canada, the strike would have been unlawful from day one, and the dispute would have been settled by binding arbitration. It seemed to me that in these cases in other provinces the trade union movement did not take the position that they opposed such no-strike legislation and lay it at the door of the government in power. In Saskatchewan we had taken the position that trade unions should enjoy an unlimited right to strike, with the understanding that when there was a serious threat to the public there could be back-to-work legislation. That legislation would have to be justified in a public way in the legislature. Back-to-work legislation was sparingly used, and the arbitration provisions were uniformly fair, but its use precipitated far more hostility on the part of the trade union movement than did the no-strike legislation in all other provinces. So there was some hostility in some sections of the trade union movement.

More fundamentally, economic conditions were causing a good deal of concern in the minds of the public. Interest rates were rising sharply, soaring to 15 and 20 per cent. The government had been doing very well financially. It had balanced its budget in every year since 1971 and was, in later years, enjoying a good level of resource revenues. There was a feeling that somehow the provincial government should protect its citizens against the effects of high and rising interest rates. We were not too clear what the provincial government could do that would have much effect on soaring interest rates in North America. But, in retrospect, we should probably have done something, if only in a symbolic way, to recognize the public concern. In the eyes of some, it seemed that they were poor and getting poorer, while the government was rich, getting richer, and doing nothing.

Others have suggested that the negotiations which led up to the patriation of the Canadian Constitution in April 1982 consumed too much of the government's time and effort. And that is probably true. Both Roy Romanow and I put a great deal of effort into the endless meetings leading up to the agreement arrived at in November 1981 and the formal ratification the following April. The public seemed interested. But, as has often been said, all politics is local. People are concerned, not with the sweep of charters and resource taxes, but with the things that directly affect their day-to-day lives. I've already noted Premier Ross Thatcher's quip: 'If you ask the people of Saskatchewan what their 100 most pressing problems are, the Constitution comes in at 101.'

In any case there was no real alternative. The work on the Constitution simply had to be done. Or so I thought then and think now.

Still, when we did the opinion polling, it showed that support for the NDP was holding. A Gallup poll compiled from information gathered on the very weekend that the election was called in March 1982 showed the NDP with a 10-percentage point lead over the Progressive Conservatives. In almost all categories, the voters appeared to favour the NDP. There was one ominous exception. A majority felt that it was 'time for a change.' The answers to questions asked during polling are frequently not consistent.

The Opposition Progressive Conservative Party ran a very skilful campaign. They did not attempt to show that things were going badly. Rather, they took the position that things could be much better. Their campaign slogan was, 'There is so much more we can be.' This conveys the idea to the voters that all of the benefits they now enjoy will be preserved and that there will be further improvements. There were specific promises to eliminate the tax on gasoline and a plan to pay grants so that the effective rate on some house mortgages would be pegged at about 14 per cent. Some have suggested that our government 'was out of touch.' The media pundits who made that observation were undoubtedly right, but none of them made it before polling day.

Others suggested that a polling day in April is always bad news for the government. After having survived a Saskatchewan winter, nobody feels upbeat in April. Elections should be held in June, when Saskatchewan people are almost invariably optimistic.

The above comments hardly amount to a full analysis of why we lost the election and lost it so badly. But lose it we did. On election night the seat count was Progressive Conservatives 55, New Democrats 9. In speaking to the media on election night, I made a statement taking full responsibility for the loss. One of the people working with me as a media person was Dick Proctor, an old sports reporter who was later to become a Member of Parliament for Palliser. At the time Dick commented, 'When any party loses this badly, it can't be the responsibility of one person. It's got to be a team effort.'

Grant Devine had replaced Dick Collver as leader of the Progressive Conservative Party in 1980. Mr Collver's political perambulations comprised a bizarre series of events. He left the party of Sir John A. Macdonald, our first prime minister, who proudly declared, 'A British subject I was born, a British subject I will die.' Mr Collver formed the Unionest Party, with the stated purpose of promoting the union of Canada with the United States. He carried one caucus member with him, Dennis Hamm, the MLA for Swift Current. This is the only time in the history of the Saskatchewan legislature that we have had members advocating clearly that Canada should become a part of the United States. I need hardly say that the government did not share his views. Perhaps because of my Nova Scotia background, perhaps because of my family background, which was in the old Tory tradition as United Empire Loyalists, perhaps because the NDP frequently finds itself mildly at odds with the triumphant capitalism sometimes espoused in the United States, or perhaps because we felt that he did not reflect the visceral hopes and aspirations of Saskatchewan people, I and other New Democrats in the legislature took strong objection to the Collver fantasy, as we would have called it.

Neither Mr Collver nor Mr Hamm stood for re-election in 1982, and each disappeared from the Saskatchewan political scene. Mr Collver had links to the southwest of the United States, where, I suspect, the political and business climate of Phoenix and Las Vegas suited him better.

One would think that having the leader of your party desert the party and many of its long-established traditions would sink the party irretrievably. But not so with the Conservative Party in Saskatchewan. It should be called the Nine Lives Party. It had the great misfortune to be the leading player in a coalition that comprised the government of Saskatchewan from 1929 to 1934, a time when the province was ravaged by depression and drought. It was badly mauled in the election of 1934. It did not rise again, except for sporadic signs of life in 1960 and 1964, until the election of 1975. The reality is that since 1934 the Farmer-Labour-CCF-NDP political grouping has been dominant on the left of Saskatchewan politics. On the right has been the Liberal Party. Beginning in the mid-1970s, the federal Liberal Party, in office in Ottawa, became hugely unpopular with Saskatchewan voters and, in the course of so doing, made the provincial Liberals unpopular. The Progressive Conservatives were needed by voices on the right to stand against the NDP.

The defeat in 1982 was not the high point in my political career. I just felt sick about the defeat of some very able people. All but three of my fellow cabinet ministers went down to defeat. I think of people like Roy Romanow, the deputy premier. He ran in the constituency of Riversdale, where he has run a total of nine times. In 1982 he was defeated by fewer than twenty votes. In all other elections, he has secured more than twice as many votes as anybody who has stood against him. Since we felt that Roy's seat was totally secure, we pressed him to campaign everywhere else in the province, which he willingly did. Necessarily he neglected his constituency. After the election, a sage observer of the Saskatoon political scene commented, referring to a street running through the core of the constituency, 'If Roy had walked down 20th Street once during the campaign, I think he would have won.'

I was worried about whether some of the things we had done would survive – the children's dental plan, the prescription drug plan, and some of the resource Crown corporations. I was worried, too, about how the new government might deal with some of the many able people who were in the public service and who had done such a first-rate job for the people of Saskatchewan. And personally, I wondered whether I should stay on as the leader of the party. If so many of our key people had not lost their seats, I would have felt that it would be wise of me to step down. I had an attractive offer of employment that tempted me, but eventually I decided there was a tough rebuilding job to be done, and since I had got the party into its then current mess, I should see what I could do to get it out of the mess.

After the 1982 election, the legislature proved to be the next thing to a zoo. Some of the new members had received very bad advice and felt that it was appropriate to shout down Opposition members when they were speaking. I found that I could not speak off the cuff. Because of the noise level, I couldn't hear what I was saying, and so I had to prepare my remarks in detail and deliver them even though I could not hear my own voice. This performed no useful purpose in the legislature itself, but it meant that because of the audio system in the legislative chamber anyone who watched the televised proceedings could see me and hear the message I was delivering. This was a new experience for me. In my more than twenty years in the legislature in government and opposition, I had not known a time when Mr Speaker permitted such a level of uproar. Conduct in the house improved somewhat but never regained the level of civility of previous years. I was pleased to note, however, that over time a number of the new members on the government side came to recognize that the legislature had an important function to perform that could not be done well unless the rules developed over the centuries in the parliaments in Westminster and in Canada were observed.

My job over the next four years was to rebuild. The party could be depended upon, with a little boost from our few elected MLAs, to rebuild itself. It has deep roots in the political soil of Saskatchewan. It was my job to convince people that we had a strong political future. In particular, I had to approach many dozens of people to see whether they were willing to stand as candidates for the party in the next election. I spent endless hours on the telephone and travelling about the province talking to potential candidates. Not since the 1934 election had so many seats been held by another party. So, for the election expected in 1986, many new candidates had to be recruited. A few members of the old guard would be reoffering – people like Ed Tchorzewski and Roy Romanow – but the overwhelming number of our candidates for the coming election would be new.

We weathered the battering in the legislature, and as the new government gained a track record, we had an easier time of it. From my partisan point of view, they were an incompetent government, and this became increasingly clear to the public. We were able to mount a highly credible election campaign in 1986. But we fell short. We garnered 45 per cent of the vote to 44 per cent for the Progressive Conservatives. But some of our votes were in the wrong place, and the seat count turned out a disappointing 38 for the Progressive Conservatives and 25 for the NDP. But there was no doubt that the New Democratic Party had been rebuilt and was a clear contender for office.

Once the results of the 1986 election were clear, I told the officials of the New Democratic Party that I would be stepping down as leader, at a time that was best for the party and for me. They urged me to stay on until the renewal of the party was still more advanced. I stayed until 1987. The Saskatchewan NDP elects its leader for a one-year term. I announced early that I would not be a candidate for election as leader at the 1987 party convention in November. There was a leadership contest that proved to be no contest. Roy Romanow, deputy premier from 1971 to 1982, had been re-elected in 1986 and was elected leader by acclamation. He is the only person who was ever elected leader of the Saskatchewan CCF or NDP by acclamation in its history – unlike his predecessors George Williams, Tommy Douglas, Woodrow Lloyd, or me, and his successor, Lorne Calvert. Roy led the party brilliantly to a convincing win in the election of 1991.

The Conservatives made a very rapid rise from near oblivion in 1971 to government in 1982. They then had the misfortune of being a less than competent government for nine years from 1982 to 1991 and being caught up in a number of scandals, some petty and a few not so petty. This led to their crushing defeat in 1991. It was so pronounced that they decided to suspend operations as a political party for, as I recall, ten years. The NDP was back in office. The federal Liberals were again in office at Ottawa, and feelings against them were still high, so that it was very difficult for the provincial Liberals to resume their place as the standard-bearer of the right in opposition to the NDP. So the Conservative Party, in effect, rose from the ashes, this time with a new name, the Saskatchewan Party. The Conservative members in the legislature and the party organization joined with a few disgruntled Liberals to form a party of the right. This grouping did not affiliate with any federal political party because it clearly wished to woo supporters of both the Reform Party (later the Alliance) and the federal Progressive Conservatives. The difficulty in this regard has been removed since the union of the Reform Party (renamed the Alliance) with the federal Progressive Conservative Party into a new Conservative Party of Canada. I somehow doubt that the Saskatchewan Party will become formally affiliated with any federal party.

I regard it as unfortunate when political parties do not have both a federal and a provincial wing. The federal government must take action from time to time that may not be well received in a particular region of

Canada. I believe it to be helpful if there is a provincial political party in each region of the country that feels some obligation to make the case for the governing·party in Ottawa. It's too easy to fall into the stance of always bashing Ottawa and failing to consider why some national policies, unpopular locally, may be necessary. Provincial political parties without any federal affiliation, and therefore any need to develop a national perspective, are further evidence of the disturbing drift to regionalism in Canada. We have a Parti Québécois and a Yukon Party; we do not need a Saskatchewan Party.

One of the happy things about the political life is being able to be elected to form a government and to be able to go ahead with some projects that you feel will be good for the province. Conversely, one of the sad things about the political life is to see things that you set in place and that you feel were good for the province dismantled by a succeeding government.

I look back with satisfaction on some of the major innovation of our government: a single agency for northern Saskatchewan – DNS; a new (for North America) occupational health and safety regime; the Land Bank – our attempt to deal with the problem of getting farmland into the hands of the next generation of family farmers; the children's dental health plan – a method of dealing with a shortage of dentists and lack of preventive dentistry; the prescription drug plan – an attempt to deal with the then emerging problem of the high cost of prescription drugs; the Saskatchewan Oil and Gas Corporation, Potash Corporation of Saskatchewan, and Saskatchewan Mining Development Corporation – our attempt to get the best possible return for Saskatchewan people when our natural resources are extracted; the beef and pork price stabilization boards – our efforts to provide some stability for livestock producers; our efforts to defend the subsidy to farmers implicit in the Crow's Nest Pass freight rates; and a good number of other initiatives. Most are now gone. A few, such as the occupational safety laws and a radical reform of workers' compensation, have been adopted by most other provinces and are part of the general Canadian labour law regime.

Some of the changes that we made were meant to be temporary. We had intended to reintegrate parts of the Department of Northern Saskatchewan into the general government structure as conditions in the North became more like those in the rest of the province. I feel that the Devine government which succeeded us disbanded the department too soon and that this resulted in a long delay in bringing economic and social conditions in the North to a level closer to that of the provincial average. Following 1991, the Romanow and Calvert governments have renewed the positive contribution of mining to employment for Aboriginal people in the North. The idea that the provincial government has a role to play in allowing young people to enter farming by taking over their parents' land holdings has largely been abandoned. The Land Bank is gone. In the public mind, it was clearly flawed. There has been no successor. In the 1970s there was a fear that money from Europe and the Arab oil states was seeking a safe home in North America and there would be a major move to buy Saskatchewan farmland. There were some purchases by offshore money. Restrictions were placed on the foreign ownership of farmland. The Cold War died; so did the threat, and in due course the restrictions.

The children's dental plan was dismantled for no good reason. I would regard it as still a very sound and cost-effective way to deal with the dental needs of Saskatchewan children and with the looming shortage of dentists in rural, small-town, and small-city Saskatchewan. The prescription drug plan was scrapped. It was replaced by a simple and limited cost reimbursement plan that, unlike the drug plan, does little to keep costs down for consumers. What is now needed is a national prescription drug plan along the model of the original Saskatchewan plan.

I am not upset when an idea that I championed has served its purpose and passed from the scene. I'm not very upset when an idea I've championed is discarded in favour of another approach which someone feels will work better. I am upset when changes are made which don't make any sound business or sound government sense but, rather, are made largely on ideological grounds. The moves to privatize the resource corporations, I feel, fell into this category. Before turning to the horror stories of uranium and potash, I will recite the small tale of sodium sulphate.

Saskatchewan Sodium Sulphate was set up in the late 1940s. It competed with several private sector plants in Saskatchewan and elsewhere in North America. It had no customers in Saskatchewan. For upwards of fifty years, it operated successfully. It developed the most sophisticated production methods in the industry, produced a product of a quality unsurpassed in the industry, and made money consistently under governments of different political stripes. It returned to the provincial coffers many times its original cost and kept its plants in top condition. It provided solid and, in one case, crucial support for the economies of several Saskatchewan villages. It was sold for a price many times its original investment. It still operates. Perhaps it made sense to sell this little golden gosling, but no reason was ever advanced other than the bald assertion that government should not be in business. This is clearly a reason based on faith. The evidence and the cash all pointed in the other direction.

The case of uranium and the Saskatchewan Mining Development Corporation was another story. It had had a very impressive record following its creation in June 1974. In preparation for sale by the Devine government, it was converted into a standard joint stock company under The Companies Act. Shares were given value and sold at a price of $11.75 a share in 1988. In November 2007 those shares would be worth $250.00 each. Similarly the Potash Corporation of Saskatchewan was privatized. Shares were sold for $18.00 each. In November 2007 those shares would be worth $340.00 each. In the 5 December 2007 issue of the Saskatoon *Star Phoenix*, the CEO of the Potash Corporation of Saskatchewan is quoted as saying that, as a privatized entity, the corporation had brought 'a 4,300 per cent gain for investors since the initial public offering.' Admittedly much has happened in the last fifteen years or so. But I cannot help but believe that these resources of the people of Saskatchewan were sold at fire sale prices to satisfy an ideological belief that governments should not own resource companies. Setting up an income trust or some other vehicle for the benefit of, say, post-secondary education – universities and technical institutes – now comes to mind as an option that might have been pursued. But it's too late. I realize that in the late 1980s these companies were not the mature organizations that they are now. But if these corporations were regarded as having the purpose of building an endowment fund for post-secondary education rather than providing immediate annual income, then the fact that income flows were uneven would be of no great consequence. The great U.S. universities, such as Harvard and Yale, have endowment funds in the tens of billions of dollars. The celebrated economist John Maynard Keynes made a fortune for his college, King's College Cambridge, by managing their investments. One might hope that the University of Saskatchewan and its sister institutions could have enjoyed similar success. Simply holding the shares as a passive investor would have provided billions to post-secondary institutions and would have met the desire to get the government out of the business of managing resource companies. The people of Saskatchewan deserved a better return than they got on the disposition of the resource companies they owned.

Hindsight is 20/20. Foresight is not. But I believe that our citizens deserved more than the 20/200 foresight they received.

The old order changeth. And it is in the nature of old politicians to deplore some of the changes. But if one can content oneself with the belief that you did reasonably well in your day and age, then that should be enough. In any case, that's all there is.

21

Academe and Beyond

I left elected politics in March 1988. I recall my last day at the legislature. Once it is clear that you are finally leaving, friend and foe alike find kind words to say about you. And kind words followed – after twenty-eight years.

My wife and I went on an extended trip to Greece, Egypt, Italy, France, and Britain for six weeks – the longest holiday trip of our marriage. I then went on to teach at Osgoode Hall Law School at York University in Toronto. Osgoode is Canada's largest law school, with the finest law school library. Dean James MacPherson, now a judge of the Ontario Court of Appeal, arranged my appointment there. He was part of the constitutional law team of the Saskatchewan government in the early 1980s and is a first-class lawyer. I've kept in touch with him in the years since.

I stayed on for a second year, teaching constitutional law. I taught legal relations between federal and provincial governments in Canada. I was able to bring to the classroom some experience, which I believe was useful to students. Canada is a federation, which is a bit complex as a system of government. The citizens of a country choose one central government to do some things on their behalf and several (in Canada, thirteen) provincial, territorial, or state governments to do other things on their behalf. It makes perfect sense to have one central government to look after such things as foreign affairs, the armed forces, railways, the Canadian dollar and banking, for instance, and to have provincial governments to look after roads, the school system, and local parks, which are better handled locally. But inevitably there are problems in drawing the lines around the areas in which each government should operate.

A rich body of law and practice, formal and informal, has grown up dealing with the division of powers, as the lawyers call it. I'll give an example. The federal government is given power to make laws and rules governing the armed forces. The provincial government of, say, Ontario is given power to make laws and rules governing highways and traffic on highways. Suppose that, in the course of army manoeuvres and training, a convoy of military vehicles is proceeding down Highway 400 north of Toronto. Is the convoy required to obey ordinary traffic laws made by the government of Ontario, or do only the federal rules about the army apply? In Canada we have dozens of such problems of overlapping laws. Most are worked out in a common-sense way, but occasionally a dispute arises and the courts have to decide where to draw the line.

I recall one such puzzle during my time as premier. Uranium mines are always a conundrum. The provinces are the governments that make rules about mining and mine safety. But there is an obscure provision of the Constitution, section 92(10)(c), which allows the federal government to declare that a mine or other undertaking is to be regulated by the federal government for the good of all Canada. Uranium mines were so declared to be a federal responsibility during the Second World War, and this declaration had never been changed. The question then arose: which government was responsible for mine safety in uranium mines? People in both the federal and Saskatchewan governments got together and agreed on a set of safety regulations. Each government passed those regulations. The province's inspectors were on the ground enforcing mine safety and checking on environmental matters. Environmental matters and worker safety are closely related. So each government gave authority to the mine inspectors to enforce the regulations on its behalf. If a mining company claimed, as they sometimes did, that the provincial inspector had no authority to enforce the rules, the inspector would reach into his pocket and produce his federal appointment, and the problem was solved.

I can remember musing to others that we should present the problem to the courts in a friendly lawsuit and get our answer. But somehow it never seemed a top priority item, and I don't believe it has ever been resolved in a legal sense. It's just one of the dozens of ways we have found to make the Canadian federation work. And it works about as well as any large federation in the world.

While at Osgoode, I taught a course at the York University School of Public Administration on management in the public sector. I taught with a lively academic, Sandford Borins, who now teaches at the University of Toronto. Sandford and I produced a book, *Political Management in Canada*, which is something of a primer on the problems of managing a

smaller provincial government. Again it was an area in which I had quite
a bit of background and experience.

While in Toronto for two academic years, I gave some lectures at the
University of Toronto and at Wilfrid Laurier University. I have a very clear
recollection of agreeing to give a lecture to a master of business administration (MBA) class taught by Jim Fleck at the University of Toronto. He
asked whether I would give a seminar on 'the potash cases.' To me these
were two high-profile legal disputes with the potash industry, each of
which had gone to the Supreme Court of Canada when I was premier in
the 1970s. I went to the class in downtown Toronto and arrived about fifteen minutes early, prepared to teach about these legal cases and to give
them a 'business' slant. Most of the students were young business people
in their thirties. When I got there, it became apparent that they had a
book of business cases illustrating problems that might be faced by managers in given business situations. The book contained two cases about
relations between the potash industry and the government of Saskatchewan. Neither had much to do with the legal cases. I had just enough time
to read the two 'cases' to find out what issues I was to address, but I had
no time to prepare anything in response. So I was on my own. I thought
I did reasonably well and we had a good discussion, but I made a clear
mental note to myself that the next time I agreed to speak, I would find
out just what topic I was to speak on.

At Wilfrid Laurier the professor of business administration was showing some films as a prelude to discussing the potash issues. A few people
who were not students in the MBA class had come along as well. The professor asked me to be a part of the non-student group and remain completely unidentified. He gave a review of the issues and showed a film of
a phone-in television show run in Saskatchewan by the potash industry at
the height of the dispute. He then showed a half-hour interview that I
gave to Patrick Watson, the distinguished Canadian broadcaster, giving
the government side of the dispute. Students were asked to comment on
the issues and the television presentations. They said some less than
complimentary things about the industry and its television presentation
and about the government and my television interview.

After a brief break, the professor said that he would ask someone who
was familiar with some of the issues to join the class, and called me from
the back of the room. It was a bit of a low blow to the students, who had
spoken freely. I, of course, did not mind. I had had a good deal worse
things said about my position than anything uttered by the students. We
had a lively discussion, from which, I believe, the students profited.

I liked living in Toronto. It is a vibrant city, with music, theatre, and a great range of restaurants and organizations to fit every taste. Anne and I chose to live in downtown Toronto, even though I taught at York University on the northern fringe of the city. But I had a lot to learn about the logistics of living in a great city. I remember recounting a tale of being stuck in a traffic and people jam on Spadina Avenue. My listener asked, 'When?' I replied, 'Saturday morning.' He looked at me pityingly and said, 'Don't you know you can't use Spadina Avenue on a Saturday morning? It is Chinese market day and is always totally impossible!' As a matter of fact, I did not know, but I was learning fast. I was able to do some work with organizations that interested me – such as the newly emerging Public Policy Forum in Ottawa, and others. Anne did not like to drive in Toronto but found the public transit system just excellent, and the Toronto Public Library a great resource for work she was doing.

We enjoyed our two years in Toronto but were happy to return to Saskatchewan, where I taught at the College of Law at the University of Saskatchewan in Saskatoon. The dean was Peter MacKinnon, now the very able president of the university. It is a welcoming, collegial college, where I have continued to make my academic home since stepping down from teaching after two years. At Saskatoon I again taught constitutional law, specifically issues related to federalism.

I gave up teaching because I accepted an appointment to the federal Royal Commission on Aboriginal Peoples. I served for about two years and then stepped down. The role of the commission was to study relationships between Aboriginal and non-Aboriginal peoples in Canada, and to make recommendations to improve our lives together in the years ahead. We will be living together as a society for many decades, probably centuries, to come. There are those on the Aboriginal side who prefer to believe that they can live separate and apart from mainstream society. And there are those on the non-Aboriginal side who profess to believe that Aboriginal people will before long integrate into the non-Aboriginal economy and culture and there will no longer be an 'Aboriginal problem,' as they are pleased to call it. I don't believe either of these positions is correct.

I left the commission because of a difference with some of the other commissioners on what we should be about. Some of them felt that the commission should be documenting the conditions under which Aboriginal people live, should be examining the very real grievances that Aboriginal people have with non-Aboriginal society, and should make recommendations to governments on what they might do to deal with these living conditions and grievances.

I felt that much of that work had already been done. Rather, I wanted the commission to identify the specific next steps forward that Aboriginal leaders wished to take and to suggest what governments could do to assist the process.

As an example, we heard a number of calls for the repeal of the Indian Act. I would have liked to have helped Aboriginal leaders to have a draftsperson draw up a revised Indian Act that included the things they wanted left in and excluded the things they wanted out. This would have identified specific issues and problems that could be tackled. Admittedly, such an approach would have put pressure on Aboriginal leaders. They would have needed to descend from generalities to specific objectives. But equally it would, perhaps, have produced a steady stream of small victories, if governments had agreed to one proposal and then another.

Leaders of any disadvantaged people have a difficult role. I've referred earlier to approaches to this issue by Saul Alinsky in his book *Rules for Radicals*. It is necessary to organize the disadvantaged group, in our case Aboriginal people, against a common adversary. In our case, this is indifferent white society. The common adversary needs to be identified and, if necessary, demonized. We are all familiar with these organizing techniques. We see them in wartime when the enemy is demonized, in trade union disputes when the call is to 'fight back,' and in many other circumstances when people need to be organized and energized. This type of organization is essentially negative. It is easier to get a disparate group to agree on a common adversary or a common peril to be resisted than it is to get the same group to agree upon the next forward step that they should take.

Listing the grievances held by Aboriginal people against white society, however justified, is essentially a negative activity.

The next step for a disadvantaged group is to decide upon some clear attainable step forward. It is important that small victories be achieved. In the words of an old hymn, 'each victory makes easier some other to win.' I felt that the time had come for Aboriginal groups to identify some small steps forward, steps which governments might be persuaded to accept and help along. A major problem with concentrating on grievances is that it focuses attention on who was at fault for creating the grievance. That might be an important issue, but discovering the culprits does next to nothing to remedy the problem now existing.

Certainly there can be a point to dwelling on grievances, to practising the politics of victimhood. It might well create a sense of guilt – I've sometimes called it constructive guilt – that causes the offending parties to help in dealing with the grievance. But it is quite unlikely that the offending parties, in our case white society, can solve the problems suffered by Aboriginal people. Only Aboriginal people can solve those problems. When I was premier, I used to speak to many Aboriginal groups. As earlier noted, my message was consistent: 'You people have problems. I really don't fully understand your problems. You do. I can't solve your problems. You can. Not all at once. But step-by-step. And very likely I can help. The government will certainly look at any forward step that you decide might work and that you are prepared to pursue.' I believed that then. And I believed that when I was a member of the royal commission. I hoped the commission might be able to identify some concrete steps forward, and to see whether governments would accept some or all of them. If the commission could do some marketing of particular proposals before we presented our report, then perhaps the report could be welcomed as a constructive start, limited objectives could be achieved rapidly, and a process of incremental progress could be set in motion.

I was conscious of the fact that I was proposing a role that might be filled by governments rather than a commission of enquiry. But I felt that it was worth a try. It was not to be.

Outstanding leaders of disadvantaged people are sometimes able to point to a broad vision of a better future – not specific, but visionary. And then they are able to convince their followers that individual small steps are steps on the road to a better future.

I think of Martin Luther King. He created a vision. He spoke of a promised land, a dream of a genuinely desegregated American society. And then he was able to convince African Americans in a northern city like Chicago that desegregating the seating on public transport in Alabama was a step toward that dream, even though these people had never seen a segregated bus in their lives.

Aboriginal people have yet to determine whether their future lies within the institutions of the economic and cultural mainstream, or whether separate institutions such as Aboriginal schools, universities, credit unions, nursing homes, or whatever, are the best path for the future, or whether it should be some of both. It is likely that they will experiment with both models. In this way, they will begin to flesh out the concept of Aboriginal self-government, which is now serving as the organizing dream being put forward by Aboriginal leaders.

Aboriginal peoples in Canada are extraordinarily diverse. I do not expect that the same approaches will be used by each of the different peoples. But if they are able to move forward, they will, perforce, make decisions about their future. I've written elsewhere about some of these challenges. But it is clear that we in white society must stand ready to assist our fellow Canadians of Aboriginal background as they improve their lot and make an even greater contribution to our common future. Our actions will be for their benefit and for ours.

22

Overseas

One of the happy side benefits of retirement is that it becomes possible to pursue some interesting new challenges. I remained at the University of Saskatchewan as a visiting scholar, giving a few lectures in political studies and constitutional law, but was now free to pursue some international activities.

In the 1990s the Canadian government had an enterprising project in South Africa. It was operated through an agency called the International Development Research Centre (IDRC), which is an arm of the Canadian International Development Agency (CIDA). In 1993, IDRC was advising the African National Congress (ANC), the political party headed by Nelson Mandela, on how they might deal with some of the problems of government they would face if they were successful in being elected in the first national elections in the new South Africa to be held in April 1994. The ANC were in negotiations with the National Party (NP), headed by Frederik Willem (F.W.) de Klerk, about the shape of the new South Africa. The negotiations produced an agreement to set up a federal-style government – a type of government that South Africa had never experienced since it became a Dominion in 1910.

The ANC decided to ask groups from the United States, Australia, Germany, Canada, and elsewhere to give them some thoughts on federalism. The IDRC launched a project from its office in Johannesburg headed by Albert (Al) Johnson, my friend of long standing who, among other jobs, was once president of the CBC. Al asked Canadians – ex-politicians, academics, and public servants – to go to South Africa to give talks, participate in seminars, and the like. I was on the list. I went to South Africa on five occasions and met with groups of South Africans in Canada perhaps half a dozen times. This was a fascinating experience.

The ANC officials and, later, the provincial officials whom we met had a general understanding of the parliamentary system, so that we had some common ground. They had no knowledge of federalism. They liked Canadians, not because of our sterling character or sunny dispositions, but because of our almost unconsciously pragmatic approach to politics.

I was in Johannesburg in November 1993 when the new Constitution was being negotiated. I was not participating in the negotiations but was one of a group talking with ANC leaders about some of the issues that would arise if the Constitution provided for a federal structure with a central government and eight or nine provincial governments, as seemed likely. The ANC people were sceptical about a federal structure. They wanted a strong central government. But concessions had to be made if an agreement was to be achieved with President de Klerk's National Party. Perhaps because I had lived with federalism, perhaps because I had seen the ability of federalism to defuse inter-group tensions, I thought the federal model was a good one for South Africa.

The old South Africa was a highly stratified society. On the top level were the whites – British and Afrikaners. The former were the descendants of the British who settled in South Africa after Britain seized the Cape of Good Hope area from the Dutch in 1806. The Afrikaners were descendants of people who settled in South Africa while it was held by the Dutch prior to 1806. The British in South Africa had maintained contact with Britain over the years well into the twentieth century, as was common with British settlers in 'the colonies,' as the British would put it. The Dutch, on the other hand, had largely lost contact with Europe and had developed their society in isolation from strong European influence. They are sometimes referred to as the 'white tribe of South Africa.' These were the top-rung whites.

The next rung was occupied by people with ethnic roots in the Indian sub-continent. These Indians, as they are called, are centred in the province of KwaZulu/Natal but live throughout the country.

The third rung consists of people who are referred to as 'coloured.' They are mixed-blood descendants of unions between white settlers and indigenous blacks two hundred years ago. They identified sometimes with the whites, sometimes with the blacks, and, as might be expected, were not fully accepted by either.

On the bottom rung were the blacks, the indigenous people of Africa. They were composed of many tribal and linguistic groups and have no long tradition of acting as a unified group.

The Afrikaners for the last fifty years had their power base in agriculture, government, the army, and the police. The British had their power base in agriculture, industry, business, and commerce. The Indians had a strong mercantile class and were prominent in business and commerce. To the coloureds and the blacks fell the more menial jobs that abound in any society. Many skilled trades were regarded as the preserve of the white working class. This is an over-simplification but is sufficiently accurate to illustrate the kind of broad problems that would emerge when this system was toppled.

Some very rough numbers would be useful. In 1995 the population of South Africa was perhaps forty million. The numbers are necessarily very approximate since the statistics are acknowledged to be inaccurate. Of that number, some five million were white, one million were Indian, three million plus were coloured, and thirty million were black.

South Africa had been in a state of civil war for a decade, and the level of violence was something I had never experienced. The African population had been brutally oppressed by the National Party–led apartheid government. Africans were deprived of any right to vote or participate in government except in the so-called homeland areas set aside for them. These areas included none of the major cities or major centres where there were jobs. The Africans resisted by armed force, and there were many clashes between the African resistance organized by the ANC and the police and armed forces of government.

As the years of conflict continued, both sides committed atrocities and the level of resentment grew. It seemed that there was no path for the future that could avoid a bloodbath. Out of this almost hopeless situation, two people of remarkable qualities of statesmanship appeared. The intellectual and symbolic leader of the ANC was Nelson Mandela, a lawyer of great character and ability who had been convicted of high treason and had been imprisoned for twenty-seven years at a notorious prison colony on Robben Island, twelve kilometres off the coast from Cape Town. F.W. de Klerk became president in 1989 and came to realize that there could be no hope of peace while the five million whites attempted to exercise virtually total control over a country of forty million.

De Klerk decided to see whether he could break what appeared to be an insoluble problem of growing violence. In dramatic fashion on 2 February 1990, he released Mandela from prison and removed the ban on the ANC and on the South African Communist Party. Mandela, upon his release, was called upon to show similar statesmanship by convincing the ANC that their best interests would be served by negotiating with the National Party government and not seeking a military victory. Mandela believed and preached that the future of South Africa lay in building a multiracial society in which all groups, African, white, coloured, and Asian, could find a home, a 'rainbow' country as he called it. Mandela and de Klerk set about to negotiate a constitution with which this would be possible, and to set up mechanisms to reconcile the bitter disputes within South African society. A new Constitution was negotiated, replete with compromises, yet holding out a strong vision for the new South Africa. The first elections under the new Constitution were held in April 1994. Following the elections, Mandela became president and de Klerk, vice-president.

Soon thereafter they, together with another remarkable and practical visionary, Bishop Desmond Tutu, established what must be the most unusual institution ever devised in the course of nation-building. They created a Truth and Reconciliation Commission, with Tutu as chairperson. It was based on the principle that, except in extreme cases, people who came before the commission and outlined what they had done in the course of the previous struggle and expressed remorse – if what they had done were illegal or unconscionable – would be forgiven and would not face prosecution. Only those who attempted to hide their involvement for past atrocities would be pursued. There was to be no vengeance by the victors. And, in a very large measure, there was not. One cannot feel anything but awe for the ability of the people of South Africa to let bygones be bygones and to start afresh.

Certainly the world community has been in awe. Nobel Peace Prizes have been awarded to de Klerk, Mandela, and Tutu.

But the aftermath of centuries of oppression, fifty years of sharp division since the election of the first National Party government in 1948, and many years of violence on a major scale, commencing with the Sharpeville Massacre of 1960, could not be completely eliminated. The culture of violence would take longer to eradicate. A generation of young Africans had known virtually nothing but violence. The election of the Mandela government meant that there was no longer a justification for general violence, but for some of the young people who had little education and fewer prospects, the descent into violent crime was almost inevitable.

I have vivid recollections of the indications of continuing violence.

I recall on one occasion when I was travelling to South Africa, from Canada perhaps for the third time, I arrived at the airport at Johannesburg and telephoned my contacts at IDRC. They said they would be right out to the airport to pick me up. I replied: 'Don't bother, I will just pick up a cab at the airport and take it to the hotel. It's the same one where I stayed on an earlier visit.' The reply was immediate and peremptory: 'You will not pick up a cab at the airport. You will never pick up a cab at the airport. You will not pick up a cab on the street. You will not pick up a cab at your hotel. If you want a cab at your hotel, ask the desk to call one and get them to give you the name of the cab company. When the cab from the named company arrives, you will ask the driver whom he is picking up. If you do not hear your name, do not enter the cab.' All of this was delivered in the sternest tones. My initial reaction was to reply: 'All right and excuse me for living.' It was clear that they felt it absolutely necessary that I understand in the clearest terms the security situation in Johannesburg and that I never fall back on my habits acquired in Saskatoon or Toronto or London.

I thought that this reaction was perhaps a bit of overkill until I saw in the Johannesburg newspaper a vivid story which featured a half page displaying 365 coffins in rows. The story went on to say that 365 was the number of police killed in South Africa in the last twelve months. I tried to think what the reaction would be in Canada if 365, or for that matter 36, policemen were killed in a year in the line of duty. Yet this was the situation in South Africa. The story went on to say that most of the policemen were killed so that the assailants could retrieve the guns and protective gear that police ordinarily had. I certainly could understand a society where lawless groups would seek to get weapons. I could not understand a society where it was the custom to acquire the weapons by killing policemen on a wholesale basis.

It was very much a garrison society. On one occasion I went to visit a friend of mine from Oxford days, Bob Plewman, a Rhodes scholar from South Africa, who had become a mining engineer and then went on to teach engineering at the University of the Witwatersrand, in Johannesburg. He lived in a house overlooking the city with a spectacular view and had another residence on his property. A high wall topped with razor wire surrounded the two residences. The entrance was through electronically controlled gates. Plewman was sympathetic with the changes going forward in the Mandela era but was sad to see the breakdown of public order that was accompanying the painful transition. .

Prior to the 1994 Constitution, political power had effectively resided with the whites. After the new Constitution was adopted and the first elections held in April 1994, political power resided with the blacks through their chosen political party, the ANC, led by Nelson Mandela. The ANC, very naturally, sought to seize the levers of power. They made few changes in agriculture, except with respect to the right to own land. They made few changes in industry, business, and commerce. So the power bases of the British and the Indians were only marginally affected.

But the ANC, again very naturally, moved their people into the public service, the army, and the police. The change was not wholesale, but it was certainly marked. The power base of the Afrikaners was sharply eroded. Their political party, the National Party, has fared badly. As my friends in South Africa tell me, 'They just carry too much baggage from the apartheid era.'

So the political problem is to open doors for the blacks, to equip them to take over some of the reins of government, and to ease the transition for the whites, particularly the Afrikaners, into a new role – still economically comfortable, but politically very much less dominant.

I could not detect any high level of discontent among any of South Africa's racial groups, except among some blacks who were unhappy at the rate of change. I did not regard this as threatening, since to give oppressed people political freedom and relief from the daily petty humiliations of legal apartheid goes a long way to satisfying immediate hopes and aspirations.

I was disappointed that the new government was not able to launch a major campaign to respond to the needs of the poorest. It seemed to me that the extra resources available to the government were consumed in improving the position of middle-class blacks. Again, to oversimplify, what we saw was the old South Africa with five million whites relatively affluent, one million Indians also somewhat affluent, and thirty-five million coloureds and blacks who were poor, transformed into a new South Africa with whites and Indians more or less unchanged in status, but with a new group of a few million blacks and coloureds who were now well off, or reasonably so. Thirty million blacks and coloureds were still poor.

This new South Africa was bursting forth with energy and hope, but was beset by monumental problems in dealing with even the most elementary tasks of government, such as maintaining law and order. This is the country we were attempting to assist with our advice. In some ways, we Canadians were competent. In others, we simply had no experience that would allow us to say anything useful.

At times I was struck with just how useful our Canadian experience was and why we seemed to be so welcomed. We were certainly not the only advisers about. There were academics and government people whom I met from time to time from the United States, Australia, Germany, India, and Spain, all of them federations. Their approach generally seemed to be to describe how particular problems were dealt with in their countries and to express the hope that their approaches might be of some use to South Africans. Canadians tended to do the same but ended their comments by asking, 'But what's your problem?' A Canadian academic, Richard Simeon, and I were visiting Northern Cape Province and its new legislature in Kimberley. A legislative committee to consider changes in the Constitution was meeting, and we asked if we could sit in. We sat quietly at the back of the room, and before long the committee of six or seven members began asking us how problems were dealt with in Canada. We replied briefly and with some diffidence. Shortly thereafter, they asked us to pull up chairs around the table. The problem they were dealing with was to find a way for the Afrikaner community to have their own schools. Around the table were legislative members from the ANC, from the NP, and from the Freedom Front, a right-wing nationalist group. It was understood that there could be private schools that could limit enrolment to a racial or cultural group. There was also early agreement that no public school could possibly limit enrolment to any group defined by race. Rights defined by race were what the old apartheid regime was all about and were, on every count, impossible under the new regime.

Being a typical Canadian, I asked whether there wasn't another way to achieve the same result. Could you not set school boundaries that included areas where the great majority of people were Afrikaners? I said that where I lived in Saskatoon, most of the schools drew their students from a defined geographic area. I was assured that this was not possible. The group was too dispersed. I then said: 'How about language? Could you have a school for people who speak Afrikaans?' I mentioned that we had some schools where I lived that drew their students from the French linguistic group in the city. They said this would not work because many coloured people spoke Afrikaans and they would not be welcomed in the proposed school. My next comment was: 'Well, how about religion?' Where I live, we have schools that draw their students on the basis of the family's religious affiliation. I suggested that the coloureds were not likely to be members of the Dutch Reformed Church. So could students be drawn from families that adhered to the Dutch Reformed Church? There then ensued a discussion of the four branches of the Dutch Reformed Church and whether it would be possible for them to agree on anything with respect to schools. The chairman of the committee, a member of the Democratic Party, called the discussion back to order, and we never did resolve the point.

Later someone asked me whether, in the city where I lived, there were schools paid for by the public in which student bodies were selected, some on the basis of geography, some on the basis of language, and some on the basis of religion. After I answered 'yes,' they asked me how we made that mess work. My answer was that we didn't really think of it as a mess. With a little give and take, we could make it work. This was in many ways a typical Canadian approach, and one that they very much appreciated in wrestling with some of the nearly insoluble problems they were facing.

Canadians were not totally alone in this. I remember that some of us were having a discussion with a person who had been a judge on the Spanish Constitutional Court. We were talking about the Spanish federation and the powers that the individual regions have. He outlined a package of powers and then went on to say that two of the regions, those in Catalonia and the Basque Country, had additional powers. I asked why these two regions would have extra powers. His answer was, 'It was the only way we could make it work.' That sounded very Canadian. In Canada some provinces, notably Quebec, but not only Quebec, exercise powers not exercised by other provinces such as Saskatchewan. We manage to make it work, and in so doing, we show that devising a workable constitution for a country is not an academic exercise, but rather an exercise in practical statecraft. Very recently, Canadians have adopted a treaty that provides a structure for governing the Nisga'a First Nation of British Columbia. I am not sure whether or how it fits in with the current Canadian Constitution, but I have no doubt that with goodwill we can make it work.

In the course of my time in South Africa, I came to know a small number of people well. I met a number of their premiers and had many dealings with one, Patrick 'Terror' Lekota, then premier of the Free State, which is the old Orange Free State. Terror did not get his name from any rebel activities with the ANC, but rather because of his prowess on the soccer field. Terror has visited with us in Saskatchewan. He has gone on to be the chair of the National Council of Provinces (South Africa's second chamber) and, later, minister of defence.

The South African experiment, which commenced with the remarkable Mandela–de Klerk partnership, has been an outstanding success. It has achieved a peaceful transition from a repressive colonial-style government to a popular government in which all elements of the nation participate. It has not avoided all violence, but the violence is of a criminal nature, rather than organized violence between sectors of the population.

It has survived the succession from Nelson Mandela as president to

Thabo Mbeki, someone hand-picked by Mandela as his successor and renowned for his political skills and diplomatic experience. He does not have the record of imprisonment and sacrifice in the struggle for freedom possessed by many of South Africa's leaders, including Mandela.

There have been many successes, but there remain huge challenges. South Africa, like much of the continent, is being ravaged by HIV and AIDS. Tens of thousands of people in their early working life are dying, leaving shortages of skills and massive social problems.

Some of the promise of what might have been is not being achieved. It was perhaps too much to expect, but I had hoped to see the new South Africa take what surplus money it could acquire above the cost of maintaining minimum government services and direct it to the most pressing needs of the nation. I judged them to be economic development, improvements in rural education, and a program for urban housing. There has been some progress in each of these areas, but a depressing amount of money has been diverted to improving the status of a relatively small African and coloured middle class.

Archbishop Desmond Tutu has expressed outrage at the relatively high salaries of the new parliamentarians and the new African public servants. What we are seeing is the development of a significant African middle class based on government and industry. What we are not seeing is a frontal attack on problems faced by the rural Africans. Certainly these rural poor are enjoying an increase in dignity and in participation in public affairs, as evidenced by their very high voter turn-out at election time. But we are not seeing a sharp increase in their economic well-being. Perhaps it was too much to expect.

There are further grounds for unease. The election of 1994 showed the ANC to be in an overwhelmingly dominant position and in firm control of the national government and at least six provinces. The Zulu-based party, the Inkatha Freedom Party, won control in the province of KwaZulu/Natal, while the NP formed the government in the province of Western Cape, both of them strong and populous provinces. So each major party had a power base and, accordingly, some stake in the system. An immediate crisis was avoided. But the ANC is too dominant. In the 1994 elections, of the 19.5 million votes cast, the ANC received 12.2 million, while the National Party got 4.0 million and the Inkatha Freedom Party 2.1 million. No other party received as many as a half million votes, and together the remaining sixteen parties received just over one million votes. Since 1994 no credible opposition to the ANC has emerged. It is no bad thing in the early days of a revolution (for that is what has occurred in South Africa) to have a dominant party able to shape the public agenda. But, as time goes on, there must develop a credible vehicle for discontent to manifest itself and threaten, or at least influence, the dominant group – otherwise absolute power will begin to corrupt. There is time enough for things to develop in South Africa, but I would be happy to see another political party emerge that had solid support among the African voters.

The true miracle in South Africa is the transfer of power from a repressive racial minority–based regime to a regime based upon broad popular support. This was done peacefully and by agreement that there would be no reprisals for the atrocities committed by the white minority regime or by the ANC rebels (or freedom fighters, if you will) who were waging guerrilla warfare against the regime. The device used to allow grievances to be vented without a bloodbath of revenge was the Truth and Reconciliation Commission referred to above. I can think of no transfer of power in such difficult circumstances that has been done anywhere in the world with less bloodshed and more success.

Rural poverty is still deep, and urban township poverty is still very troubling, but there has emerged an identifiable black middle class involved in government, the army, the police, and to some extent in industry, business, and commerce. Perhaps that is the way it must develop.

The Former Soviet Union

I had opportunities to go to other countries to talk about government. The year 1991 saw the break-up of the Soviet Union into fifteen republics, five of them in central Asia. One of these is Kyrgyzstan. I had been serving on the board of Cameco Corporation, a Saskatchewan mining company operating a gold mining project in Kyrgyzstan in partnership with the government. The University of Saskatchewan had an agreement with an educational institution in Kyrgyzstan to provide classes in business and economic development. It worked out that I could go there with a delegation from the university and visit the gold project at the same time.

Kyrgyzstan was just emerging into independence. It was clearly a traumatic change. Not only did they have to devise institutions of government, but, much more troublesome for them, they had to create an economy separate from the command-and-control, centrally planned economy of the former Soviet Union, an economy which had now vanished.

I recall giving some lectures that were translated into Russian. I spoke slowly and wrote keywords on a blackboard, so that the translator could better convey what ideas I was trying to get across. But I made frequent errors. It is said that teaching is attempting to lead your students' minds from A to B. The B is easy. You know what idea you want to leave them with. The A is more difficult. Sometimes you don't know just where their minds are when you start. That certainly was my experience.

I recall one occasion when I was trying to tell a group of thirty-to-forty-year-old men, intelligent and seasoned administrators, how the new government would likely develop. I said that the public would want many things – economic development, education, health services, roads, and the rest. And they wouldn't want to pay for it. That is standard. I repeated: 'It's a balance between what the public wants and the taxes they are willing to pay.' I paused for questions. The first one was: 'What are these things called taxes?' I asked: 'When you go to the store to buy something, is no tax added on?' Answer – no. 'When you get your pay cheque, is nothing taken off for the government?' No. I ask: 'Where does the government get its money?' 'Well, it gets it from the manufacturing industries.' I say: 'But these industries that manufactured for the Soviet economy are no longer operating.' They answered: 'Yes, we know that.' I ask: 'But where will the government get its money now?' They replied: 'We don't know. We hoped you would tell us.' I answered: 'It will be from taxes. Get used to the idea of taxes.'

It's not easy to talk about how to operate a modern non-communist government to intelligent people, experienced in government, who have never known direct taxes. I just didn't understand where their minds were.

This happened to me a second time. We were talking about what things the new country would need to import – petroleum, some farm machinery, and other items – and what they might export. There was gold that Cameco was producing at the mine, which was the largest economic project in the country. I asked what else they could manufacture. They listed some items. I then asked: 'And where would you sell those?' It was quickly apparent to me that for them this was a totally different question. They made no connection between producing a product and finding a buyer for it. They had never lived in a market economy and simply did not have the mindset that there was no point in manufacturing a product if nobody would buy it. We acquired this idea as part of the nature of our world. They had so much to learn about the new world into which they had been thrown. I concluded that I would have to spend more time learning their background and patterns of thought before I could really connect with them.

I recall yet another occasion when I was talking about building a public service. I was using the chalkboard, so that the interpreter could have more time to see the English words I was using and translate them into Russian. I was saying that for the most part public servants should be chosen on the basis of merit – the first question is: do they have the technical skills to do the job? But I noted that there are other considerations. It would not be a good idea to have all of the public servants come from the capital city and none of them from the countryside. There should be some geographical representation. I also made the point that some effort should be made to provide jobs for disabled people. I got a nod of agreement. And for women. I got an icy stare. Too late I recalled that this is a Muslim country. I then said that some people get their jobs because of the politicians they know. Again came a nod of agreement. I said that this should be kept to a minimum.

I then said that some people get jobs because people in their family already work for the government. When translated, this produced a great gale of laughter. And they shouted: 'Put that at the top of the list!' They explained to me that Kyrgyz society is dominated by family clans and that getting jobs for your family clan members is considered to be a clear duty of anyone in the public service. I said this should be discouraged. But I was struck by a feeling that if I did not understand some of these key factors in Kyrgyz society, I was probably not going to be able to say much that was useful to them in dealing with their problems.

I spent some of my time in Bishkek, which now looked rather run-down but had clearly been a city with a good deal of charm. It had wide streets and some handsome buildings. Statues of Lenin and the hammer and sickle emblem of the old Soviet era still remained. I asked about this because in some parts of the old Soviet Union (Ukraine, for example,) this was not true. Symbols of the old Soviet era had been pulled down with gusto. It was explained that there was still fondness for the Soviet days. The Soviets had arrived in the early 1920s and rescued the people from what was a feudal system. I was surprised that the old khanates of central Asia had survived that long.

The war memorial in Bishkek was the most affecting I have ever seen. It was set in a green area. At one end there was a statue of a woman, careworn and anxious. Perhaps a hundred yards away across the green sward was a soldier in uniform, a little tattered with a bandage about his head and a rifle in his hand, struggling toward the mother figure. It was a celebration, not of victory, but of peace and family reunification, powerfully done.

Cameco's gold mine was a partnership with the Kyrgyzstan government, with the government having a two-thirds interest and Cameco the remainder. The deposit was twelve thousand feet above sea level and in a very mountainous area. The logistics of building a mine and mill were daunting. Machinery and supplies had to be imported from Canada and Europe. Some was moved through the port of St Petersburg (formerly Leningrad) and across the Trans Siberian Railway. Some was sent to Turkey and moved by truck convoy on dubious roads and with armed guards riding shotgun across Turkey, Iran, Turkmenistan, and Uzbekistan to Kyrgyzstan. Yet the project was completed on time and within budget limits, except for one item – an engineering calculation error made in Canada. Such is life. The mine produced a large part of the gross national product of this isolated country and provided the best paying jobs in Kyrgyzstan.

I also travelled to Russia in an advisory capacity, but I doubt my efforts were of any use. As in Kyrgyzstan, I simply did not understand the mindset of the people, mostly legislators, to whom I was talking. I was in Moscow and in Kazan, a city of over one million, about 600 kilometres east of Moscow. Kazan is on the Volga River, still a wide, deep river even 1,100 kilometres from its mouth at the Caspian Sea. I was struck with how much the land around Kazan looked like parts of Saskatchewan and how much the farming methods differed. There were scores of people seeding or weeding by hand or using antiquated machinery. A Saskatchewan farmer can farm for a month without touching the soil except to walk to his tractor or combine.

23

The Future

Superannuated politicians, and others, are often given to speculation on what the future will bring and how much better it would unfold if they were in charge.

We can predict that much in the future will be depressingly the same as the past. But much will not be. This is sometimes equally depressing.

What does the future hold for Canada? We will continue to wrestle with the problems and issues that have faced us since Confederation.

We will search for the best basis for good relations between francophones and anglophones in Canada. There are many hopeful signs on this front. I have always felt that the driving force behind the desire of many Québécois for Quebec to be a separate nation state was the sense of bitter resentment that many of them felt at the lowly status given to things French and Québécois in Canadian society. During the 1950s and 1960s, in the halls of commerce, even in Quebec, the dominant language was English. In major banks, such as the Royal Bank of Canada, which until recently had its head office in Montreal, the senior management was English, and the language in which business was conducted at higher levels was English. This was by no means confined to banks. I read in the autobiography of Eric Kierans, a man I greatly admired, that in the Montreal of the 1960s it was entirely possible to operate in business circles without a working knowledge of French. It is small wonder there would be resentment. This has changed markedly. Today the Quebec business establishment is well populated with people born and educated as part of francophone Quebec.

The leadership of francophone Quebec is, of course, more confident of their ability to go it alone. One would be foolish to suggest that Quebec could not function, and function well, as a separate state. That may be a source of concern for believers, as I am, in a united Canada.

But for Quebec and for the rest of Canada there are many benefits to remaining a single state. And the opportunities for Québécois to become 'maîtres chez nous' (masters in our own house), any more than they now are, are not extensive. No small nation state in the world is truly independent. Each is constrained by trade agreements such as those of the World Trade Organization (WTO), by diplomatic alliances such as the North Atlantic Treaty Organization (NATO) and North American Aerospace Defence Command (NORAD), and other regional pacts; by international institutions such as the United Nations; and by the realities of power politics dominated by a small number of powerful states. Most of this is good, and all of it is very difficult for a small country to influence. So for Quebec nationalists, being part of Canada is not all bad. Similarly there are real benefits for Canada economically, culturally, and politically to remain united.

And there are less obvious benefits. I believe that Canada has a contribution to make to the world by providing a working example of civic nationalism, a nation state not based on a single dominant ethnic group but rather a nation state that accommodates more than one language and a range of ethnic and cultural groups. The world is difficult enough to govern with 200 nation states. If all significant ethnic groups were organized as separate nation states, the number would be 600, or several thousand, depending on one's definition of significant, and the world would be far more difficult to govern. For the world to move forward, some countries must be seen to be successful multicultural, multi-ethnic, nation states. Canada has been a star performer. South Africa is doing well in its first decade of democracy. Russia is having real difficulty accommodating some minorities in Chechnya and Dagestan. Yugoslavia has dissolved in a welter of violence, leaving ethnic minorities that were once within one nation state now scattered among several nation states, where they are a fruitful source of continuing unrest.

Canadians seem a little better able to accommodate different cultures than many countries. We should hone our skill in this regard and provide an example of successful multiculturalism, even if it means a Canada markedly different from the one that I grew up in. The emerging Canada should allow francophones, anglophones, Aboriginal Canadians, and newer Canadians from many lands to live in harmony, enjoy a large measure of cultural independence, and still share a range of values sufficient to allow us to create a united, prosperous, and sharing Canada.

Canada has known strains between the political and economic power of the heartland – southern Ontario and western Quebec – and the relative powerlessness of all other parts of the country, east, west, and north. These strains are still evident with respect to Atlantic Canada and the North. They are evident in a different form in western Canada. As Alberta and British Columbia grow in population and prosperity, their position in Canada will improve. Ontario will continue to be the heartland but will be under pressure as its manufacturing base declines. Secure as the financial centre of Canada, Toronto will continue to overshadow Montreal. Its rivals will be Calgary and, I expect, a rejuvenated Vancouver.

The four Atlantic Provinces will continue to be hinterland, lacking in power and wealth. Ontario will be heartland, but not as dominantly so. Alberta and probably British Columbia will be a new western heartland, with wealth and increasing power. Manitoba will struggle. Saskatchewan will swing between wealth and penury, but like the Atlantic Provinces and Manitoba, will be relatively powerless.

We as a country have agreed to provide equalization in several forms to Atlantic Canada and the three northern territories of Yukon, Northwest Territories, and Nunavut to provide for public services at a roughly equal Canadian standard. (I'll say more on this later.) Their combined population will not exceed three million, less than one-tenth of the Canadian total. Less well off areas in Ontario, Alberta, and British Columbia get services roughly comparable to those in wealthier areas at the expense of their provincial government. Saskatchewan is sometimes as wealthy as the national average and sometimes not, but rarely a disproportionate recipient of equalization, broadly defined. Manitoba is less favoured but is likely to fall only modestly short of national averages. Quebec is, I believe, a different case. The economic powerhouse that was Montreal is declining in relative terms. It is less able to provide a high level of services for the large areas of Quebec that are clearly hinterland. Federal equalization for Quebec will become more and more a necessity. Already Quebec receives close to half of the funds paid out in the formal equalization program (approximately 43 per cent in 2005/2006). This is likely to increase. Federal government support for industries key to the Quebec economy, for example, the dairy and poultry industries, will continue to be important.

The challenge for future federal governments will be to retain support

for broad equalization among Canadians living in Ontario, and especially in Alberta and British Columbia, as Quebec's relative economic
and political power wanes and that of Alberta and British Columbia
grows. In this context, it may be no bad thing, at least in the short run, to
see political alliances between western Canada and Quebec to counter-
balance Ontario dominance. Not only might such alliances temper hostility to the federal government, so often expressed in Quebec and parts
of western Canada, but also it might cause western Canadians to appreciate more fully the economic and cultural challenges faced by Quebec.
To have, say, a Calgarian in federal office plead in Calgary and Vancouver
the cause of Quebec in the federation could be solidly positive.

Along with French-English relations, and heartland-hinterland tensions, the third abiding theme in Canada's past and Canada's future is
relations with the United States.

I find myself at odds with prevailing opinion on this issue. It seems to
me that the popular view is that greater and greater economic integration with the United States is desirable and, in any case, all but inevitable.
I am less certain that this integration is inevitable, and I feel that its desir-
ability is a mixed bag. The United States is a large, wealthy, powerful, and
remarkably insular nation. It will not continue to be the only dominant
power in the world. It will increasingly need to share hegemony with the
European Union, China, and perhaps India. But it will continue to be
the most dominant country for many decades to come. A smaller European Union might have been a serious rival. But as the EU expands into
eastern Europe, as it is in the process of doing, it will become a more
powerful trading bloc but, I believe, a less powerful political bloc. I do
not think it can be welded into a coherent political force speaking with
one voice for many decades to come. I could see French, Germans, and
Spaniards becoming a coherent political force in the near term, but not
French, Greeks, and Estonians.

So I would see the existing nation states continuing to be the political
voice of Europe, and a weaker voice than if the western European
nations had chosen to try to form a tight economic and political bloc.
China will become a superpower. But it will display largely economic
power. China has not in recent centuries been an expansionist political
power and is unlikely to become a nation with armed forces distributed
around the globe in a manner similar to the United States. And, as its
economic well- being increases, there will be growing pressure to democ-
ratize (in some form) its governmental structures. In this, it may do well
or do badly. But these internal issues are likely to consume its time and

talent. India is a large country with tens of millions of well-educated people, but it would have many hurdles to overcome to achieve the status of
world power.

So the United States will remain a dominant power, and Canadians
must live with that. The United States could, if it wished, conquer Canada
in short order. But it does not follow that Canada should seek economic
integration. Canada should certainly remain a member of such world
trading pacts as the World Trade Organization (WTO). In such an organization, we have a chance to put forth our point of view and to have the
organization's dispute resolution mechanisms work in a way that is reasonably fair to us. I do not see that Canada has the same level of influence
in the North America Free Trade Agreement (NAFTA). The position of
the United States is simply too dominant. In addition, the terms of
NAFTA, and particularly chapter 11, have a much greater possibility of
interfering with Canada's internal governmental decisions than do the
terms of the WTO agreements. I would see a trade regime with the
United States governed not by NAFTA but by the terms of WTO agreements, and probably some sectoral agreements such as the former auto
pact, and doubtless a sectoral agreement on trade in energy – particularly
oil, natural gas, and electricity. These would be bargained. In the course
of the bargaining, we would not be without some powerful arguments.

Closer to home, I would see Saskatchewan as having a modestly prosperous future, without large gains or losses in population calculated
over a time span of several years. The farm economy will employ a
decreasing number of people, tempered only by the possible development of intensive livestock operations. Resources will continue to flour-
ish in the longer run and will continue to be subject to shorter-run ups
and downs.

There is a possibility of major development in the general nuclear
area. It would be prudent for Canadians to develop a disposal site for
spent fuel rods from nuclear reactors – something like the one being
developed by the U.S. authorities at Yucca Mountain, Nevada. The federal government agency examining this issue, the Nuclear Waste Management Organization (NWMO), believes that the best site would be in
Precambrian rock that has been stable for hundreds of thousands of
years. Northern Saskatchewan is a good site for such a facility. We have
the geology, the workforce, and a public who are familiar with nuclear
issues. As concerns about global warming grow, as I believe they will,
there will be increasing interest in generating power by using nuclear
fuel rather than fossil fuel. As oil prices rise there may well be an oppor-

tunity to use surplus or off-peak uranium-generated electricity to manufacture hydrogen for motive fuel. These are possibilities only, but they
illustrate that in these areas of development Saskatchewan has some substantial advantages.

The single greatest issue in Saskatchewan's future is the development
of relations between Aboriginal and non-Aboriginal people. The proportion of the total population of the province who are Aboriginal is increasing. This is happening because birthrates among Aboriginal people are
higher than among non-Aboriginals and their out-migration rate is
lower. Their in-migration is probably lower as well, but not enough to be
significant. Aboriginal life expectancy is lower than non-Aboriginal life
expectancy, but that gap has been narrowing. The effect of these tenden-
cies is to increase the proportion of Aboriginals in the total population.
Aboriginal people, for a variety of reasons, have, on average, lower formal education attainments than the general population. This limits their
opportunities to participate in economic mainstream occupations and
their ability to capture the fruits of such participation.

Aboriginal and non-Aboriginal people have very different roots. Plains
Indians have been very largely rural, hunting-gathering societies with
some agricultural pursuits. They have not been influenced by the ancient
Mediterranean cultures. Non-Aboriginals are largely the inheritors of
European cultures and moulded by the earlier Greek, Roman, and Chris-
tian influences. Non-Aboriginals came to what is now Saskatchewan to
partner with Aboriginals in fur gathering. During that period there was a
relationship of mutual respect. As widespread agricultural settlement
came in the last 125 years, Aboriginal people have been dispossessed. We
non-Aboriginals have removed the wildlife, particularly the bison, on
which they depended for food, and we brought diseases foreign to the
Aboriginals, which wreaked havoc – wiping out a large proportion of the
Aboriginal population. These diseases we regarded as an act of God.
Aboriginal people regarded them as 'gifts' from the invaders.

Treaties were signed by which lands that are now Saskatchewan were
surrendered for settlement. These were signed generally in the last
twenty-five years of the 1800s. There is no agreement about the meaning
of the treaties. The written treaties do not contain the whole of the
agreement. There is a large measure of concurrence on this. But what
else is included is a matter for lively dispute. Aboriginal people from
time to time assert that the treaties include this or that further benefit
based upon what elders now say was said one hundred years ago. Non-
Aboriginals tend to scoff at the accuracy of this oral history. More funda-

mentally, Aboriginal people frequently assert that the treaties established a relationship that is ongoing, and accordingly what was intended
in, say, 1874 in specific terms is not relevant. The relationship created by
the treaties is said to bind non-Aboriginal society to provide what is
required in today's terms for, say, the health and education of Indians. As
an example, the federal government would deny that there is any treaty
right to post-secondary education for Indians. Indians would assert that
university education is a modern-day interpretation of the treaty commitment to provide a school on an Indian reserve.

So there will continue to be disagreement. The disagreements fuel the
arguments used. They have little other relevance to the basic issue – what
should today's and tomorrow's relationship be?

As I have already noted, I start from the premise that governments –
federal and provincial – cannot solve all or most of the problems facing
Aboriginal people. Aboriginal people themselves will have to identify
what the problems are and what are the most practical first steps toward
solutions.

I have observed that more and more Aboriginal people are moving to
urban centres, as is true of non-Aboriginal people. Now more than half
of all Aboriginal people in Saskatchewan live in towns and cities. I
believe it is time that the provincial government helped them to take
greater control over their future there. If Aboriginal people show interest (and with possible participation by the federal government), I would
like to see an Aboriginal social services board, an Aboriginal school
board, and an Aboriginal housing board elected in, say, Saskatoon by
residents who declare themselves to be Aboriginal. These would be
formed in a way similar to the way that separate school boards are
elected. I would expect the social services boards to operate child welfare services and social services for Aboriginal seniors by agreement with
government agencies. I would expect the school board to operate
schools, or perhaps make agreements with existing schools to infuse
more Aboriginal content in the curriculum. I would expect the housing
board to operate housing programs by agreement with the provincial
housing corporation.

Some of these things are happening now. I would like to see the more
formal structure that I have suggested. These boards (or it could all be
done by one board) could provide a recognized voice for Aboriginal
people while they become part of the life of our urban centres. The
boards would serve to reduce the sense of disconnectedness that many
Aboriginal people feel in urban centres. The boards would probably be

temporary and wither away as Aboriginal people became increasingly part of the economic mainstream. That would depend, in part, on the extent to which they became part of the cultural mainstream.

These proposals for governance are little more than transitional tinkering. The chief task is to improve economic opportunities for urban Aboriginals. Here I put reliance on education. We all recognize that calls for education to solve all problems are very familiar. But while these calls are often overblown, they are also often partly true. And many Saskatchewan Aboriginal leaders recognize that. As I have mentioned, they are often heard to say, 'Education is the new buffalo.' It should not be beyond our combined intelligence to devise educational programs that equip Aboriginal people to participate in the economic mainstream, if they so desire, and still leave scope for Aboriginal culture. Clearly there is overlap between how we earn our living and how we live, but I believe that a substantially Aboriginal lifestyle and participation in the mainstream economic pursuits are not incompatible.

Some Aboriginal people seem to take the position that since Saskatchewan was 'their' land, it is reasonable for them to require non-Aboriginal society to provide them with the wherewithal to live on a scale comparable to the average non-Aboriginal, without them making a living in the mainstream culture. I do not think non-Aboriginals can be persuaded to do this – whatever the fair and equitable course of action may be. Certainly, Aboriginal people will be supported, but only at a near subsistence level, which is disturbing to them.

Non-Aboriginal people simply do not know all of the barriers to economic integration for Aboriginals. We should not assume that all Aboriginal people want to be 'well off,' but we expect that some would. There is no single course of action that can solve the issues of Aboriginal/non-Aboriginal relations. But our best prospects would seem to be along the following lines: Some Aboriginal people, largely in northern Saskatchewan, can still pursue the traditional way of life – hunting, fishing, trapping, and the quasi-traditional pursuits of sports guiding and the production of Aboriginal arts and crafts – and they may wish to do so. They should be helped by giving them first call on the fish and game resource. The claims of the tourist industry, which provides a good bit of employment for Aboriginal people, will need to be accommodated. This balance has been achieved in the past and can be managed into the future.

Some Aboriginal people will wish to stay on reserves. I am not persuaded that reserves in Saskatchewan can be developed to provide significant employment. The report of the Royal Commission on Aboriginal Peoples seems to suggest that the reserves can be made robust economic centres. For almost all non-urban reserves, I disagree.

Even if the size of the reserves was doubled or tripled, I have trouble envisioning the economic development that would provide commercially viable jobs for all of the people requiring them. What can be done should be done. But I do not see these efforts as an effective alternative to equipping Aboriginal people who live on reserves with the education and skills to join the off-reserve (or urban reserve) economic mainstream.

Increasing numbers of Aboriginal people will live in urban centres in Saskatchewan. Many will readily become part of the economic mainstream. They require only minimum assistance. It is those who feel that the reserve offers little for them and their children, who move to urban centres, but who often have difficulty becoming part of the economic mainstream, who should be the focus of non-Aboriginal assistance. I have suggested a way to give them a voice and an identified leadership corps through elected boards. I would expect that cultural organizations would develop which would lessen the sense of isolation that must accompany the strange new surroundings. And I have suggested vigorous efforts to strengthen education and training opportunities at all levels through culturally sensitive institutions.

A substantial number of Aboriginal people have made the transition from reserves to off-reserve economic life. I have no doubt that this movement will continue. I do not wish to minimize the extent of the adjustment from an Aboriginal way of life on a reserve to a way of life that involves participating in the economic mainstream. But it is not easy to see what the alternative is. Transfer payments from governments can ease the transition, but I do not regard them as a permanent approach to the issues. They will simply provide a blighted future for Aboriginal people and generate resentment among non-Aboriginals.

Equalization

My warm friend Albert W. (Al) Johnson developed a proposal for equalization when he was a public servant with the government of Saskatchewan. He renewed the proposal when he went to the federal government in 1964. The idea became a proposal for national public policy when put forward to a federal-provincial meeting by federal finance minister Mitchell Sharp in September 1966. From that point, the concept quickly became accepted. It was set out as a principle of Canadian federalism in 1982.

The Constitution accepted by Canadians in 1982 provided that Parliament and the government of Canada are committed to the principle of equalization. The federal government from its tax resources will make payments to some provincial governments so that they will have enough money to provide levels of public services comparable to those in other provinces with comparable levels of taxes.

Equalization does not provide that the government of one province transfer any money to any other province. Some federations do have schemes whereby money is transferred among provincial governments. Not so Canada. Ours is a wholly federal scheme. There is no simple way to distribute equalization money. The current distribution formula, based on representative taxes, has become very complex and is producing serious distortions. The problems do not ordinarily arise when trying to calculate how much money a province has available to it from taxes – on income, property, retail sales of goods or gasoline or alcohol or tobacco. The problems come when provinces receive money from the sale of minerals – money for the sale of mineral property or from royalties from each unit of production. It would be generally agreed that if the province of Quebec privatized Quebec Hydro and received a substantial sum of money, this would not be income. It is simply trading one asset for another. The provinces that produce oil and natural gas say that the same rules should apply when they sell oil and gas resources. It is a one-time sale of an asset and not income. Other provinces resist this argument. If a province sells these resources year after year and uses the money to provide public services, then, they say, this money should be counted in calculating equalization payments if the idea of equalization is to provide money so that the people in all provinces can enjoy comparable levels of public services. Or so it is argued.

It seems to me that to the extent that proceeds of the sale of assets – be they electric utilities or oil resources – are used to provide other assets not ordinarily classed as public services, then they should not be counted as income for equalization purposes. To the extent that the proceeds are used to provide public services to the people of the producing provinces, on a current basis, they should be counted for equalization purposes.

This proposition is easier to state than it is to apply. If money from petroleum land sales is supplied to a university for its operations, this is clearly using it for a public service. If the money is paid into an endowment fund for universities, then other arguments can be made. It can be argued that this is simply trading one asset for another. The better argument would be that the income from the endowment fund used to provide current services would be income to the province and that income from the sale of petroleum lands would not.

An equalization formula based on this principle would not be simple. But no equalization formula can be simple. As with so many activities of government, particularly tax regimes, they can be reasonably fair or reasonably simple but not both.

I am a warm supporter of equalization. There are those who contend that these types of programs delay the necessary economic rationalization of Canada. The argument is that because of equalization people are encouraged to remain in areas of stagnant economic activity when they should be moving to jobs in growing economic areas. We have had equalization for several decades. Yet the movement of people from the four Atlantic Provinces, and from Manitoba and Saskatchewan, has been swift and substantial. And the inter-provincial figures mask the intra-provincial movement. There have been major population shifts within those provinces to St John's, Halifax, Moncton, Winnipeg, Saskatoon, and Regina. The emptying out of rural Canada in these six provinces and in Quebec, and perhaps parts of Ontario, Alberta, and British Columbia, has proceeded apace, even with the equalization plan.

As I would see it, these shifts need not proceed any faster. The costs of this emptying are high, in terms of stranded social capital – schools, hospitals, and roads – and in human terms. I am unconvinced that Canada would be better off with an accelerated rationalization process, and so I am not persuaded by the force of this attack on equalization.

In any case, governments should not have as their primary objective the increase of the gross national product. The primary objective should be the increase in the well-being of its citizens. While well-being is more difficult to measure and while increases in GNP often add to the well-being of citizens, they are by no means identical measures. If they were, more Canadians would live in Toronto or Los Angeles or Dallas. There are many values that contribute to richness of the lives of all Canadians. The equalization plan contributes to these values.

Social Programs

I think many of us are familiar in a general way with how liberal democracy and social democracy came into being. For the most part, they came to Canada from Britain, with some influences from the United States and northern Europe. In Britain, the world of 1750 was a world of status. It was largely an agrarian society with modest manufacturing and trading sectors. People enjoyed their status in society in accordance with well-established rules of class. By 1850 much of that had changed. The Industrial Revolution saw the development of the steam engine and railroads, and with them a burgeoning manufacturing and mining economy. There developed a belief that decisions in social policy should be left to the market to decide, the theory being that if everyone pursued his own enlightened self-interest, all of society would be best served. From this there flowed the idea that governments should not interfere with what was thought of as free competition. But this approach proved unacceptable. The ideas that the hours of labour in a mine should not be twelve hours a day if people can be persuaded to work fourteen, or that one should not employ men when women and children can be hired to work for less, did not commend themselves to ordinary people, whatever the tenets of economic theory.

Society reached the conclusion that it did not want goods and services at the lowest possible cost. Not at the cost of leaving employees who worked at producing and distributing these goods without adequate incomes and increasingly without protection against the risks of injury and the infirmities of old age.

So governments stepped in to regulate employment in mines, factories, and elsewhere. There has blossomed in Canada, in the twentieth and twenty-first centuries, a matrix of laws regulating whole ranges of human activity. We have seen building codes, vehicle operation codes, employment and safety codes, environmental regulation, and many, many other regulations. And some governments set out to provide goods and services to their citizens by directly providing sewer services, electricity, telephones, natural gas, postal services, ferries, canals, roads, railroads, airlines, bus services, schools, universities, television-radio, pensions, hospitals, nursing homes, medical and dental insurance, agricultural products selling agencies, disaster insurance, protection services such as fire, police, ambulance, prisons, armed forces, and others.

There is widespread public support for most of these activities. Indeed, if one looks at an election campaign in Canada, the debate will usually be, not whether the state should be providing roads or medical care or universities or postal services, but whether or not they should be providing all these services to a better standard.

Think tanks still put forth the idea that markets will solve social problems and that government should not use programs like equalization to interfere with market forces. But this surely is a tunnel view of society. In his book *Remembering*, Eric Kierans said this: 'Markets cannot fix the problems of our schools and universities, nor provide all our people with the health care and employment that they need. Governments have had to broaden their activities to provide housing, help for the poor, and money to clean the environment. We organize ourselves, our land and people, to meet the needs of all members of the community. An economy is a social organization.'

So a major role for governments at all levels has been acknowledged, with occasional calls for privatization or deregulation, on the one hand, or calls for a new service to be provided by governments, on the other. There are differences in opinion about whether governments should attempt to curtail the power that is exercised by large private corporations, national and multinational. I believe that as giant corporations gather power and as governments hesitate to challenge them, more influence in society is transferred from governments and the people who elect them to corporate management and their shareholders – a small group drawn from the broad public. A corporation like Wal-Mart sets out to procure goods in, say, China at the lowest possible cost and to have them distributed in Canada by employees paid the lowest wages that will retain them. Prices paid by customers are low, often lower that that offered by the competition. But the consumers receiving the benefit of these lower prices are going to incur the social costs generated by employees who are paid low wages and have inadequate pension and welfare benefits. As I see it, society would work better for all if all major sectors of the economy paid fair wages, so that all groups of employees could provide for themselves and their families.

What are fair wages? Generally speaking, these are wages bargained by a responsible employer with a responsible union representing the employees. When an employer uses every available device to resist the unionization of its staff, this often indicates a desire to drive down wages. Not always. Some employers – one thinks of Japanese automakers, steelmaker Dofasco, and others – have paid 'going rates' but hoped to avoid dealing with unions. But some employers – one thinks of Wal-Mart – hope to avoid paying the level of wages and benefits that have been paid by competitors such as Safeway for many years. Low prices, paid for by having poorly paid workers all along the production and distribution chain, carry with them social costs that we all will pay.

Again, I find myself sharing many of the views set forth by Eric Kierans

in his autobiography. He expresses real concern about the growing influence of major corporations. Regarding global markets, Kierans says: 'I
am no fan of ... global markets. The financial system, it is true, has
become international ... But that is a paper world in which the multipli-
cation of financial products creates an arena for gambling, not investment, and in which speculation on sunspots and time periods replaces
real investment in the production of goods and services.'

Kierans goes on to say that proposals by John Maynard Keynes, professor of economics at Cambridge in the 1930s, and James Tobin, professor
of economics at Yale in the 1970s, to limit the speculation by imposing a
transfer tax on such transactions, have been studiously ignored. Kierans
adds that this 'is because we have been persuaded, against logic and
moral sense, that the institution that most needs our support these days
is not society, not the human community, but the global corporation.'

I disagree profoundly with the view of the economy and the role of
business organizations in that economy made famous by Milton Friedman, the Chicago economist. Eric Kierans, in his book, uses the following quote from Friedman:

> There is one and only one social responsibility of business – to use its
> resources and engage in activities designed to improve its profits so long as
> it stays within the rules of the game, which is to say, engages in open and
> free competition, without deception and fraud ... Few trends could so thor-
> oughly undermine the very foundations of our free society as the accep-
> tance by corporate officials of a social responsibility other than to make as
> much money for the stockholders as possible ... This is a fundamentally sub-
> versive doctrine.

Thus, if one corporation acts responsibly concerning the environment
and a competitor does as little as the law requires, it is the first corporation and not the second that is acting improperly and whose directors
should be censured. As Eric Kierans says in the work cited, 'The trouble
with this argument, besides its moral obtuseness, is that it assumes that
the only legitimate motive for humankind is greed.'

These types of views, widely held and often articulated – I think of Terrance Corcoran, formerly of the *Globe and Mail* and now of the *National
Post* – would be dangerous enough if applied to corporations operating
within Canada. Governments can make laws and restrict the worst rav-
ages of this piracy, but only at the cost of more and more regulation,
often with high compliance costs. But these views are far more danger-

ous when thought of as the guidelines for transnational corporations. For many activities of transnationals there is no effective governing regulator; no 'rules of the game' are enforced. We are left with the law of the jungle. As business guru Peter Drucker has put it, transnational corporations put economic decisions 'beyond the effective reach of the political process and its decision makers, national governments.'

Unless we find effective ways of governing the activities of transnational corporations in the way that the people of Britain found to govern the activities of intra-national corporations in the nineteenth century (and which we have copied and expanded), the forces of global economic integration must be resisted. Kierans says: 'As a liberal, I reject any global order or commercial world view. Globalism and corporatism block intellectual growth and cultural and political freedom. An open-ended future for mankind demands the pluralism and diversity that are the hallmarks of a true liberalism.'

I am less a liberal, in that sense, than is Kierans. But for a former president of the Montreal Stock Exchange, he has a clear idea of the role of the modern corporation in an increasingly global society. I believe it will take more than 'true liberalism' to make sure that the economic engine which is the modern corporation, which has proved so effective in allowing us to organize and produce goods and services, is harnessed to the cause of fair distribution of those goods and services. I would say that we require the approaches of social democracy.

Definitions are imprecise, but in general this means popularly elected democratic governments dedicated to doing their best to see that the fruits of our economic system are distributed in the fairest possible way. Of course, there will be differences about just what is fair. But they should not be fuelled by myths that our economic system is free and competitive. The well-known late economist J.K. Galbraith said of the U.S. economy of the 1950s that fully 60 per cent of people enjoyed the advantages of some legal or *de facto* monopoly to improve their income. We could all make a long list in Canada. They would include professionals such as doctors, lawyers, dentists, architects, engineers, nurses, pharmacists, teachers, accountants, and many others, all of whom are given forms of legal monopoly. Included also would be banks and bank employees, airlines and airline employees (protected against non-Canadian competition), and many more. And anyone who believes that retail gasoline prices are set on the basis of free competition throughout the system is unusually naïve.

There are good reasons for many of these monopolies and quasi-monopolies. But they destroy any notion of unrestricted free competition. I am not asserting that these protections are unwise. I am asserting that they make nonsense of any assertion that the market provides a fair way to distribute the fruits of our economic system. It provides a start but must be supplemented by steps to deal with the imperfections of our system. That is what social democracy is about.

Sometimes it means providing opportunities to enrich the future of individuals and society (elementary, secondary, and post-secondary education). Sometimes it means intervening in areas of significant market failure (for example, low income housing). Sometimes it means that government directly provides goods and services. This is true for electric power in much of Canada. Often it means income support for persons who are casualties of the system (employment insurance and social welfare) or who might be casualties if action was not taken (old age security and income supplement).

All of these and like measures need to be reviewed and adjusted regularly to see that they contribute to the objectives of meeting the moving target of a fair distribution of the fruits of the economic system.

We are all aware of the pleas of the well-to-do and their institutional voices that efforts to improve the way that goods and services are distributed will reduce the amount of goods produced. But there is scant evidence that, on balance, this is true. Rather, the evidence seems to be that as wealth is more evenly distributed, more money is spent. As the economists would say, the poor have a greater marginal propensity to consume than the rich. This spending is more often local. And this extra spending more than offsets any disincentives that the higher taxes to finance redistribution may create. This accords with my own observation. As suggested earlier, I have known several periods when business was doing well and when lower wage employees were doing badly, but few, if any, periods when lower wage employees were doing well and business generally was doing badly.

I sometimes feel that society needs more ways to measure our performance. We have a ready and popular way to measure the quantity of goods produced – the gross national product. We should have a similarly popular measure of the effectiveness of our system of distributing goods. There are, for example, some measures of child poverty. Canada's record in this regard is disgraceful when measured against the Scandinavian and some other European countries. We do reasonably well in the commonly used health measures – infant mortality and longevity. On literacy our record is tolerable. The United Nations has an index of gen-

eral well-being. But no index is generally accepted as a measure of how
well we are doing on distribution, the way that the GNP is accepted as a
measure of how well we are doing in production. If we had such an
accepted measure, it would serve to focus the attention of legislators,
academics, journalists, and the public on some of the key issues which we
face – some of which I have referred to above.

Our challenge for the future will not primarily be to produce more
goods, but rather to distribute the goods more fairly. It is not simple.
There will always be those who urge that we produce more and that the
market will look after distribution. But that has worked relatively poorly.
When governments have intervened to distribute education, health, and
many other services at low or reduced cost, society has been the better
for it. This approach is not a panacea. Most areas are not appropriate
areas for government intervention. But there are still areas for action. A
look around the world tells me that where able and active governments
(and there are many) intervene on behalf of people with special needs
or lower incomes, society works best. There is no magic bullet, although
many continue to seek some formula that will relieve them from thinking. Nobody believes in the public ownership of all the means of production, distribution, and exchange. I doubt whether they ever did. Nobody
believes all major economic decisions should be left to the market to
decide. I doubt whether they ever did. What is needed is a more nuanced
approach.

On the economic side, we need a judicious mix of private, public, co-
operative, and non-profit ownership of the means of production, distribution, and exchange. Such a system could operate within rules set by
democratic government and be regularly reviewed to make all the trade-
offs needed to protect the environment and to assist in the task of fair
distribution. Some countries in some periods have done reasonably well
in the production of goods, but we have only rarely done well in sharing
the wealth. Here we need some principles, not easy to agree upon, and
some markers and indices to measure our success.

I have not dealt with the important environmental questions facing
Canada and the world. I have not done so because they are the subject of
lively public discussion to which I can add little. That the globe is under-
going warming cannot reasonably be denied. That this warming is partly
caused by human activity in releasing carbon dioxide into the atmosphere is firmly established. Whether there are other factors causing global warming not related to human activity has not been established but
has not been clearly rejected. As the evidence mounts, ordinary pru-

dence would suggest that Canada should join the forces calling for a substantial reduction in carbon dioxide and like emissions. It is said that until major nations – the United States, China, India – join a campaign to reduce such emissions, Canada's actions will mean little. I believe this discounts the influence which Canada can have in joining with European countries to show how a modern industrial economy can lower its greenhouse gas emissions and still retain a standard of living in line with what we have enjoyed. On these issues, my experience does not give any more insights than those of my neighbours.

Added to these economic approaches, we as a society need to encourage the other human activities – spiritual, charitable, cultural, and recreational – that nourish the human spirit. I am far from despairing. Of course, we could do better. I'm confident that we will do better. But even with its warts, Canada is a good country. We have much to be proud of. Our children will have the opportunity of showing how much more we can be.

Index

Bolstad, Wes, 5
Bowerman, Ted, 73
Bridgewater, 9–11
British North America Act (1867),
174
Broadbent, Ed, 137
Brockelbank, J.H., 27, 73
Burton, John, 144
Bury, Dr John, 89

Cadbury, George, 24–5
Callaghan, James, 182
Calvert, Lorne, 209
Cameco Corporation, 7, 230–7
Canadian Bill of Rights 1960, 176, 198
Cardinal, Douglas, 110
Carter, Mary, 18
Carter, Roger, 18, 115–16
CBC, 194
central time, 34–5
Charter of Rights and Freedoms, 176,
179, 199–200; and private power,
180–1; violation of, 179–80
Children's Dental Program, 87–8,
210; dismantled, 88, 207, 211
Ching, Don, 91
Chrétien, Jean, 181; Constitution;
187–9; freestanding section 28, 192;
Section 34 (now 35), 193
Clarkson, Dr Graham, 89
Cluff Lake, 112, 158, 163
Coldwell, M.J., 34, 37
Cole, G.D.H., 20
College of Physicians and Surgeons,
30–2
Collver, Dick, 206
Community Capital Fund, 122
Constitution: Alberta, 177; amending
formula, 174–6, 178, 181; Gang of
Eight, 175, 181; history, 174; lan-
guage rights, 176; National Action
Committee on the Status of Women
(NAC), 192–5; Parliamentary Com-
mittee, 178–9; patriation, 173–4;
public opinion, 178; Queen Eliza-
beth II, 173, 190; Romanow telex,
192–3; Saskatchewan, 176–7; Sec-
tion 15, 192; Section 28, 192–3; Sec-
tion 34 (now 35), 193; Section 92A,
136–7, 189; September 1980 con-
ference, 173; Supreme Court of
Canada, 176, 179; Victoria Charter–
type formula, 175–6
Cooper, Marjorie, 29
Corcoran, Terrance, 247
Cowley, Elwood, 146
Coyne, Deborah, 194
Creighton, 107
Crow's Nest Pass rate , 5, 119, 125, 210
Curtis, George, 18

Dalgleish, Dr Harold, 47, 60–1
Dalhousie Law School, 3, 10–14
Davidson, Davidson & Blakeney, 139
Davis, Bill: Constitution negotiations,
84–5, 134, 187–9; federal-provincial
conference, 5; Grey Cup, 134
Dawson, Robert, 11
Department of Northern
Saskatchewan (DNS), 108–12; and
northern development, 110–14
Devine, Grant, 206
Diefenbaker, John, 36; Bill of Rights,
179; Douglas defeat, 56; federal
election, 36, 45; Emmett Hall, 119;
health services, 48; hospital care
insurance, 46; Otto Lang, 79–80;
Prince Albert, 96
Douglas, Thomas Clement (Tommy):
background, 40; federal defeat, 56;